Internationalizing Higher Education

CERC Studies in Comparative Education

1. Mark Bray & W.O. Lee (eds.) (2001): *Education and Political Transition: Themes and Experiences in East Asia*. Second edition. ISBN 962-8093-84-3. 228pp. HK$200/US$32.

2. Mark Bray & W.O. Lee (eds.) (1997): *Education and Political Transition: Implications of Hong Kong's Change of Sovereignty*. ISBN 962-8093-90-8. 169pp. [Out of print]

3. Philip G. Altbach (1998): *Comparative Higher Education: Knowledge, the University, and Development*. ISBN 962-8093-88-6. 312pp. HK$180/US$30.

4. Zhang Weiyuan (1998): *Young People and Careers: A Comparative Study of Careers Guidance in Hong Kong, Shanghai and Edinburgh*. ISBN 962-8093-89-4. 160pp. HK$180/US$30.

5. Harold Noah & Max A. Eckstein (1998): *Doing Comparative Education: Three Decades of Collaboration*. ISBN 962-8093-87-8. 356pp. HK$250/US$38.

6. T. Neville Postlethwaite (1999): *International Studies of Educational Achievement: Methodological Issues*. ISBN 962-8093-86-X. 86pp. HK$100/US$20.

7. Mark Bray & Ramsey Koo (eds.) (2004): *Education and Society in Hong Kong and Macao: Comparative Perspectives on Continuity and Change*. Second edition. ISBN 962-8093-34-7. 323pp. HK$200/US$32.

8. Thomas Clayton (2000): *Education and the Politics of Language: Hegemony and Pragmatism in Cambodia, 1979-1989*. ISBN 962-8093-83-5. 243pp. HK$200/US$32.

9. Gu Mingyuan (2001): *Education in China and Abroad: Perspectives from a Lifetime in Comparative Education*. ISBN 962-8093-70-3. 252pp. HK$200/US$32.

10. William K. Cummings, Maria Teresa Tatto & John Hawkins (eds.) (2001): *Values Education for Dynamic Societies: Individualism or Collectivism*. ISBN 962-8093-71-1. 312pp. HK$200/US$32.

11. Ruth Hayhoe & Julia Pan (eds.) (2001): *Knowledge Across Cultures: A Contribution to Dialogue Among Civilizations*. ISBN 962-8093-73-8. 391pp. HK$250/US$38.

12. Robert A. LeVine (2003): *Childhood Socialization: Comparative Studies of Parenting, Learning and Educational Change*. ISBN 962-8093-61-4. 299pp. HK$200/US$32.

13. Mok Ka-Ho (ed.) (2003): *Centralization and Decentralization: Educational Reforms and Changing Governance in Chinese Societies*. ISBN 962-8093-58-4. 230pp. HK$200/US$32.

14. W.O. Lee, David L. Grossman, Kerry J. Kennedy & Gregory P. Fairbrother (eds.) (2004): *Citizenship Education in Asia and the Pacific: Concepts and Issues*. ISBN 962-8093-59-2. 313pp. HK$200/US$32.

15. Alan Rogers (2004): *Non-Formal Education: Flexible Schooling or Participatory Education?* ISBN 962-8093-30-4. 316pp. HK$200/US$32.

16. Peter Ninnes & Meeri Hellstén (eds.) (2005): *Internationalizing Higher Education: Critical Explorations of Pedagogy and Policy*. ISBN 962-8093-37-1. 231pp. HK$200/US$32

Order through bookstores or from:

Comparative Education Research Centre
Faculty of Education, The University of Hong Kong, Pokfulam Road, Hong Kong, China.
Fax: (852) 2517 4737; E-mail: cerc@hkusub.hku.hk; Website: www.hku.hk/cerc

The list prices above are applicable for order from CERC, and include sea mail postage; add US$5 per copy for air mail.

No.7 in the series and Nos. 13-15 are co-published by Kluwer Academic Publishers and the Comparative Education Research Centre of the University of Hong Kong. Kluwer Academic Publishers publishes hardback versions. No.16 onwards are co-published with Springer.

CERC Studies in Comparative Education 16

Internationalizing Higher Education

Critical Explorations of Pedagogy and Policy

Edited by

Peter Ninnes & Meeri Hellstén

Comparative Education Research Centre
The University of Hong Kong

Springer

First published 2005
Comparative Education Research Centre
The University of Hong Kong
Pokfulam Road, Hong Kong, China

© Comparative Education Research Centre

ISBN 962-8093-37-1

Contents

List of Abbreviations

ABC	Australian-born Chinese
ADS	Australian Development Scholarship
AusAID	Australian Agency for International Development
AVCC	Australian Vice-Chancellors' Committee
CDU	Curriculum Development Unit
CVCP	Committee of Vice-Chancellors and Principals
DE	Distance education
DEST	Australian Department of Education, Science and Training
EAP	English for academic purposes
ELICOS	English language intensive courses for overseas students
EU	European Union
FCAE	Fiji College of Advanced Education
GATE	Global Alliance of Transnational Education
GATS	General Agreement on Trade in Services
GDLN	Global Development Learning Network
GU	Guangdong University
ICT	Information and Communication Technology
IELTS	International English language testing system
IMF	International Monetary Fund
IT	Information technology
MIT	Massachusetts Institute of Technology
MoE	Ministry of Education
NESB	Non English speaking background
NGO	Non Government Organization
NYU	New York University
OECD	Organisation for Economic Cooperation and Development
OIS	On-shore international students
PNG	Papua New Guinea
TESOL	Teaching English to speakers of other languages
TOEFL	Test of English as a foreign language
TVET	Technical and Vocational Education and Training
UNESCO	United Nations Educational, Scientific and Cultural Organisation
VCP	Virtual Colombo Plan
ZU	Zhongshan University

Series Editor's Foreword

The internationalization of higher education is a theme of great significance, and this book makes a major contribution to understanding of the phenomenon. The Comparative Education Research Centre (CERC) at the University of Hong Kong is thus delighted to include the book within its series CERC Studies in Comparative Education.

The book owes its origin to a conference organized by the Australian and New Zealand Comparative and International Education Society (ANZCIES). This explains the emphasis within the book on perspectives from Australasia and its neighbors. The ANZCIES is one of the 32 constituent societies of the World Council of Comparative Education Societies (WCCES), of which CERC is the secretariat. This professional linkage within the field of comparative education provides an additional reason why CERC is glad to include the book in its series, promoting the work of the ANZCIES in the wider arena.

Australia, in particular (and more visibly than New Zealand), has become widely known for its aggressive recruitment of overseas students and for export of services through campuses of Australian universities in other countries. The book notes that in 2002, Australian public higher education institutions enrolled 185,000 students compared with just 29,000 twelve years previously, and that the international students in 2002 comprised over 21 per cent of the total student load. One third of these international students were in 'offshore' programs, and studied entirely or largely within their own countries. This activity generated over AUS$2 billion for Australian universities, and further substantial amounts were spent by international students and their families in living expenses when resident in Australia. For these reasons, Australian interest in international student flows has been particularly strong, and Australian scholars have made major contributions not only to literature specifically concerned with Australia but also to the broader arena. It is a pleasure to make some of this literature available in the present book.

Moreover, in addition to the work that focuses on Australia the book contains other perspectives. These include an instructive case study of the internationalization of a major comprehensive university in China; a wide-ranging analysis by scholars in the United Kingdom of global commodification of teaching and learning; and a view from Fiji of international policy convergence in higher education.

As might be expected, much of the commentary in other books, particularly ones emanating from official sources, has been very positive. The present book, however, sets out to problematize the phenomenon. As explained by the editors in the Introduction, the volume aims to "peel back taken-for-granted practices and beliefs". The book has indeed succeeded in this task. It has brought together an outstanding group of contributors, and presents analyses on this complex topic which will attract broad interest not only from countries which, like Australia, are exporters of higher education but also from countries which are importers.

Mark Bray
President, World Council of Comparative Education Societies;
Chair Professor of Comparative Education;
Dean, Faculty of Education, The University of Hong Kong

Introduction: Critical Engagements with the Internationalization of Higher Education

Peter Ninnes and Meeri Hellstén

For the academic with a taste for adventure, an insatiable desire to know and experience a wide range of exotic 'others', a willingness to board the entrepreneurial bandwagon, a hankering after airport departure lounges, and an immunity to the effects of long term exposure to radiation at 10,000 metres above sea level, the internationalization of higher education is an enticing and intoxicating cocktail of possibilities. From teaching intensive residential schools off-shore in the 'glitz and glamour' of Hong Kong, to educational consultancies in remote Kingdoms 'lost in time', to the mad cap intellectual menagerie of massive academic conferences in Montréal, to the exquisite pleasure of witnessing the graduation of one's on-shore international students, the internationalization of higher education appears to provide increasing opportunities for academics to become global travellers, makers of difference, effectors of personal change, and facilitators of social progress. Indeed, if some programs are to be believed, it provides elusive opportunities to be peddlers of poverty alleviation practices and dispensers of sustainable development. Under internationalization, the world is our oyster, or perhaps, our garden, in which we sow the seeds from the fruits of our academic labours: powerful knowledges, proven (best) practices, and established systems of scholarship, administration and inquiry. Of course, the preceding description is only one reading of the internationalization of higher education, and the main purpose of this volume is to trouble such unproblematized notions and to provide more critical readings and explorations of the process.

Internationalization has been the subject of study and comment in a range of academic fields, including comparative education. The relationship between internationalization and comparative education is both complex and dynamic. For decades, comparative educators have been concerned that the field of comparative education

1

should contribute to international understanding, peace, and global interconnectedness. Demiashkevich (1931: 45), for example, expressed a desire that the field would contribute to the enhancement of intercultural relations and the sound conduct of international relations, and would contribute to the avoidance of war as nations learned about each other. Kandel (1933: xxv) hoped the field would contribute to a rational internationalism that would enhance "the work and progress of the world". Similar sentiments have been expressed by Moehlman (1951), Ulich (1954), Schneider (1955), Woody (1955), Paplauskas-Ramunas (1955), and Butts (1973).

As well as debates over the role of comparative education in promoting internationalism, the field of comparative education has at various times tried to differentiate itself from international education. Kandel (1956: 2), for example, argued that comparative education

> should not be confused with the aim of international education, which seeks to promote a common aim – good-will, friendship, brotherhood, peace and so on – among the peoples of the world. The study of comparative education may have a contribution to make towards this aim by showing where and how it may be implemented but it is not itself international education.

In a similar vein, Bereday (1964: ix-x) argued that because of the unique combination of methods and concepts that comparative education employed, it "cannot simply be a part of history of education or of sociology of education or of international education", although he did suggest that it could contribute to "international understanding" (Bereday 1964: 9). In a later work, Bereday (1967) suggested that there was some overlap between comparative education and international education. Noah and Eckstein (1969: 185-186) suggested that while the early aims of comparative education such as promoting international brotherhood and cooperation [were] "highly laudable" they were "inadequate bases to sustain a field of study". Later authors, such as Lawson (1975) and Wilson (1994), also sought to strictly differentiate comparative education from international education. Yet other writers, such as Collings (1956: 126) argued that one of the relevant issues for comparative education was "international cooperation for economic and social development, particularly through technical assistance". Much of this technical assistance occurred through student exchanges such as the Colombo Plan (Auletta 2001), which are often considered a component of international education. Others argued that international education is a subset of comparative education (see, for example, Fletcher 1974), while Arnove (1980: 62), in introducing world systems theory into comparative education, argued that such a move restored the international element to comparative education. It could also be argued that Arnove's (1980) introduction of world systems theory into the field of comparative education presaged the later emphasis on globalization. More recently, Rust (2002) has editorialized that articles on international education have a proper place in comparative education

Arnove – World Systems Theory

journals, as long as they meet certain academic criteria regarding conceptual framing, methods, and originality.

The acceleration of globalization in the last two decades has to some extent rendered obsolete the debates about the differences between comparative and international education. Cultural, economic and political globalization has resulted in, if not the breakdown, then the increased porosity of the nation state, which many comparative education researchers have used and continue to use as a unit of analysis. However, the notion of the discrete nation state able to be studied and compared with other nation states becomes less meaningful as nation states become more socially, culturally, politically, and economically integrated. In addition, the notion of international education comprising primarily international exchanges in order to learn about other countries, or to provide technical assistance in development, is also limited. While some international student exchanges still have these goals, many are based on economic motives. For countries such as Australia, international student recruitment has shifted emphasis from aid to trade. Furthermore, as Harman (this volume) shows, the international dimensions of higher education also embrace practices such as the global movement of teachers and researchers, the diversification of the curriculum, educational programs offered across national borders using new technologies, bilateral and multilateral agreements between universities and the commercial export of education. This appears to be a broader set of activities than envisaged by Knight (1995), who defined international education in terms of incorporating international or intercultural elements into teaching, service and research. The implication for comparative education research is that, as part of its engagement with globalization (see, for example, Stromquist & Monkman 2000, Jones 1999), there needs to be an increased emphasis on the academic study of international education as a practice and of the diverse processes of internationalization. It is this emphasis to which the current volume contributes.

The increasing pace of the internationalization of education is a response to a diverse set of conditions. As Bauman (2002: 231) observes, we live in a "fast globalizing world of crumbling state borders and a worldwide supranational network of capital, knowledge, and knowledge capital". This has created a perception that international perspectives in all levels of education are imperative, as have global events such as terrorism and protracted regional disputes focused on issues of ethnicity and religion. At the same time, changes to funding regimes for higher education have forced many institutions to engage globally through off-shore programs and increased recruitment of international students. Yet education is an increasingly contested domain as the processes of global destructuring and restructuring continue to empower and disempower a range of education stakeholders. Furthermore, these changes have produced uncertainty at the micro level, or in the everyday practices of systems, institutions, academics and learners. There is now a questioning of the character and quality of the products of the rapid internationalization of education. At the unglamorous ground levels of office and classroom, it could be argued that the internationalization of higher education is currently experiencing a moment of exhaustion brought on by increasing workload demands and seemingly insoluble pedagogic and ethical dilemmas. Many programs are simply being sustained by academics' goodwill and passion for teaching. Thus there is a great need for review, renewal and critical insight into current practices of internationalization.

In this volume we attempt to peel back taken-for-granted practices and beliefs (McHoul & Rapley 2001), and "alienate" normalized notions (Søndergaard 2002). Rather than provide a manual on how better to internationalize higher education institutions (see, for example, Cavusgil & Horn 1997, Mestenhauser & Ellingboe 1998, Speck & Carmical 2002), we seek to be intentionally critical of teaching, learning, research and policy. By "critical" we mean that we seek to explore the gaps and silences in current pedagogy and practices, and to address the ambiguities, tensions, unevennesses and contradictions in internationalization. We aim to foreground, and consider the unintended consequences of, the taken-for-granted, and to ask unsettling questions about whose interests are served by the processes of internationalization.

Welch (2002) attempts to distinguish internationalization from globalization, as do Edwards and Usher (2000). In the former case, Welch employs Knight's (1995) relatively narrow definition of internationalization mentioned above, and hence sees internationalization as a relatively benign or positive process, in contrast to globalization and especially "the unfettered global competition of industries and institutions, including the knowledge and culture industries" (Welch 2002: 434). Edwards and Usher (2000), in contrast, view internationalization less benignly, arguing that it comprises "the spread of Western institutions, culture and practices", while globalization is concerned with issues such as hybridity, space and the global-local nexus (Edwards & Usher 2000: 20). This colonial characterization of internationalization is revealed in several of the chapters is this volume. At the same time, many of the works collected here reject these dichotomistic approaches and show how internationalization and globalization are entangled with, rather than distinct from, each other. The space-time compression, electronic information networks, global spread of ideas, cultures, and values, economic integration and so on that many writers identify as aspects of globalization (McGinn 1997, Edwards & Usher 2000, Rizvi & Lingard 2000, Stromquist & Monkman 2000, Langhorne 2001, Carnoy & Rhoten 2002, Torres 2002, Singh 2004) simultaneously aid and are intensified by processes of internationalization. Thus, while the space-time compression of the teaching and learning process is aided by, for example, the existence of web based educational delivery systems, the development and improvement of such systems is driven in part by universities' desire to internationalize their operations. As a result of this entanglement, many of the chapters in this volume frame their analysis of internationalization in terms of processes of globalization.

This book arose from ideas generated at the 30th annual conference of the Australian and New Zealand Comparative and International Education Society (ANZCIES), which had as its theme "Internationalizing Education in the Asia-Pacific

Region: Critical Reflections, Critical Times" (Ninnes & Tamatea 2002). A number of the chapters are revisions of work first presented at that conference, while the other chapters have been specifically commissioned for this volume.

The chapters proceed through two stages, dealing successively with pedagogy and policy issues. The first set of chapters commences with Michael Singh's exposition of how internationalization and globalization provide opportunities for creating new kinds of teaching and learning in universities. Drawing on the findings of a major research project with international students, Singh shows how academics can work with/in the incomplete and inadequate concepts and practices of internationalization to construct meaningful and powerful learning communities. In chapter 2, Rajani Naidoo and Ian Jamieson unsettle some of the taken-for-granted assumptions about the pedagogical desirability of virtual learning. They argue that many of the recognized characteristics of effective teaching and learning are difficult if not impossible to reproduce in cyberspace, because virtual learning systems are designed principally to deliver a commodified educational product rather than to engage the learner in deep and profound cognitive or affective change. In chapter 3, Cathie Doherty and Parlo Singh trouble some of the familiar routines and performances of English language classes for international students. Their insightful presentation of data from a research project conducted in Australia and Indonesia demonstrates how practices of internationalization that apparently seek to empower international students are inadvertently contributing to westernization. Next, Anne Prescott and Meeri Hellstén disrupt some of the assumptions about the process of transition of international students into the academic cultures of their host institutions. They argue that the ways in which many international students interpret their initial experiences are quite different to the host academics' expectations, and Prescott and Hellstén call for a re-thinking of pedagogies that are meant to aid and include international students' transitions.

The following two chapters provide a case study of internationalization and a review of Australian literature on the process. The case study in Chapter 5 is provided by Rui Yang and focuses on a major Chinese university. His work shows how internationalization policy has impacted on research agendas over three quarters of a century. Of particular interest is the way in which his research reveals the unevenness of internationalization between academic departments, and how internationalization benefits some parts of the university at the expense of others. In the following chapter, Grant Harman provides a rich and detailed review of research into internationalization, pedagogy, practice and policies, conducted in Australian universities. The chapter shows the various approaches that have been used, the kinds of results found, and also the gaps and silences that currently exist in the issues, frameworks and topics that inform contemporary research in this area.

The final chapters of the book explore specific issues pertaining to internationalization policies. In chapter 7, Peter Ninnes presents an alternative reading of a government aid program designed to involve higher education institutions in international development. His analysis shows how the program inadvertently creates overly flattering representations of Australia's capabilities and characteristics, while simultaneously representing Australia's neighbours as essentially lacking. Pam Nilan's analysis of an overseas aid scholarship program follows in chapter 8. Nilan reveals how the scholarship recipients use the program for their own purposes, which may be at odds with the purported aims of the program. Furthermore, despite its best intentions, the program contributes to the maintenance of social stratification in the recipient country. In chapter 9, Jan Schapper and Susan Mayson explore a number of management policies and practices related to internationalization in one major university. Their work identifies the ways in which these policies and practices contribute to a deskilling and marginalization of academics and a homogenization of the curriculum. Finally, in chapter 10, Katarina Tuinamuana discusses the implementation of international management practices at a higher education institution in Fiji. Her analysis is particularly important in showing how international practices intersect and interact with local institutions, academic cultures, and bureaucracies with unexpected and unintended effects.

Barring a full-scale revolt by jaded and jet-lagged academics, the internationalization of higher education is likely to continue at an increasing rate. Our hope is that in a small way this volume will contribute to a thoughtful and critical approach by academics, policy makers and administrators to teaching, learning, research and policies of and within the internationalization of higher education.

References

Arnove, R.F. 1980. "Comparative Education and World-Systems Analysis." *Comparative Education Review* 24(1): 48-62.

Auletta, A. 2000. "A Retrospective View of the Colombo Plan: Government Policy, Departmental Administration and Overseas Students." *Journal of Higher Education Policy and Management* 22(1): 47-58.

Bauman, Z. 2002. *Society Under Siege.* Cambridge, UK: Polity Press.

Bereday, G.Z.F. 1964. *Comparative Method in Education.* New York: Holt, Rinehart and Winston.

Bereday, G.Z.F. 1967. "Reflections on Comparative Methodology in Education, 1964-1966." *Comparative Education* 3(3): 169-187.

Butts, R.F. 1973. "New Futures for Comparative Education." *Comparative Education Review* 17(4): 289-294.

Carnoy, M. & Rhoten, D. 2002. "What Does Globalization Mean for Educational Change? A Comparative Approach." *Comparative Education Review* 46(1): 1-9.

Cavusgil, S. & Horn, N. 1997. *Internationalizing Doctoral Education in Business.* Lansing: Michigan State University Press.

Collings, D.G. 1956. "Comparative Education in the Work of the United Nations and UNESCO." In *Comparative Education in Theory and Practice: Proceedings of the*

Third Annual Conference on Comparative Education, edited by W.W. Brickman. New York: School of Education, New York University.

Demiashkevich, M.J. 1931. "Why Comparative Education?" *Peabody Journal of Education* 9(1): 41-45.

Edwards, R. & Usher, R. 2000. *Globalisation and Pedagogy: Space, Place and Identity.* London: Routledge.

Fletcher, L. 1974. "Comparative Education: A Question of Identity?" *Comparative Education Review* 18(3): 348-353.

Jones, P. 1999. "Globalisation and Internationalism: Democratic Prospects for World Education." *Comparative Education* 34(2): 143-155.

Kandel, I.L. 1933. *Studies in Comparative Education.* London: George G. Harrap..

Kandel, I.L. 1956. "Problems of Comparative Education." *International Review of Education* 2(1): 1-13.

Knight, J. 1995. "A National Study on Internationalization at Canadian Universities," in *Strategies for Internationalization of Higher Education: A Comparative Study of Australia, Canada, Europe, and the USA*, edited by H. de Wit. Amsterdam: European Association for International Education in association with the Program on Institutional Management in Higher Education of the Organization of Economic Cooperation and Development.

Langhorne, R. 2001. *The Coming of Globalization: Its Evolution and Contemporary Consequences.* Basingstoke: Palgrave.

Lawson, R.F. 1975. "Free-Form Comparative Education". *Comparative Education Review* 19(4): 345-353.

McGinn, N. 1997. "The Impact of Globalization on National Education Systems." *Prospects* 27(1): 41-54.

McHoul, A. & Rapley, M. eds. 2001. *How to Analyse Talk in Institutional Settings: A Casebook of Methods.* London: Continuum International.

Mestenhauser, J. & Ellingboe, B. eds. 1998. *Reforming the Higher Education Curriculum: Internationalizing the Campus.* Westport, CT: Oryx Press.

Moehlman, A.H. 1951. "Comparative Education in Various Cultures." In *Comparative Education*, edited by A.H. Moehlman, & J.S. Roucek. New York: Dryden.

Ninnes, P. & Tamatea, L. eds. 2002. *Internationalizing Education in the Asia-Pacific Region: Critical Reflections, Critical Times.* Proceedings of the 30th annual conference of the Australian and New Zealand Comparative and International Education Society. Armidale, NSW: School of Education, University of New England and ANZCIES.

Noah, H.J. and Eckstein, M.A. 1969. *Toward a Science of Comparative Education.* London: Macmillan.

Paplauskas-Ramunas, A. 1955. Comparative Education in the Canadian Universities. In *The Teaching of Comparative Education: Proceedings of the Second Annual Conference on Comparative Education*, edited by W.W. Brickman. New York: School of Education, New York University.

Rizvi, F. & Lingard, B. 2000. "Globalization and Education: Complexities and Contingencies." *Educational Theory* 50(4): 419-426.

Rust, V. 2002. "The Place of International Education in the *Comparative Education Review.*" *Comparative Education Review* 46(3): iii-iv.

Schneider, F. 1955. "The Conception of Comparative Education." In *Comparative Education. An International Meeting held from 12-16 April, 1955, at the UNESCO Institute For Education, Hamburg.* Hamburg: UNESCO Institute for Education.

Singh, P. 2004. "Globalization and Education." *Educational Theory* 54(1): 103-115.

Søndergaard, D. 2002. "Poststructuralist Approaches to Empirical Analysis." *Qualitative Studies in Education* 15(2): 187-204.

Speck, B. & Carmical, B. eds. 2002. *New Directions for Higher Education. Internationalizing Higher Education: Building Vital Programs on Campus.* San Francisco: Jossey Bass.

Stromquist, N.P. & Monkman, K. eds. 2000. *Globalization and Education: Integration and Contestation across Cultures.* Lanham, Md.: Rowman & Littlefield.

Torres, C.A. 2002. "Globalization, Education and Citizenship: Solidarity Versus Markets?" *American Educational Research Journal* 39(2): 363-378.

Ulich, R. 1954. "Some Observations Concerning the Study of Comparative Education." In *The Role of Comparative Education in the Education of Teachers: Proceedings of the First Annual Conference on Comparative Education*, edited by W.W. Brickman. New York: School of Education, New York University.

Welch, A. 2002. "Going Global? Internationalizing Australian Universities in a Time of Global Crisis." *Comparative Education Review* 46(4): 433-472. .

Wilson, D.N. 1994. "Comparative and International Education: Fraternal or Siamese Twins? A Preliminary Genealogy of Our Twin Fields." *Comparative Education Review* 38(4): 449-486.

Woody, T. 1955. "Futures in Comparative Education." In *The Teaching of Comparative Education: Proceedings of the Second Annual Conference on Comparative Education*, edited by W.W. Brickman. New York: School of Education, New York University.

1

Enabling Transnational Learning Communities: Policies, Pedagogies and Politics of Educational Power

Michael Singh

Introduction

In responding to and giving expression to contemporary geopolitical shifts, universities around the world are increasingly entangled in intersecting local, national, and global relations. Transnational students are using the internationalization of higher education to extend and deepen their capacity for thinking and acting globally, nationally and locally in order to enhance the viability of their life trajectories. In doing so they find competing university systems offering contrasting perspectives on, and pathways through, the contours of this ever-changing global/national/local-scape. This chapter explores the problematic connections between university imaginings of the internationalization of higher education and transnational students' uses of international education to enhance their life opportunities as global/national/local citizens, workers/employers and learners.

Adopting a transformative perspective, this chapter contributes to the burgeoning debates about the possibilities of bringing forward, reinvigorating and reinventing those traditions which have enabled education policies, pedagogies and politics to respond responsibly to the fiery imperatives of the past. Through the examination of the global/national/local connectedness of particular students, this chapter opens possibilities for discovering how other students—local and international, bilingual and monolingual, majority and minority world alike—may offer important media through which to learn about and develop the attributes required for dealing with the imperatives, uncertainties and complexities inherent in the structures and (il)logic of contemporary transitions in globalization.

To ground this project socially, this chapter is based on an analysis of interviews with students from the People's Republic of China who were enrolled in the final year of their undergraduate degree, mostly in disciplines related to business, science and technology, at a range of Australian universities. The interviews explored these students' views of how their formal and non-formal learning experiences in Australia deepened and extended their transnational education begun in China, and how they expected to use the learnings they had so far accumulated in their life. The students did not offer a homogenous narrative on the internationalization of higher education, nor did they represent anything like typical transnational students. Each student had her or his own different and particular transnational educational history, and they had highly variable accounts of how they were using their education in Australia to elaborate their pre-formed identities as transnational workers/employers, global/ national/local citizens and worldly learners. Further, in itself this focus on trans-national students from China reflects and gives expression to a notable reorientation of economic globalization in Australia as elsewhere. From the beginning of the 21st century, Australian considerations of transnational capitalism and politics have extended to China, displacing but not marginalizing an earlier focus on Japan. Moreover, this focus on Chinese students also invites consideration of the role of non-Europeans in inciting innovations in university teaching and learning in Australia, a country still struggling with its legacy of White Australia politics (Singh 2001).

This chapter contributes to exploring the educational significance of re-presenting and engaging all students as media of transnational global/national/local connectedness, rather than as merely sources of revenue or sites of English language deficiencies or "empty vessels" to be filled with Euro-American knowledge. Marketing models have often framed the meanings assigned to the internationalization of higher education in Australia (Caruana, Ramaseshan & Ewing 1998, Gatfield, Barker & Graham 1999, Jolley 1997, Kemp, Madden & Simpson 1998, Lafferty & Fleming 2000, Marginson 2002, Mazzarol, Choo & Nair 2001, Mazzarol & Hosie 1996). Debates and struggles over the sustainable management of the risky commercial trade in higher education have a privileged position in educational policy, pedagogy and politics. This is not surprising given the Australian Government's disinvestment in the education of an Australian public as well as the systems required for producing its 'human resources' and 'intellectual capital' (Dobson & Holtta 2001, Taylor & Henry 2000). Further, where debates over the socio-political, economic and multicultural purposes of internationalizing higher education arise, much attention is given to compensating for presumed deficits. This is especially with respect to English language education and the imagined allures of 'Anglo-American knowledge' (Ballard & Clanchy 1997, Bradley & Bradley 1984, Cleverley & Jones 1976). Alternatively these debates over the purposes of internationalizing higher education have dwelt on the psychosocial imaginings of 'absolute differences' in the learning strategies of students from Asia and Australia (Watkins & Biggs 1996).

A significant gap in all of this research into the internationalization of higher education is the missed opportunities to engage contemporary theories of cultural globalization and the insights they offer into the history, ideological and local practices of internationalizing higher education. This chapter represents a small contribution to generating an interpretation that brings a sense of complexity to the foregoing approaches, interrupting any assumption that they give the fullest possible meaning to the internationalization of higher education. They have been replaced in this chapter by a perspective that brings to the fore considerations of students as media of complex transnational connectivities. Taking Appadurai's (1996: 33) notion of "global cultural flows" as a point of departure, it might be argued that the global/national/local movements of transnational students (and academics), and their imaginings about moving, constitute a key feature of the current transitions in the practices of globalization. This opens up opportunities for bringing to the front of the imagination possibilities for responsive and responsible educational policies, pedagogies and politics. How might education policy actors enable transnational students' learnings?

This chapter grounds the nebulous and contested notion of internationalizing higher education in the movements of transnational students. They are seen as agents shaping their own life trajectories, as well as agents in stimulating the transformative re-imaginings and re-workings of policies, pedagogies and politics for internationalizing higher education. What then might it mean for the policies, pedagogies and politics of internationalizing higher education if the local and international, bilingual and monolingual, majority and minority world students (and staff) present in universities were regarded as productive media of global/national/local connections? What innovative possibilities could arise for higher education policies, pedagogies and politics if the presence of transnational students—in all their complex connectivities—was seen as a day-to-day manifestation of the nation-state's responses to and expressions of contemporary transitions in globalization? Admittedly, this way of framing the question of internationalizing higher education is as confronting as it is productively stimulating.

By working critically with the compromised conceptual resources of Clifford (1997) this chapter reflects on the evidence concerning how and why students from China are extending and deepening their movements into the circuits of transnational communities of learning and work. In doing so, it explores possibilities for pedagogical innovations that involve re-inventing ethnographic practices of fieldwork. The sections that follow seek to provide practical conceptual resources for making innovations in education policies, pedagogies and politics through the internationalization of higher education. This work is necessary even as education itself is being subjected to, and engages in crass marketization, individualistic consumerism and technological commodification. This is perhaps nowhere more evident than in Australian higher education, which is increasingly dependent on the cash-flow derived from international fee-paying students.

Reconstituting Ethnographic Fieldwork as a Pedagogical Practice

What might it mean to formally and explicitly incorporate transnational students' travels into a cluster of pedagogical practices derived through reconstituting ethnographic fieldwork? The following comparisons of the transnational students and the ethnographic fieldworker may suggest ways of tapping into the former's observation about globalization in Australia, providing a pedagogical vehicle for turning private musings into collective ethnographic knowledge. Like fieldwork, transnational students' travels typically require co-residence, collaboration and advocacy, and involve conducting interviews, making surveys and composing reports about people and their place (Clifford 1997: 59). Usually fieldworkers and transnational students are required to physically leave their 'home' (however that is defined), and to travel to and from, in and out of some place which may be imagined as being distinctly different. The fieldworker is required to engage in intensive or 'deep' interactions by living in a community for an extended, if inevitably temporary, time; so too does the transnational student. By re-making ethnographic fieldwork as a method of teaching, the world's geopolitical shifts might be represented to, by and through the learning experiences of transnational students. Students-as-fieldworkers could investigate global/national/local economic, cultural and socio-political flows, including the import-export of higher education in which universities are already enmeshed, to reveal what questionable habits are being taken for granted.

To get a sense of the possibilities that the internationalizing of higher education has to offer the elaboration of transnational identities, students were asked about the connections they had made in Australia. By actively occupying, and moving through and around space, these students were able to discursively map the field. They built networks with students from elsewhere in China and from other countries. This extension of their participation in a transnational learning community was constituted via their first language or by using an English dialect to make connections across different languages. However, they all had hopes that such a community would be inter-ethnic, including Anglo-ethnic and Other Australians as well as non-Chinese students from other nations.

Languages and Cultural Understandings

The student-as-fieldworker has to learn the local language or dialect in order to speak and listen for her or him self. One student in our study, Ke Chen, learnt about the differences between US/American textbook English and Australian spoken English:

> When we are in China we learn from the textbook, "How do you do?". When I came here the Australians said, "How are you" straight away. That was really confusing. When you read the textbook it says that only when you are very good friends do you say, "How are you?" straight away, otherwise you don't say that. Well, one guy said, "How are you?" straight away. I didn't even know this guy. I had to think, "How come Australians do not follow the textbook?"

The student-as-fieldworker learns to speak the language to a level of vernacular proficiency so as to engage in complex, often political negotiations without the aid of "cosmopolitan intermediaries" (Clifford 1997: 23). This was more than language education. For Ke Chen this involved learning cultural understandings:

> My education is not just from the university. … I've learnt more cultural things. Sometimes I don't understand what Australians are talking about, and I speak English very well. The words can be understood but I still don't know what they are talking about. That's the cultural understanding I'm learning.

The existence of multiple Englishes was something that Peng discovered: "In China our English tests are mostly for writing and reading. We had few opportunities to speak English. Our listening was from British or American English; it is different from Australian English." Likewise Yang recognized that "English" is not one bounded whole, but a complex tapestry of dialects, if not languages:

> In China we learnt American English, which is quite different from Australian English. It was not easy for me to pick it up, but now I … learn English from the lectures, the university and also from my work. … The more you speak and the more you listen the more you pick up … about routine or everyday life words.

The students know they cannot rely on interpreters or translators as in the case of short-term contacts; extended dwelling in the field requires bilingual communicative competence. However, despite preparatory English language education, Ying experienced the shock of language failure:

> Sometimes I failed some subjects here. I never thought I would fail subjects. My mum said that everything couldn't always be good for me. … I was really confident that I could at least get a credit. But I failed. In China I felt that my English is good. … I never failed a subject. When I came here, even if I studied hard, I would talk to the teachers and study the whole book, I could not … really understand. I also felt that some of the local students are laughing at me. … I have no expression on my face. I'm so confused. … I'm unbalanced (Ying).

To mitigate this sense of failure students used various strategies. For instance, Ying elected to learn English through her interactions with a friend from another Asian country: "I live with a Korean. … Her English is really good … we always communicate and talk in English. We're from different cultures so I have learnt a lot from her." Multicultural mediators helped Su to learn this other English:

> I made friends with some ABCs [Australian-born Chinese] … because I wasn't afraid as they have a Chinese face but they act like Australians. … after that, I hoped I could communicate with other Australian people. The ABC's … can easily understand my problem. So I can say to them, "Can you please speak

slowly, I can't understand you?"

As in fieldwork (Clifford 1997: 57), discursive practices are crucial to the translation, definition and re-presentation of both the 'transnational student' and the 'field' into scholarly knowledge claims. However, questions about the bilingual oracy, writing, listening and speaking of transnational students, along with those concerning the rise of multilingual knowledge economies, tend to be erased. The project of internationalizing higher education seems to be pre-occupied with the commodification of English in language laboratories, something they can do in their home country. There seems to be a lack of preparedness to explore English-only policies, pedagogies and politics in ways that engage bilingual students in more intimate interactions with Anglophone students as part of their day-to-day higher education studies.

Enhanced Deep Learning with Critical and Creative Thinking

Standing in opposition to superficiality, the transnational student-as-fieldworker is oriented towards the production of deep knowledge. Through the educative efforts of academics, Jun learnt that her 'job' involves not only ensuring a deep understanding but also producing knowledge:

> In China the teaching method is more teacher-centred. The teacher talks too much in front of the class and the students keep silent. They sit there and take notes. If they memorise the notes they can pass the exam. But in Australia it is quite different. The teacher stimulates the student's critical thinking and wants the student to become an independent learner.

The students were not provided merely with descriptions of the fields being studied but also with interpretive tools that opened meaningful spaces wherein they produced their own knowledge. That is, teaching and learning are co-joint knowledge producing endeavours that build 'fields' for multicultural translations and give 'work' its critical meanings. The idea of becoming a worker able to produce knowledge was a source of enjoyment for Xiang:

> In China we only learn something that the teacher has told you. ... In Australia the teacher only speaks to tell you a little bit, and then you have to do research. ... I like the Australian style better because you can do something you like, you can spend more time on it and do things for yourself.

Transnational students used their fieldwork to generate empirical data that puts socio-political, multicultural and economic theories of globalization/localization to the test. This interrelationship between deep understanding and knowledge production underlined Che's comment:

In China you need to write it down, memorize information, and you get good marks. In Australia ... you must analyse the information and figure things out. You need a logical way of thinking to come to your own conclusion. It's a little bit hard for me.

These students have acquired a range of learning strategies. They include those that emphasize the memorization required for a deep understanding of knowledge as well as those needed for the critical and creative generation of knowledge. Their fieldwork grounded their theoretical interpretations through enabling them to generate empirical evidence (Clifford 1997: 52-53).

Group-based Multidisciplinary Projects

Lectures provided Su a scaffold for undertaking team projects in which all members participate:

Teamwork is very important for you to learn to communicate with others. In the group you have to give your own opinion. As other people have their opinions this can help you to think in other ways to improve confidence. ... I made friends with students ... from places like Hong Kong, Singapore and Malaysia because we were doing the same assignments and projects.

Academics were regarded as crucial to the students' learning processes. However, these practices are constituted by distance and displacement as much as by focused, disciplined attention. The academics created situations where Riu was able to take advantage of his contacts, facilitating both the representation of different world-views and the emergence of new relationships:

In Australia, teachers pay more attention to teamwork ... and small group discussions ... In China ... even though it has a big population there is still no teamwork. Having to work with other people is very good experience.

Team-based projects provided Xiang opportunities for building transnational connections: "I work with people from different countries. I met people in Australia ... from Malaysia, Hong Kong, Indonesia, Japan and India." Likewise Junwen found that her group assignments provided the basis for creating an extended learning community:

I made some friends when we were doing group assignments and we keep in touch although we've finished the assignments. Most of my friends come from China and other countries ... India, Indonesia and some Australian students.

Lectures stimulated Peng's interest by creating a framework for doing the detailed collaborative work of developing informed discussions involved in investigating problems. Xin also recognized the benefits of group work: "We did an assignment and formed a group, then we got along with each other and became very good friends. We help each other." However, Xianlong noted some of the complexities of teamwork:

> The course requires you to do group work. Sometimes it's hard to make a group. Several Aussies are in one group while "Asians" are in another group. ... They have an advantage with language over us.

As an embodied spatial practice, these transantional students expected that international education would be constituted by various modes of border crossings, temporary if intensive dwelling away from home, travel, and few boundaries. They expected that universities would deliberately promote and en-skill inter-ethnic teamwork. Their concern about boundaries, about the isolationism of Anglo-Australian students, were reinforced by Ying:

> Some of the groups arc all local students; some of the groups are all overseas students. ... From the first year until now every group I've been with has been overseas students. I have never had a chancc to be in a gioup with local students. ... I really feel upset about this because the Australians want to be separate from the overseas students.

This separation by Anglo-Australian and international students reinforces presuppositions about there being a spatial distinction between a pure, absolutely different home, and home as being a place of transnational discovery. Li made a similar point:

> During the lectures and tutorials we don't talk to each other. So most of my friends are from Asian countries. Sometimes we have group assignments. They don't want to join the Asian students for the group.

While fieldwork was once largely an exclusively Western European practice for knowledge generation, this is no longer the case. Transnational students are observing Anglo-Australians, most of whom have yet learn to think of themselves as Others.

Learning through Part-time Jobs

For these students, learning in Australia was not only informed by their formal education, but also shaped by the informal learning they acquired through day-to-day life, and especially through part-time employment. Many of the students secured part-time work in order to obtain additional income but also as a deliberate tactic to secure significant learning experiences. Junwen designed internet web pages for friends, Jiang worked for an e-business, while Jing worked in an Internet café as a receptionist. Most students, like Li understood the Australian government's visa restrictions on overseas students working for no more than 20 hours per week during semester and also acknowledged that their parents did not want them to work, preferring that they concentrated on their studies. While tuition fees were paid for by parents and other family members, Yan worked part-time for money to cover additional living expenses. Likewise, while most families made major sacrifices to pay their children's university fees, Ying worked part-time in a Japanese restaurant to supplement her living allowance. However, not liking this type of work, she was looking forward to the cooperative work experience program planned and organized by her university as an accredited part of her course for the following year. Nevertheless, her current job provided her with useful learning experiences:

> I have to work because … I have to challenge myself to deal with different people. … Sometimes the customers are rude. "Can I maintain my balance? How can I do better as a waitress?"

While we are all participant-observers to some degree and at some times wherever we find ourselves, fieldwork is a special kind of localized dwelling. For Yuan, work experience in Australia was a beneficial part of her education: "I didn't have any experience in working before coming here … it's been useful to have some work experience here." Ming, a telemarketer, provides some insights into what is learnt through part-time jobs about the alienating culture of some forms of work:

> I try to annoy people every day. That's a terrible job. Before I came here I never imagined I would be sitting beside a phone every day, trying to smile on the phone in order to persuade people to give me some money. It is very hard. Every day you meet different customers. Some people are very nice. They say, "Sorry Ma'am, we really don't have the money to help you." But others … they receive these kinds of phone calls every day and they are very angry so they swear at me. It's not my problem. It's just a job I have to do. Everyone has different jobs to make a living. I hope they can understand that. I don't really want to disturb them but what can I do?

Ting worked in a hotel in order to communicate with people in different situations. Working part-time provided Su with the opportunity to improve her English, ability to communicate with others, confidence and independence, and her writing skills. Keifung worked in a restaurant because

> The first few years I just said, "Yes" or "No." I am just shy and scared … but I want to learn … then I thought if I want to improve my English then I better work – so I now have a part time job … the good point is that I have to take orders from the customers in English, so I can pick up the language and test my listening … the customer ordered … I couldn't understand so I kept saying, "Pardon, pardon me." Finally the customer felt annoyed, "How come this waiter can't take the order?" At that time I lost my confidence to talk.

To make extended observations the student-as-fieldworker participated by being 'adopted' by locals, learning their culture and language, thereby creating a home away from home. A job as a door-to-door salesperson gave Riu range of learning experiences:

> I found this job so I can practice my English. It's very good. ... I make friends locally, talk to them, and share ideas. I actually see that this is really a multicultural country, people are from all over that come here.

The students' work in the field involved more than the work of observing. For instance, the fieldworker might learn that any sense of being a nuisance to the locals may be mitigated by practices of reciprocity. Part-time work for Jiang created opportunities to make friends and learn about and from Greek- and Indian-Australians. Similarly, Xianlong worked for, and learnt from a Jewish-Australian family who owned a retail jewellery business. Due to Australia's multilingualism, Liu and Jun were able to teach in community language schools, working with children and adults. In providing childcare for three children, Jianguo learnt more than she anticipated about Anglo-ethnicity when she took this job which first she saw as:

> an opportunity to learn English. But then I feel a little bit strange with their version of family life. I thought that being Australian, the man and woman would be very equal. But in their family the wife didn't work, instead the husband works to supports the whole family.

These transnational students lived full-time in a global village, sharing the life of those with whom they studied, and those who were under study. They used part-time work to enable them to conduct serious, relatively unobtrusive, and almost panoptic participant-observations (Clifford 1997: 20-22). The students regarded their diversity of work experience in Australia as very important for their future career prospects. However, for these students to grow and develop in multicultural competence they are likely to benefit from inter-ethnic work/language learning experiences that are structurally facilitated by universities.

Pedagogical Reworkings of Ethnographic Fieldwork

Most Australian universities are the products of the power and history of White Australia politics, being limited to nation-building institutions rooted in specific metropolitan or rural centres. These universities are now promoting various transnational experiential teaching/learning practices ranging from study abroad, student exchanges, international internships and overseas field studies. Ideally, such practices provide deep, extended and interactive teaching/learning encounters. However, there is wide variation in criteria and actual experiences governing the length of engagement, the mode of interaction, opportunities for repetition at deeper levels, and grasp of languages. For education policy actors the question is how might these experiences and knowledge gained by transnational experiences be reconstituted as public knowledge of educational benefit to all?

Transnational student mobility and the industries that it sustains, do not point universities in one historically predetermined direction. Responding to student mobility creates opportunities for innovative approaches to education policies, pedagogies and politics. Innovative forms of multi-local, multi-centred education policies, pedagogies and politics now seem necessary to do justice to the global-national-local political, economic and cultural forces that traverse and constitute not just universities through their many transnational students, but also nation-states. The purpose of enabling transnational learning communities is to provide education policies, pedagogies and political strategies that "accommodate ex-centric residents and travelling culture-makers" (Clifford 1997: 25).

Despite the problems incited by economic reductionism, Australian universities are still sites where academics engage in bringing forward and remaking worthwhile educational traditions. In the face of corporate managerialist resistance, academics are gleaning what they might salvage from a multiplicity of good educational practices, rearticulating them for the changes wrought by contemporary globalization (Pratt & Poole 1999, Reid 1996). There is no pure stance that is possible or desirable in the face of either the dominating neo-liberal ideological project or the resistance and resentment manifested in regressive, parochial politics. At the very least, enabling transnational learning communities could represent a renewal and re-articulation of the responsiveness and responsibility of education to engage the imperatives of these changing times.

Changing Fields, Changing Workers

Historically, ethnographic fieldwork practices of making and unmaking mono-cultural meanings were framed by Euro-American colonialism, but since 1945 contests against continuing imperialisms have contributed to "decolonization" (Clifford 1997: 3). Ethnographic fieldwork has been criticized because of its colonialist history and its positivist legacy that defined the 'field' as a 'laboratory' wherein privileged Euro-American males made their 'discoveries'. Anti-colonialist struggles, postcolonial discourse analysis and critical anti-racist theories/practices have de-centred, but not marginalized, the dominating constructions of ethnographic fieldwork which were the privileged work of White, Euro-American men (Clifford 1997: 63-69).

Following Hooks (1992: 338) we can observe that there is no official body of non-European-Australians whose central ethnographic project is to study the power of Anglo-ethnicity and White Australia politics. However, some non-Europeans present in Australia do develop a collective, but largely unwritten, knowledge of these matters. As the transnational students' interviews above indicate, this is because such knowledge is necessary for them to extend and deepen their transnational trajectory. More than this, such knowledge remains an important source of lessons and insights for all students studying in Australian universities into contemporary practices of globalization. As argued below, there is work to be done to reinvent ethnographic fieldwork as a practice for enabling transnational learning communities to speak to the disjointed and uneven transitions in contemporary globalization. Currently, ethnographic fieldwork is predicated on in-depth Euro-American interactions with racialized difference. The reworking of ethnographic fieldwork is necessary for innovative knowledge-producing pedagogies to be generated as part of the work of realigning education policies, pedagogies and politics to push through the limitations of neo-liberal globalism. This would necessarily include developing collective ethnographies of the lived knowledges of non-European Australians.

Inherent in the work of re-inventing ethnographic practices that enables transnational learning communities is the pedagogical engagement of all students as media of global/national/local connectedness. Pedagogically, this involves the shift in focus (i.e. power) from the ways in which Anglo-ethnics perceive the non-European presence, to actively expressing interest in explicit representations of Anglo-ethnicity in the non-European imagination. While Clifford (1997) is optimistic about shaking off the colonial legacy of ethnography, there are difficulties concerning the subject position of Anglo-Australian students. Even though White Australia politics may not have the apparent legal or ideological force in Australia it once had, and this is debatable, the political habits for cultivating, upholding and maintaining it linger. When listening to the observations gleaned from the study of Anglo-ethnics by non-Europeans, how might Anglo-ethnic students react? Addressing a similar question in the USA, Hooks (1992: 339-440) found:

> Usually, white students respond with naïve amazement that black people critically assess white people from a standpoint where 'whiteness' is the privileged signifier. Their amazement that black people watch white people with a critical 'ethnographic' gaze, is itself an expression of racism. ... Many of them are shocked that black people think critically about whiteness because racist thinking perpetuates the fantasy of the Other who is subjugated, who is subhuman, lacks the ability to comprehend, to understand, to see the working of the powerful.

This shift in focus (i.e. power) to representations of Anglo-ethnicity in the non-European imagination, challenges Anglo-ethnic desires to assert control over the gaze of non-Europeans. It also suggests that their imagined invisibility to non-Europeans is no longer safe; learning to relinquish this security blanket is a challenge. Moreover, enabling transnational learning communities implies that Anglo-ethnics are aided in bringing to an end their imaginings that there are no representations of Anglo-ethnicity or White Australia politics in the imagination of non-European students other than how they prefer to appear. Consider for a moment the likely challenges to their identity such knowledge could pose. Writing in the early 1990s, Hooks (1992: 341) discussed the Black American representations of "whiteness as terrorizing," as being a response that emerged from:

the traumatic pain and anguish that remains a consequence of white racist domination ... black folks associated whiteness with the terrible, the terrifying, the terrorizing. White people were regarded as terrorists ... They terrorized by economic exploitation. ...Their presence terrified me ... they looked too much like the unofficial white men who came to enact rituals of terror and torture. ... To name that whiteness in the black imagination is often a representation of terror.

A renewed pedagogy of quasi-ethnographic fieldwork that enables transnational learning communities could generate such powerful and thought-provoking insights as those offered by Bell Hooks in the early 1990s. It is possible that the transnational student presence in Australian higher education might even help in efforts to re-invent ethnographic fieldwork, freeing it from at least some of its "history of European, literary, male, bourgeois, scientific, heroic, recreational meanings and practices" (Clifford 1997: 33). Despite an ambiguous inheritance, pedagogies of quasi-ethnographic fieldwork might be reworked along the lines indicated below so as to be useful in enabling transnational learning communities that give form and substance to a new generation of trans-national workers/employer, global/national citizens and worldly learners.

Pedagogies of Quasi-ethnographic Fieldwork

Ethnographic fieldwork is being or could be reworked in a number of ways. First, pedagogically, ethnographic fieldwork is no longer the exclusive or privileged method of White, Euro-American men. Now, the Other is coming to study Europeans, Americans and Australians (Clifford 1997: 29, 52-53, 60). The global political eco-nomy, and especially the market in international higher education, is creating pres-sures and opportunities for renewing fieldwork. What is proposed here is that the internationalization of higher education might be used to create opportunities for students-as-fieldworkers to turn to Europe, North America or Australia as a field to study (multi)cultural, economic and socio-political globalization, using the diverse relational approaches of ethnographic and historical investigation. Here it is important to be mindful that some transnational students, both local and international, could have ancestors who were once more likely the object of ethnographic fieldwork. With the internationalization of higher education, the range of possible venues for fieldwork has expanded dramatically. The geopolitical location for fieldwork has been challenged, and is no longer secured solely by the Euro-American interests. The borders defining both the 'field' and the 'worker' are destabilized and made the subject of renegotiations as a result of the global mobility of transnational students. Who are the insiders and outsiders in the global economy? Who feels at home or in a foreign place when confronted with the cosmopolitanism of cultural globalization? These boundaries are being challenged by transnational student mobility. The contemporary lack of clarity concerning what now counts as ethnographic fieldwork opens up a range of spatial practices for innovative academics. Fieldwork is no longer a matter of a White, Western European:

> (worldly) traveler visiting (local) natives, departing from a metropolitan center to study in a rural periphery. Instead, [the fieldworker's] site opens onto complex histories of dwelling and traveling, cosmopolitan experiences (Clifford 1997: 2).

Such teaching/learning experiences may lead to new knowledge being produced for the benefit of the rising generation.

Second, the balance of power has, or is shifting the "worker" and the "field" (Clifford 1997: 41). Pedagogically the focus is on the ethical questions of rapport and reciprocity. For instance, to undertake ethnographic fieldwork among Indigenous communities now, the ethical question "What's in it for us?" puts reciprocity on the agenda from the very start. Thus, expectations regarding reciprocity are raised by students-as-fieldworkers producing knowledge about globalization. This is because enabling transnational learning communities is a both-ways educational practice involving the use and collaborative production of knowledge. The practice of reciprocity may take various forms such as providing opportunities for work experience in revitalizing linguistic diversity through bringing languages forward or contributing to a history project exploring changing global/national/local interconnectedness. Questions of ownership that were once elided in ethnographic fieldwork or subsumed under the patrimony of making a contribution to Euro-American knowledge would be the subject of explicit curriculum negotiations. Pedagogies of ethnographic fieldwork shift the focus/power from developing rapport to making explicit ethical concerns involved in negotiating transnational learning communities.

Third, co-residence for extended periods has had considerable authority in defining ethnographic fieldwork (Clifford 1997: 55-60). The length of stay by mobile transnational students, and the depth and intensity of the interactions between transnationally mobile and immobile students are changing. With developments in high-speed communication and transport, fieldwork as an instance of a situated transnational learning community may involve extended dwelling as much as repeated visits to engage in collaborative work. Increasing transnational mobility means that the time in the 'field' (in both the disciplinary and spatial sense) is short irrespective of whether the fieldwork involves localized dwelling for an extended period or a series of encounters. Sometimes this leads to an Australian Permanent Residence Visa and thus the opportunity to travel and work more broadly than on their original passport.

Fourth, the ethnographic quest for a theoretical framework that grasps the complex realities of any given field or site has proven elusive (Clifford 1997: 48-49). The quest for a single, all-encompassing theoretical framework resulted in fieldworkers feeling trapped by the difficulties of their interpretive task given the complexities of customs and their environments. Pedagogically, we not only expect our analytical concepts to crumble but we are interested in just how far they can be taken before doing so. Then our interest turns to what has overwhelmed these conceptual tools, what was left out of our overly neat formulas and what is the basis of their incompatibility with other interpretative schema, if any. No longer being able to clutch at conceptual keys like 'culture' as if it is a single thing, the student-as-fieldworker wrestles with her/his role as theorist/knowledge producer of multicultural, socio-political and economic globalization. Fieldwork then helps students to learn just enough to know what vast empirical and conceptual levels remain to be produced. However, without some theoretical scaffold to map the interacting, multi-level patterns in the data, and the interpenetration of the local by the national and global, any hope of deepening our knowledge and generating alternative understanding escapes.

Fifth, the power relations of ethnographic fieldwork are being reconfigured as ever-advancing technologies are being deployed (Clifford 1997: 58). Pedagogically, these new technologies may broaden the range of people engaged in the co-production of knowledge and extend students' access to funds of community knowledges. A disembodied fieldwork is made possible by digital communications technologies, providing opportunities for participant observation of extended (multilingual) communities of knowledge on-line. This means transnational students do not necessarily have to leave their first language/s at home. Notions of travel, boundary, co-residence, interaction, inside and outside that have defined the field and the worker may be challenged as they are reworked through innovative knowledge producing pedagogies using new technologies of information sharing and on-line emotional support. To minimize the dangers of reproducing the inherited boundaries of previous eras of globalization, pedagogies of ethnographic fieldwork could be used to document those dimensions that have been historically erased or marginalized. This involves group-based multidisciplinary projects investigating the social forms of life upon which transnational learning communities depend. These include the technological means of transport and communication; the city and its global/national/ local connectedness; weak (parochial) and strong (global/national/local) senses of home among students; the sites of linguistic interpretation; and the relations of multicultural translation.

Challenges that Extend the Students' Cosmopolitan Outlook

The neo-liberal university offers an image of the world market in education as one of transnational student mobility. However, student travel is not new but has long-established and complex histories. For some of these students from China, their friends or relatives moved to Australia because of wars or in the quest for money and jobs. Others know that their forebears were denied the opportunity to do so, and so they stayed in China or moved elsewhere. This suggests the likelihood of greater continuities than discontinuities in the staging of an 'international student' identity as part of the trajectory in forming the new transnational worker, global/local citizen and worldly learner. For instance, Edward Said (1999) was educated in English schools in Palestine, Egypt and Lebanon. While he completed his secondary and tertiary education in the USA, it is most unlikely that he would have gained entry into White Australia in 1951, had that been his family's desire. Edward Said's autobiography suggests that the work of creating 'international students', of developing the skills required to become an 'international student' begins in their 'homeland'. British and Australian colonialism has also made this true for students in many countries throughout Asia. However, conceptualizing international student mobility in terms of 'travel' raises complex problems.

How were the students' cosmopolitan outlook extended and deepened as a result of their education in Australia? Three issues concerning agency and control are addressed below. A major challenge for these students was engaging with multi-cultural Australia's multiple racisms. The students were aware that the Asian presence in this country offends, perhaps unconsciously, some of those Anglo-Australians (and others) imbued with a deep sense of what the Australian Federation was created in 1901 to achieve in terms of race. The interviewees also reported that there is one group of students which has not made itself part of this comospolitanism, namely local Anglo-Australian students. Their accounts suggest the reasons for this, as much as the desirability of re-locating and re-aligning Anglo-Australian students within the transnational webs of social and economic relations created by global flows of international students.

Engaging Multiculturalism and Multiple Racisms

Travel is tainted by its historical "associations with gendered, racial bodies, class privilege, specific means of conveyance, beaten paths, agents, frontiers, documents, and the like" (Clifford 1997: 39). Perhaps not surprisingly then, as part of their international education, these transnational students had to engage with Australian multiculturalism and Australia's multiple racisms. Jun's experiences of a pleasant life in multicultural Australia were important to her education. For Ke Chen's life in "Australia is very good for the old people and for young kids but not very good for the young people. It's a good country but fairly slow." Denying the assertion of absolute cultural difference between China and Australia that finds expressions in White Australia politics, Yang saw possibilities for alliances and hoping for connections:

> I heard of Pauline Hanson, such a rude lady. ... Australia is a multicultural country ... it's democratic... everyone is equal but some are just want Australia to be a white country. I think One Nation and John Howard are in that group. It's upset me. When I call my family, my mother and father they say, "It is okay because we have heard from the local newspaper that they said it's okay. It's still in the upper level of society, so it hasn't not deepened onto you." But I can still feel it in some people's eyes, their posture and language.

The topographies of White Australia politics are systematically gendered, involving powerful female symbols, the institutionalized staging of the masculine self and the marginalized representation of the racialized, sexualized other. The struggles between different interests within and across nations were hinted at by Xin:

> On China's TV they reported that many people in Australia are friendly to Asian people. I saw that as well. So I think that those people here who don't like Asians are not the majority.

Patriarchal, orientalist educational experiences intertwine roots and routes. Wu wondered about the limitations in the global education, in the Asia-literacy of Anglo-Australians adrift amidst multicultural experiences:

> Some Australians ask me if men in China still have pigtails. I felt very uncomfortable because we have done without that for over one hundred years but they still don't know. I can't understand that ... They are not very much aware of what's happening outside. I wish they could understand. Even for my lecturers who have been to Malaysia, China and Japan many times, there are still some misunderstandings.

The desire by Liu to make links between people was interrupted by conditions that undermine this possibility:

> When I was driving another man began to shout at me, "Asian man, do you want to fight with me?" He held up his fists to me and said some dirty words. I just said, "That man was crazy. Ignore him." It was very bad. But that's a very rare event.

Women "have their own histories of labour migration, pilgrimage, emigration, exploration, tourism and military travel, histories that are linked with and distinct from those of men" (Clifford 1997: 5-6). White, Western European bourgeois women travellers are marked as special in the dominating discourse of international travel. Rejecting sentimentality in assessing parochialism, Xianlong saw a need for this to be transcended:

> Some people's attitudes are really not nice to Asians. They say, "Why do those foreigners come to my country, stay here and do nothing?" ... If you want a job, you have to work hard. ... Australia is an immigration country so you need immigrants to come here.

In terms of safety the gender and race of the traveller in foreign lands is a significant consideration. Women who travel are frequently coerced to conform to normative male definitions of their experiences, or masquerade as a male, or discreetly rebel, albeit within masculine limits. The very different travel histories of women include forced sex and indentured labour. International travel is associated with heroic, educational, scientific, adventurous, noble men, whereas women are typically (but not always) situated as male companions.

Universities as Zones of Isolationism

Travellers tend to ascribe their experience to a degree of autonomy and cosmopolitanness, and downplay forms of movement that involve the forced mobility of labour (Clifford 1997: 34-35). A traveller is thought to be someone who has the security and privilege to move about in relatively unconstrained ways through unfamiliar places. *His.* more often than *her* movement is frequently represented as a matter of bourgeois independence and individualism. This travel myth emphasizes individual agency over structures of control. Their role in ensuring transnational student comfort and safety is neglected; perhaps this is because of their race or class. However, for those entering Australia at least since 1901 the agency of travellers and the structuring of their travels has been

> powerfully inflected by three connected global forces: the continuing legacies of empire, the effects of unprecedented world wars, and the global consequences of industrial capitalism's disruptive, restructuring activity (Clifford 1997: 6-7).

The political and economic pressures that control the flows of transnational students from China and elsewhere into Australia pull very strongly against an overly romantic view of their mobility. Success in the globalization of teaching and learning for Ying meant coming to know others:

> Australian students don't want to make friends with Asian students. ... I don't know why. I hoped we could be happy together and share our cultures but I really don't know how we can do that.

Most transnational students move along and within highly determined circuits. Transnational students are located along quite specific routes that are structured, if not dictated by political, economic, intercultural and global/local relations of colonialism, neo-colonialism or post-colonialism. For Keifung, globalizing teaching and learning were not matters of facilitating mechanical contact between local and international students: "Because they think we can't speak English very well, they seem to think we're idiots." That the educational formation of global/national/local citizens does not work on a blank slate was understood by Xianlong: "they are not willing to talk to me. ... It takes some effort. ... They are afraid. They don't look friendly. Maybe they are friendly but they don't look friendly." Sensing some inability among local students to create themselves as global/local citizens Ming said:

> I can't make any friends with Aussies. ... It's very hard for me. ... When I first came here my friends in China said, "You will make a lot of Aussie friends."

But it's hard. I don't enjoy the things that the Aussies do ... they go to the footy. I am not keen on that.

Ming went on to imply that the day-to-day pressures in their lives outweigh any desire they might have for building transnational relations: "I think most of the Australians are very self-protected. ... They don't want to get involved with international students because they have their own life." In considering the reasons for local students' isolation, Che implies our own self-interests must be transcended to engage the interests of others: "My colleagues from the lab are very kind but sometimes when they laugh, I don't know why they laugh. They talk about some movies or TV programs which I don't know." The desirability of creating new narratives which local and international students can share was suggested by Che: "It's alright to build relationships with them but sometimes it's difficult. I can't share the same stories with them. Some things they know, I don't." It is usual for transnational students to be assisted by companions, translators, agents, interpreters, suppliers and guides. It was difficult for Xianlong to understand how local students see the world, because of the structuring of Australian university life:

It's really hard to make friends. In China we make friends in the university because we all study and live together on campus ... Here we meet people in one class but we're not often in the same class again ... Aussie students ... make me feel that they don't want to talk to me.

Most often these people are excluded from accounts of university efforts to internationalize education. Yan implied that Anglo-Australians may be surpassed in knowledge of the changing multicultural, multilingual world that is now important to the collective success of Australia, because the imperative to self-fund the increasing costs of higher education:

In the University I feel the Asian students and the local students don't really talk a lot. ... Maybe its because most of the local students are working people or because we don't really have lots in common.

An earlier image of universities suggests a form of gentlemanly travel, during an era "when home and abroad, city and country, East and West, metropole and antipodes, were more closely fixed" (Clifford 1997: 31). Is it complacency or the intensification of work that causes the isolationism of Anglo-Australians that Yuan observed?

In China you are in the same class all the time. In Australia you are always changing your classes. ... Many local Australians are also studying or working part time. ... I got to know this local student, and then our study or work changed again and we did not meet each other again.

'Bridge building' attributes are now required of graduates to enable them to carve out spaces as mediators of economic and cultural globalization. According to Jing, transnational students are already expanding their learning in this regard, but it is not apparent that local students are doing likewise: "We don't have many Australian classmates ... they are all working, so they come to study and don't talk to you at all. ... It's quite easy to make friends with international students." Thus while universities have complex histories of travelling cultures and cultures of travel, applying the 'travel' metaphor to Anglo-Australian students is problematic because of its marked association with the privileges of class, gender, race, socio-cultural location and historical formation. How and whether this problem will be addressed remains an open question.

Mono-lingualism as a Barrier to the Transnational Labour Market

The movement of these transnational students from China is not necessarily centred on a return to their homeland. Their movement depends on how and where politics and economics generate opportunities for their life trajectories. In contrast, there is the possibility that local students' investment in English monolingualism may work to structure their marginalization in the transnational labour market. Su suggests that English may subvert the possibility of Anglo-Australian students having a key role as 'bridge builders' between China and Australia: "I was afraid to communicate with the Australians because they speak very fast. ... I don't know how to expand. They seem to rush time. ... It's very shameful to ask them to say it again." This leaves open the question of how Anglo-Australians will develop a transnational identity grounded in a knowledge and understanding of other cultures and languages.

The difficult conditions of students' cross-border mobility, which include Australia's immigration regime and a reticent government, have not quelled the deepening and extension of their transnational formation. Former fee-paying trans-national students must negotiate a flexible identity, becoming Australian permanent residents while working in China. The lack of comparable skills among Anglo-Australian students caused Ming concerns, as instanced by her comments on turn-taking in conversations:

> We need to learn that you have to express yourself. ... When I first came here I didn't speak much and just kept quiet. I think that's a reason why I can't make any Aussie friends. ... Aussies, they talk too fast, especially women. ... I don't have a chance to say anything and they talk about another topic. When I want to say something, I am already too slow.

Transnational students might reasonably expect to find that their overseas qualifications, including their work experience, will enhance their competition for a place among the materially privileged. Some do not imagine they will be so lucky. Anglo-Australians students have not, according to Ting, learnt or been taught to move beyond parochial, monolingual contexts: "When I talk to a person, they soon become not patient because I cannot express myself very fast." Even though migration and employment are crucial determinants of transnational students' mobility, Zhou was not able to observe these traits among the local students:

> The local students have rare communication with the international students. Some of them are nice. … In class the Australians are "there" and the international students are "over there" … There is rarely any communication between local and international students.

For Ying, efforts to rebind education with the changing global economy, involves small but nonetheless significant acts of re-creation: "We don't have a lot of topics to talk about with the English people." Together these concerns raise an interesting question. What if we were to regard transnational student travel as field-work, an opportunity for innovative teaching/learning oriented to formation of the rising generation of trans-national workers, learners and citizens? What would it mean for identity of those driving the revivification of White Australia politics to learn about transnational mobility from non-Europeans?

Working Self-critically with Compromised Policies, Pedagogies and Politics

There are no neutral, uncontaminated educational policies, pedagogies and politics for discussing these students' account of how the internationalization of higher education contributes to their engagement in transnational learning communities. Many of the seemingly relevant educational policies, pedagogies and politics have the inextinguishable taint of colonialism, racism, class and gender. We cannot presuppose that educational policies, pedagogies and politics that promote 'travel,' 'boundary crossing,' or 'contact' have self-evident, uncontested virtues. This is not in the least because Australian universities now include a range of European and non-European presences. What is communicated about the internationalization of higher education using these educational policies, pedagogies and politics depends upon their meanings, which have to be "actively produced, negotiated, and renegotiated" as a result of changing historical relations of power (Clifford 1997: 64).

In contrast to Clifford (1997), Tomlinson (1999: 29) argues that it is tendentious to insist that travel is the defining feature of contemporary globalization, because "a huge proportion of cultural experience is still for the majority the day-to-day experience of physical location, rather than constant movement." While travel is a pervasive feature of transnational students' experiences it is shaped, if not decisively determined, by the cultural, political and economic structures of globalization/ localization. The vast majority of the world's people are "kept in their place" by their class and gender positioning. This is made evident in the daily repression of asylum seekers from the majority world that is leading to the systematization of "global apartheid" (Falk 1999) by the minority world. Tomlinson (1999: 29) argues that while contemporary globalization promotes the restless movement of people, the key cultural impact of this mobility "is in the transformation of localities themselves." The ties of universities to their immediate locality are transformed through complex transnational connectivities. This involves the simultaneous penetration of the local casual labour market by transnational students and the dislodging of existing pedagogies of meaning making, such as group-based multidisciplinary projects, from their local anchorages to become vehicles for students to rehearse and imagine transnational learning communities based on networks of business and friendship created through inter-ethnic, knowledge producing projects.

Transnational student travel involves complex practices of border crossing. Their presence troubles linguistic as well as racial, class and gender interactions, interrupting assumptions about the authenticity of cultures or the commonality of transnational student existence. Rather than simply transferring or extending the experience of being a 'student,' practices of displacement are also constitutive of what it means to be a 'transnational student'. Gender, ethnicity and class are integral to the analysis of the freedoms and dangers inherent in transnational student movement. Male and female students dwelling and travelling reflect and give expression to gender specific, culturally mediated experiences. We need to know a great deal more about how women students travel, why some ethnic groups may elect to limit their mobility, and why many more are kept 'in their place' by forces of economic oppression or political repression.

Boundary Crossing

Boundaries are structured by historical relations of dominance and submission. As well as being places of hybridity, boundaries are places of struggle and transgression, and sites of regulated and subversive crossings. The existence of boundaries pre-supposes politically defined lines that arbitrarily separate and police practices of crossing and communication (Clifford 1997: 246). Because boundary crossings can lead to disputes, conflicts and even wars, they do not occur without policing. Many die along boundaries from exhaustion, fear or the draining of the will to envision life on the other side. The negotiation of boundary crossings is never 'free.' Boundaries are routinely reasserted, often in non-negotiable ways. Perceptions of borders are also necessary to make efforts at alliance formation. As noted above, monolingual English may function as an anti-market, boundary-policing mechanism for Anglophone students, who want to participate in transnational learning communities and the world's multilingual knowledge economies. There are, however, several powerful currents undermining, but not totally destroying, the integrity of claims that transnational student movement represents an end to the boundaries of many nation-states.

First, agents of neo-liberal globalism make use of 'boundaries' to create new political visions that reproduce a sense of their own power. Positioning themselves as subversives deconstructing binaries between one education market and another, they project possibilities for a new boundary-less sphere in which their hegemony will prevail. This is so despite university boundaries being routinely blocked by budgets and other institutionalized control mechanisms as much as the hostility of the new generation of corporate managers as they misunderstand efforts by academics to enable transnational learning communities. The latter arise, in part, because boundary "crossings are so promiscuous and overlaps so frequent that actions to reassert identity are mounted at strategic sites and moments" (Clifford 1997: 63). University restructuring is a mechanism frequently used to assert corporate managerial control over promiscuous boundary crossings within and beyond universities.

Second, the growing international character of Australian universities is evident in their press to organize markets throughout Asia and beyond. National boundaries around Australia's public universities are being torn down in order to consolidate globally oriented markets. However, because the globalization of Australian universities works both with and against national attachments, it is premature to decree either the end or the consolidation of Australia as a nation-state:

> The world (dis)order does not ... clearly prefigure a post-national world. Contemporary capitalism works flexibly, unevenly, both to reinforce and to erase national hegemonies. ... The global political economy advances, sometimes reinforcing, sometimes obliterating cultural, regional, and religious differences, gendered and ethnic divisions. ... Recurring announcements of the obsolescence of nation-states in a brave new world of free trade or transnational culture are clearly premature. But at the same time ... the stability of national units is far from assured. The imagined communities called 'nations' require constant, often violent, maintenance. Moreover, in a world of migrations and TV satellites, the policing of frontiers and collective essences can never be absolute, or for long. Nationalism articulates their purportedly homogeneous times and spaces selectively, in relation to transnational flows and cultural forms, both dominant and subaltern. The diasporic and hybrid identities produced by these movements can be both restrictive and liberating. They stitch together languages, traditions, and places in coercive and creative ways, articulating embattled homelands, powers of memory and styles of transgression, in ambiguous relation to national and transnational structures (Clifford 1997: 9-10).

Third, migration is another related challenge to efforts by universities to dissolve the racialized boundaries through which the Australian nation-state was created in 1901. Changes in the political economy of Australian universities are pushing and pulling students and staff in various directions. The Asianization of Australian universities is a sign of their uneven, non-linear integration into and appropriation of a globalizing education industry. In this process, transnational students are not mute or passive objects blown by the globalizing political and economic interests of the Australian nation-state or its universities. The expanding Asian student presence makes a difference to Australian university communities. The boundaries of nation-states are being complicated by those students who secure an Australian

Permanent Residence Visa and secure employment overseas, often in their former homeland, quite unlike the migrant labour of the 1950s.

There is, however, a fourth important boundary at issue within Australian universities that is social rather than geographic. The social distances that local Anglo-ethnic students establish to isolate themselves from transnational students are linguistic, historical and political products. Australian universities intent on aligning their curricula with the global economy are keen to find pedagogical means for enhancing the interactions among students across these socio-political and historical boundaries. There are important questions to be considered. How is a university a site of travel that makes all students transnational? How might Anglo-ethnic students be explicitly taught to negotiate productive relationships with transnational students? How are local spaces traversed from outside? To what extent is one group's 'core' another group's 'periphery'? While there may be guarded optimism about such trans-boundary teaching/learning:

> there is no reason to assume that crossover practices are always liberatory or that articulating an autonomous identity or a national culture is always reactionary. ... What matters politically is who deploys nationality or transnationality, authenticity or hybridity, against whom, with what relative power and ability to sustain a hegemony (Clifford 1997: 10).

For reformists such as Clifford (1997: 204), boundaries can be democratically negotiated. However, crossover pedagogies are neither necessarily emancipatory nor inherently regressive. The question is who uses these both-ways pedagogies, for or against whom, and who has the relative power to win in the struggle for hegemony.

Universities as Zones of Positive and Negative Contacts

Universities do not exist as a socio-cultural whole. Thus, it is not a matter of bringing a unified Anglo-ethnic student population into contact with another totally distinct socio-cultural whole, say 'Chinese students.' Rather, Australian universities are zones of multiple, contested and contradictory contacts, both positive and negative. Many have already been constituted relationally, for instance via the disputed and displaced history of the Colombo Plan in Asia and Africa. All continue to enter new enterprise relations. As these interviewees indicate, Australian universities are now, more than ever before, zones of multiple contacts that involve blockages and policing as much as permits and transgression.

The use of the term 'contact zone' to describe the internationalization of Australian universities stands in marked contrast to the notion of 'frontier' that is grounded in the European imperial expansionist perspective. 'Frontier' assumes the existence of a centre as a gathering point and a periphery that is the focus of discovery. However, the term 'contact zone' is not without problems. The idea of a 'contact zone' suggests a space of continuing historical encounters:

in which peoples geographically and historically separated come into contact with each other and establish ongoing relations, usually involving conditions of coercion, radical inequality, and intractable conflict. [The idea of 'contact zone'] invokes the spatial and temporal copresence ... [where] trajectories now intersect [and] foregrounds the interactive, improvisational dimensions of colonial encounters ... [where] subjects are constituted in and by their relations to each other. It stresses copresence, interaction, interlocking understandings and practices, often within radically asymmetrical relations of power (Pratt, cited in Clifford 1997: 192).

Australian universities, which under White Australia politics were historically separated from rather than integrated into Asia, have now come into increasing contacts with non-European students seeking to establish ongoing relations. Given the colonialist and post-colonialist encounters, these zones of multiple contacts involve coercion, inequality and conflict grounded in asymmetrical power relations.

As sites of multicultural performances, Australian universities are traversed by a diversity of students—local and international, bilingual and monolingual, majority and minority world alike. The global/national/local determinations of Australian universities drive them to work through as much as against cultural, social, economic, political and linguistic differences. Those urban universities that are tied into international transport and communication networks act as a point of connectivity and a setting for student encounters as well as sites of trans-cultural knowledge production. Those universities that frame interactions among students who to varying degrees are away from home, are challenged to develop the multicultural imagination needed to seriously rethink themselves as sites of both dwelling and travel. They are sites of hybridized trans-cultural encounters that provide the basis for the serious knowledge production that requires deep learning along with critical and creative thinking. The university is a site of ethno-cultural difference, multilingual diversity and the debates necessary to form transnational communities. It also has a shared social, spatial and historical context that "directly challenges the way these different but related peoples [are] identified" (Clifford 1997: 132).

In terms of aligning their curricula with the global economy, culture and politics this could suggest actively and explicitly displacing the thinking associated with White Australia politics by giving expression to some form of cosmopolitan multiculture (Singh 1998: 12-17). Such an educational project could trouble established controls in Australian universities that reserve the centre for Anglo-Australians and the margins for Others. Curriculum innovation by academics faces corporate managerial resistance. This is especially evident in their efforts to use ever advancing technologies as platforms for 'reusable learning objects' in order to maintain the boundary between teacher-proof knowledge reproduction and teaching-as-knowledge generation. Tactically, such multicultural actions by academics might involve:

the making and remaking of identities, [which] takes place in the contact zones, along policies and transgressive intercultural frontiers of nations, peoples, locales. [It is to be expected that] stasis and purity are asserted—creatively and violently—against historical forces of movement and contamination (Clifford 1997: 7).

Australian universities might be regarded as sites of dwelling and travelling. This creates intersecting histories of students from different places with different economic and cultural politics. Understood metaphorically in this sense, Australian universities might be taken as powerful sites of worldly knowledge production and agents in the formation of the 'new' transnational worker, global/national citizen and worldly learner. Travel, boundary crossing and contact arising out of a heterogeneous student population are important to the on-going work of Australian universities seeking to align their curricula with the global economy. Even as academics necessarily respond to and engage with neo-liberal agendas for the internationalization of higher education, the pedagogical reworking of ethnographic fieldwork suggests that there remain possibilities for innovations in education policies, pedagogies and politics.

Conclusion

Universities around the world are being de-structured in response to and as a means of engaging with neo-liberal globalism. The ideological project, the marketization of higher education internationally, frames the academic work of making innovations in educational policies, pedagogies and politics. This chapter pointed to a range of historically encumbered ethnographic practices from which might be derived work points for innovative curriculum practices. This chapter suggested that it is important to work critically with compromised education policies, pedagogies and politics in order to remake them useful in our own field of endeavour. By implication this also suggests the possibility of working critically with tools of neo-liberal globalism for they too have to be questioned, and being innovative in the meanings we make of them.

What then do the main issues canvassed in this chapter suggest for possible university action? The following idea might be worth considering and elaborating in many different directions. University funds might be re-directed to a teaching/research program that took as its charter to deliberately create pedagogies for enabling transnational learning communities. This would be a teaching/research program for students wanting to be part of the transnational labour markets as much as global/ national citizens and worldly learners. This program, operating across multiple disciplines could explore the innovative possibilities for education policy, pedagogy and politics presented by a responsive and responsible engagement with the internationalization of higher education. Perhaps the open-ended critical reworking of ideas about universities as contact zones, students as part of the transnational labour force, and inter-ethnic boundary crossing could provide the conceptual basis for generating the rationale for such a teaching/research program. Such an innovative teaching/research program could serve the university's vision of internationalizing higher education by contributing to the generation of a multiplicity of publicly available interpretations of its best aspirations. Whatever we choose, we necessarily have to work self-critically with compromised and historically encumbered education policies, pedagogies and politics.

Acknowledgement

This chapter has been produced as part of a research project funded by the Australian Research Council. Appreciation is expressed to Fazal Rizvi for critical feedback on an earlier draft of this chapter. I am grateful to Linda and Benjamin for their time during which this research project was undertaken.

References

Appadurai, A. 1996. *Modernity at Large: Cultural Dimensions of Globalisation*. Minneapolis: University of Minnesota Press.

Apple, M. 2000. "Between Neoliberalism and Neoconservatism: Education and Conservatism in a Global Context." in *Globalization and Education*, edited by N. Burbules & C. Torres. New York: Routledge.

Ballard, B. & Clancy, J. 1997. *Teaching International Students: A Brief Guide for Lecturers and Supervisors*. Deakin (ACT): IDP Education Australia.

Bradley, D. & Bradley, M. 1984. *Problems of Asian Students in Australia: Language, Culture and Education*. Canberra: Australian Government Publishing Services.

Caruana, A., Ramaseshan, B. & Ewing, M. 1998. "Do Universities that are More Market Orientated Perform Better?" *The International Journal of Public Sector Management* 11(1): 55-70.

Cleverley, J. & Jones, P. 1976. *Australia and International Education: Some Critical Issues*. Hawthorn (Vic.): Australian Council for Educational Research.

Clifford, J. 1997. *Routes: Travel and Translation in the Late Twentieth Century*. Cambridge, MA: Harvard University Press.

Dobson, I. & Holtta, S. 2001. "The Internationalisation of University Education: Australia and Finland Compared." *Tertiary Education and Management* 7(3): 243-254.

Falk, R. 1999. *Predatory Globalization*. Cambridge: Polity Press

Gatfield, T., Barker, M. & Graham, P. 1999. "Measuring Communications Impact for University Advertising Materials." *Communications* 4(2): 73-79.

Hooks, B. 1992. "Representing Whiteness in the Black Imagination." in *Cultural Studies,* edited by L. Grossberg, C. Nelson and P. Treichler. New York: Routledge.

Jolley, A. 1997. *Exporting Education to Asia*. Melbourne: Victoria University Press.

Kemp, S., Madden, G. & Simpson, M. 1998. "Emerging Australian Education Markets: A Discrete Choice Model of Taiwanese and Indonesian Student Intended Study Destination." *Education Economics* 6(2): 159-170.

Lafferty, G. & Fleming, J. 2000. The Restructuring of Academic Work in Australia: Power, Management and Gender." *British Journal of Sociology of Education* 21(2): 257-268.

Marginson, S. 2002. "The Phenomenal Rise of International Degrees Down Under." *Change* 34(3): 34-40.

Mazzarol, T., Choo, S. & Nair, V. 2001. *Australia and the Indian Postgraduate Science and Technology Market: Examining Why Indian Students Choose to Study in Countries Other Than Australia.* Canberra: Australian Education International (Department of Education, Training and Youth Affairs).

Mazzarol, T. & Hosie, P. 1996. "Exporting Australian Higher Education: Future Strategies in a Maturing Market." *Quality Assurance in Education* 4(1): 37-50.

Pratt, G. & Poole, D. 1999. "Globalisation and Australian Universities: Policies and Impacts." *The International Journal of Public Sector Management* 12(6): 533-544.

Reid, I. 1996. *Higher Education or Education for Hire?* Rockhampton, Queensland: Central Queensland University Press.

Robertson, R. 1992. *Globalization: Social Theory and Global Culture.* London: Sage.

Said, E. 1999. *Out of Place: A Memoir.* London: Granta.

Singh, M. 1998. "Globalism, Cultural Diversity and Tertiary Education." *Australian Universities' Review* 41(2): 12-17.

Singh, M. 2001. "The Admixture of Indigenous and Asian-Australians: Funds of Community Knowledge, Social Studies Education and the Dissolution of White Australia Politics." *Delta: Policy and Practice in Education* 52(1&2): 109-137.

Taylor, S. & Henry, M. 2000. "Globalization and Educational Policymaking: A Case Study." *Educational Theory* 50(4): 487-503.

Tomlinson, J. 1999. *Globalization and Culture.* Cambridge: Polity Press.

Watkins, D. & Biggs, J. eds. 1996. *The Chinese Learner: Cultural, Psychological and Contextual Influences.* Melbourne: The Australian Council for Educational Research and Hong Kong: Comparative Education Research Centre, The University of Hong Kong.

2

Knowledge in the Marketplace: The Global Commodification of Teaching and Learning in Higher Education

Rajani Naidoo and Ian Jamieson

Introduction

This chapter presents the commodification thesis as it applies to teaching and learning in higher education in the context of globalization, internationalization, and the knowledge economy. Research on higher education has traditionally veered between two approaches: on the one hand, theoretical frameworks which position universities as reflecting the configuration of forces in the socio-economic context; on the other hand, frameworks which detach universities analytically from the macro socio-political context in order to study their inner workings. Less attention has been paid to the *interaction* between macro forces such as those associated with globalization and the activities that occur within universities, including processes associated with internationalization. This chapter takes a step in this direction by examining the relationship between the 'macro' forces impacting on higher education and the 'micro' processes of learning and teaching in universities. It therefore begins by examining the extent to which contemporary ideological, structural and economic developments in higher education apply pressures on universities to commodify and internationalize the educational process. It then draws on the recent literature on teaching and learning to outline key features of effective education in order to assess the possible impact of commodification on student learning. One major approach to internationalization, virtual education, is selected as a site that is particularly vulnerable to forces of commodification. The chapter illustrates how the repositioning of virtual higher education as an international service operating mainly on the basis of economic considerations is inimical to high quality learning.

Forces Impacting on Teaching and Learning in Higher Education

Higher education in the context of globalization has been positioned as a crucial site for the production and international dissemination of economically productive knowledge, innovation and technology (Carnoy 1994). In relation to teaching and learning, there are growing pressures on universities across the world to equip greater proportions of the population with higher order skills that can be used productively in the knowledge economy. In relation to developing countries, powerful global regulators such as the World Bank formerly held the view that higher education offered lower individual and social returns than primary education. However, this view, which led to the systematic under-development of higher education, has changed. There is now widespread acknowledgement that quality higher education is essential for developing economies to escape a peripheral status in the world economy (see Task Force on Higher Education in Developing Countries 2000). In particular, in both developing and industrialized countries, there has been an increasing pressure on universities to impart to students the skills, knowledge and dispositions related to innovation and the ability to 'learn how to learn' in order to continuously upgrade their skills in tune with the demands of a changing global economy. Interestingly, these emerging expectations from government and industry resonate with more traditional understandings of high quality learning held by academics in general.

At the same time, changes associated with globalization and the knowledge economy have given rise to developments which apply pressures on universities to commodify teaching and learning and 'sell' it in the international educational market-place. A powerful ideological force linked to the rise of the New Right (see, for example, Brown & Lauder 2001) that has impacted on higher education in the present period is the expectation that public universities contribute in a relatively unmediated manner to economic productivity. According to this ideology, the performance of universities has become more central to economic success in a context where the strength of national economies is perceived to be dependent on high value goods and services, which are in turn dependent on sophisticated scientific and technological knowledge. The conception of higher education as a 'public good' has therefore become somewhat eclipsed by the redeployment of higher education as an industry for enhancing national competitiveness and as a lucrative service that can be sold in the international marketplace (Naidoo 2003a).

Structural changes have also applied pressures on universities to commodify education. There is a global trend away from forms of funding and regulation that were based on the 'social compact' that evolved between higher education, the state and society over the last century (Marginson & Considine 2000, Newotny, Gibbons & Scott 2001). For example, the belief that universities require relative independence from political and corporate influence to function optimally, which was in turn linked to the need for guaranteed state funding and professional autonomy, has been eroded. These developments, together with more general retractions in public policy away from frameworks based on Keynesian welfare state settlements, have resulted in the implementation of funding and regulatory frameworks which revolve around neo-liberal market mechanisms and new managerialist principles (Dill 1997, Deem 2001). Such frameworks are based on the assumption that the contemporary higher education system has become too large and complex for the state to sustain its position as sole regulator and funder, that market competition within and between universities will create more efficient and effective institutions and that management principles derived from the private sector which monitor, measure, compare and judge professional activities will enhance higher education functioning. There has, therefore, been a world-wide decline in state funding for research and teaching and the deployment of mechanisms such as league tables to exert pressure on universities to comply with market based regimes.

This has led to what Slaughter and Leslie (1997) have termed 'academic capitalism', which describes the 'marketization' of public higher education and the rise of research and development for commercial purposes. Higher education has also seen an influx of direct corporate involvement due to the relaxation of state regulation over the recognition of degree granting institutions (see Naidoo 2003b) and the increased potential for profit. Finally, the technological advances associated with globalization have given rise to virtual higher education. We will return to these themes in later sections. Our argument is that the forces unleashed on higher education in the present context have propelled universities to function less as institutions with social, cultural and indeed intellectual objectives and more as producers of commodities that can be sold in the international marketplace.

The Commodification of Higher Education

In order to understand the impact of pressures for commodification on universities, it is useful to turn to the work of Bourdieu (1996). According to Bourdieu, universities exist in a 'field' of higher education, which he characterizes as a conceptual space that is relatively autonomous and relatively insulated from the direct forces of political and economic pressures. Activities in higher education have traditionally revolved around the acquisition of assets invested with value in the field which he terms 'academic capital', and which are based on academic (rather than economic or political) criteria such as a contribution to knowledge, peer recognition and the intellectual development of students. The logic underlying activity in the field of higher education has therefore been historically shaped by deeply ingrained values and professional protocols which revolve around the competition for academic capital.

Forces for commodification impact on universities by altering the nature of rewards and sanctions operating in higher education and by reconceptualizing education as a commodity. Academic success therefore shifts from being measured according to academic principles to being measured according to narrow financial criteria such as the number of student customers captured and the degree of financial surplus created. Commodification in higher education can therefore be defined as the transforming of educational processes into a form that has an 'exchange' value, rather than an intrinsic 'use' value. Commodification also implies that education processes and knowledge can be 'captured' and 'packaged' in order to be bought or sold under market conditions across national boundaries and that this can be carried out independently of the producer. A related concept is that of 'commodity fetishism' which refers to the transformation of social relationships between people into relationships between things. So it is not merely knowledge that is packaged for sale but the educational relationship itself that is transformed into a relationship that is dependent on the market transaction of the commodity; the lecturer becomes the commodity 'producer' and the student becomes the commodity 'consumer'. In this way, the pedagogic relationship is disaggregated and each party is invested with distinct, if not opposing, interests (Naidoo & Jamieson 2002).

We turn now to an examination of the effects of commodification on the quality of student learning. We begin by outlining some of the essential characteristics of effective learning in higher education before assessing the effects of commodification on the particular site of virtual education.

Effective Learning

Teaching and learning is complex and it is important to acknowledge that there are still energetic academic disputes over models of effective learning. In psychology alone behaviourists still vie with cognitivists and constructivists in providing explanatory frameworks for learning, and these three groups have been joined more recently by insights from cultural psychology. For behaviourists the idea that learning occurs as a response to a stimulus (a text, specific experience, an experiment) is still a powerful one. The cognitivists are associated with models of brain processing, or more strictly information processing, and they have obvious contributions to make in areas like memory. The constructivists' major contribution has been to emphasize the importance of the learner as an active agent in understanding phenomena, and it would be fair to conclude that "most contemporary psychologists use constructivist theories of one type or another to explain how human beings learn" (Fry, Ketteridge & Marshall 1999: 22). Finally, the cultural psychologists shift emphasis away from an individualized model of learning towards one which emphasizes that a great deal of learning takes place in groups and communities, and thus learning becomes part of the process of enculturation or initiation into 'communities of practice' to use a term from Lave and Wenger (1991). Although it is useful to have an understanding of the psychological models that underpin learning in higher education, as Entwistle (1990) has argued, we have made progress in our understanding of learning in this context because we have moved beyond the application of general psychological theories of learning towards the examination of the educational process itself.

Entwistle and Tait (1989) offer a heuristic model of the teaching and learning process in higher education which specifies a range of student characteristics (intellectual abilities, cognitive style, personality and so on); a range of teaching characteristics (including teaching methods and aids); and what they call 'departmental characteristics' (such as workload, feedback, and study skills support), which are important in determining a learner's progress. Summaries of research like that of Fraser, Walberg, Welch and Hattie (1987) come to very similar conclusions: that learning is a function of student variables, instructional variables and environmental variables. Although this is a complex field, if one focuses on those variables which are in principle open to change i.e. factors relating to the process of higher education learning, and one combines research findings with what one might call 'evidenced based practice', then it is possible to build up a picture of what an environment of high quality learning and teaching looks like.

One of the most important principles to arise out of the literature is that effective learning is highly dependent on the relationships between students and lecturers and among students themselves. The quality of these relationships is crucial; ask any successful learner about significant moments in their careers as learners and they will almost certainly mention powerful teachers and supportive peer groups. In other words, the interactive dimension provided by participative teaching (Ryan & Stedman 2002) provides the pedagogic dialogue that Laurillard (1993) has argued is essential for education. We believe that it is possible to identify six key principles of high quality learning in higher education. These relate to student motivation, the active engagement of the learner, the modification of students' cognitive maps of subject domains, the use of feedback to students, effective peer support, and the use of context variation in developing transferable learning.

In a summary of research into student motivation in higher education, Entwistle (1998: 16) concluded, "for many years now, research findings have shown a fairly strong relationship between academic motivation and levels of performance in higher education". Motivation is not a unitary concept. We can distinguish extrinsic motivation, for example, students being motivated by external pressures and rewards like obtaining a good job; intrinsic motivation derived from interest in the subject matter; and finally achievement motivation, for example motivation derived from peer competition. A consistent finding, however, is that the amount of contact with faculty in and out of class is highly correlated with motivation and interest. There is also evidence to suggest that the peer group also plays an important role. Peers have a role in the process of commenting on their fellow students' models of the world and good teachers can engineer this as part of the pedagogic strategy. We also know that integration into the academic peer group is one of the most important indicators of retention and ultimate success

A further important principle to arise out of the literature is that for effective learning to occur, students need to engage in experimentation via modes of active learning, and most importantly teachers need to constantly adjust what they do to the needs of individual learners. This is in significant contrast to a model of learning which sees the task as one of essentially adding new knowledge to students. In higher education students tend to already possess cognitive maps of the fields of knowledge which they are studying, however rudimentary. The constructivist sees the process of learning as one that involves confronting those maps with new models and information so that they may be developed and in some cases completely changed (Mezirow 1991). This has important consequences for pedagogy. Teachers have a crucial role in getting students to reveal their understandings and hold them up for public scrutiny in a manner which is both supportive yet ultimately challenging. The classic model of this is the 'crit' in architecture. This is both a time consuming and skilled process. If the constructivist approach is accepted then it is also possible to understand why feedback is absolutely crucial in high quality learning. As students put forward their own versions of solutions to problems, the teacher needs to provide detailed and timely feedback on those solutions. All the evidence shows that quality and speed of feedback are vital in the development in such learning (Raaheim 1991).

There is an increasing emphasis on the development of transferable skills in higher education. The evidence base for how these are developed is as yet modest, but some elements are becoming clear. Perhaps the most important finding is that these skills are developed if the teaching programme systematically varies the contexts for learning, that is students are required to try out their knowledge and skills in a variety of different situations (Gibbs, Rust, Jenkins & Jacques 1994). The classic model of this is the internship, but there are a wide variety of other methods of doing this including specially designed projects, as well as real world and simulated problem solving. Commentators on the type of high quality learning required for the new economy also indicate that while first order learning may be standardized, second order learning or 'learning how to learn' is unpredictable and requires exposure to uncertainty and risk taking on behalf of both students and lecturers (Seltzer & Bentley 1999). This type of learning requires personal relations of trust between students and lecturers, as well as institutional frameworks based on trust between universities and other stakeholders including the state (Brown, Green & Lauder 2001).

Virtual Education

We now turn to attempts to assess some of the evidence for the thesis that the forces of commodification in higher education are inimical to high quality learning. We are aware that there is a danger in choosing sites of virtual learning in higher education to illustrate our thesis that commodification and high quality learning are incompatible. The danger is that we take for granted that virtual learning automatically leads to commodification. This is not our argument. Numerous international examples such as the Open University in the United Kingdom, the doctoral programme at the Open University of Catalonia and Brazil's teacher training programme 'TVEscola' attest to the fact that virtual education can provide a high quality learning environment and can overcome many of the barriers faced by off-line teaching. Castells (2001), for example, has advanced the idea that developing countries may be able to use information technology to 'leap-frog' the development process. He argues that the longer-term process of improving the education system by developing a high quality indigenous teacher base is too slow for urgent development needs in a world where the 'core' appears to be spinning away from the 'periphery'. He proposes that this process can be speeded up by using information technology and distance education in innovative and pedagogically sound ways to disseminate knowledge and skills.

However, we argue that virtual education in general is particularly vulnerable to the tendency for commodification to creep in. One of the reasons is that virtual education primarily holds out the promise of more efficient ways of learning in higher education. It does this for a variety of reasons. First, once the material (the commodity) has been produced then it would appear to be relatively easy to send this out electronically to the learners. The learners can be located anywhere with an internet connection, thus offering potential savings in space. Furthermore, tutoring and assessment can in principle be delivered more cheaply by adopting some of the techniques of mass production. The flexibility offered by such an approach, both to 'producers' and 'consumers' is attractive. Universities are very often attracted to such forms of learning and teaching because they are being squeezed financially by governments, such that any opportunities to produce teaching more cheaply are seized upon (see also Schapper & Mayson, this volume). And once having made the required investment in eLearning universities become keen to expand their virtual student numbers in order to spread their costs. Interestingly, Noble (2002) argues that many universities develop eLearning initially for some of their non-core business, for example their short course provision or overseas distance operations. There is almost a suggestion here that their core on-campus provision needs to be protected from an essentially commodified offering, although Noble goes on to argue that increasing cost pressures almost inevitably push this into core teaching.

The advent of eLearning and the spread of the internet have also attracted for-profit corporations into the higher education sector, for several reasons. The number of people in higher education is growing rapidly, not only because the fraction of the age cohort entering higher education is growing in most countries, but also because the number of older people returning to higher education to acquire new skills and knowledge, or at the very least to refresh them, is growing. And many in this second category are relatively 'cash rich' and 'time poor', which makes them ideal potential candidates for corporate higher education. Finally, the corporate world is interested because it sees itself as having a comparative advantage over universities in at least two respects. First, the relatively high barriers to entry for mass eLearning play to the strengths of corporate capital; secondly, large corporations are invariably international and are well used to tackling international markets.

This is not the place to detail the advance of corporations into higher education and in particular their focus on various eLearning models. The reports for the Observatory of Borderless Education do this very well (Ryan & Stedman 2002, Garrett 2003). The brief facts, however, are startling. Couturier (2003) estimates that there are now over 2000 corporate universities worldwide, that is, over 2000 corporations offering a 'university service' to their students directly in competition with public institutions. Some of the country statistics are equally striking: there are over 200 for-profit higher education corporations in Poland; 600 in Malaysia; and 625 in the USA. Examples of global companies include the Apollo Group, which runs Phoenix University, and also universities in the Netherlands, Germany and Brazil; Sylvan operates on a similar basis in Europe, but also in Mexico and Chile where it has bought a number of private universities. Adtech is a major player in South Africa, whilst Amnet has a major operation in China.

Apart from these corporations who offer a 'full university service' to their 'customers' there are major corporations that are offering partial services. These services can be concerned with the necessary IT capability e.g. the supply of the required IT platform or other elements of software support (Skillsoft, Serebra); or they can be as a partner offering whole programmes, typically, but not exclusively in the IT domain. It is also possible to see major publishers joining in as they seek new outlets for their content. A good example is Thompson, which is a partner in Universitas 21, a global partnership of major universities collaborating together to offer on-line content.

Three overall trends are clear. First, the reliance on the public university that sees post-compulsory education as a public good is under attack on an almost global scale. It is primarily accused of being inefficient i.e. too costly, too slow to change, and too inflexible. Secondly, this is a global trend that is accelerating under the twin influences of the GATS, which decrees education as a commodity which can be traded globally, and global corporations which are turning these claims into a reality. Thirdly, the development of eLearning technologies using the internet is greatly assisting this process. It is our contention that all three of these trends are resulting in the gradual commodification of higher education.

The Effects of Commodification

What have been the consequences of these trends? Is there evidence that the process of commodification has produced problems for the quality of learning in higher education? It is not easy to pick up direct evidence of the quality of learning since little research has been conducted in understanding the pedagogic implications of virtual education (CVCP 2000). Indeed, Harris (1998), one of the founding members of the Journal *Internet in Higher Education,* concludes, "I have not been able to uncover any systematic evidence of careful consideration to questions of the 'effectiveness' of various pedagogical approaches. Neither faculty or students seem interested in the question of the 'quality' of the learning experience" (Harris 1998: 248, quoted in Hall 2001). However, the available evidence indicates that pressures for commodification in virtual higher education have the potential to erode the quality of learning in higher education.

When we talk about commodification in higher education it is useful to think about three inter-related processes. The first concerns knowledge itself, that is the ways in which knowledge can be assembled and packaged for the potential learner. This is usually in some form of text, whether it be a conventional textbook, specially constructed text based distance learning materials, audio-visual material, or some form of eLearning. The second element is usually summed up by the concept of pedagogy, that is the processes that go on between the teacher and the student in the context of learning. This can be synchronous, as in face-to-face learning and some modes of eLearning, or it can be asynchronous, as in the most common forms of eLearning. An integral part of pedagogy is the process of assessment, whether it is formative or summative. It is a commonplace to argue that models of assessment tend to have an independent effect on learners and learning. These three elements react in complex ways in the learning-teaching nexus; it is clear that following the work of Biggs (1996), all the elements of the learning-teaching nexus have to work together in what he calls a 'constructive alignment'.

Knowledge and information are often perceived as interchangeable. Our thesis is that attempts at the commodification of information are probably less problematic than attempts to commodify knowledge, pedagogy or assessment. Information in its unprocessed form is readily accessible to large numbers of people, except at the very frontiers of some subjects in science and technology. It is of interest to note that an institution like the Massachusetts Institute of Technology (MIT) is prepared to put all of its subject content on the internet as open source material. This is in recognition of the fact that what MIT adds to this is its distinctive pedagogy and its assessment of learners. All knowledge has to be processed into pedagogically effective formats, or into pedagogic content knowledge (Shulman 1987). This is not an unproblematic process for universities that have invested heavily in IT infrastructure and e-course development and who need mass markets in order to recoup their investment. The essence of commodification is that it necessarily involves a great deal of standardization of knowledge, resulting in a model of learning which sees the task as essentially one of adding new knowledge to students. In some subjects, particularly in the sciences, it might be argued that this is easier to achieve since there is an inbuilt logical linearity to the subject discourse. In this model, the logical linearity in the text needs to be represented, while at the same time having regard for knowledge of cognition, for example, how easy it is to follow and remember material displayed or represented in a certain way. However, as Crook (2002: 121) argues, "research on the effective design of such materials is scarce and some of what is known might be taken to suggest that these apparently laudable ambitions of designers are misguided". It would appear that the key issue is learner engagement, that is the ability of the text to engage the learner actively with the material such that they begin to construct or reconstruct their own models of the world according to the discipline being studied. As Crook (2002) hints, the consequences of this might be that some of the more comprehensive and logical texts are rather less good at this than texts which are good at setting students puzzles and provocations which they have to work at to solve. But even in areas like basic science this is problematic; and in areas like the humanities where cultural issues come to the fore, it is even more problematic. In addition there are some areas of knowledge and skill, particularly the soft skills, where it is very difficult to see the development of virtual solutions.

The temptation in the virtual world where one is trying to develop income via the economies of scale, is that one is producing a standardized product and generic content which can be used anywhere. This is likely to be a particular problem in the context of developing countries where national governments do not have the resources to develop indigenous higher education systems. The rebranding of higher education as an exportable commodity has led to a stampede by private for-profit providers, European and American universities and international development organizations to implement distance and other forms of profitable education provision. Commentators from the developing world such as Moja and Cloete (2001: 247) have raised fears that weak regulation and the perception of higher education as a lucrative global export could lead to developing countries being viewed as mass markets for the dumping of low quality knowledge. Hall (2001), drawing in particular on the example of the World Bank's African Virtual University, has raised concerns that virtual education in combination with forces pushing higher education towards further commodification may harden the divide between high quality, high cost learning available to the elite, and standardized low quality packages of information delivered at low cost with little interactivity or national relevance to many parts of the developing world. They note that such initiatives are likely to stunt indigenous capacity in research and education.

Commodified approaches to learning also often place a very large reliance on learning resources, simply because this is the simplest and easiest option. They can also represent an attempt to teacher proof delivery which can be important if institutions are attempting to use less qualified, less experienced and thus cheaper staff. While it is likely that some texts will be more effective than others, it should be clear that the provision of appropriate texts, in whatever format, is unlikely to be effective by itself. There are limits to what can be acquired even by the very able by passively engaging with texts. Noble (2002) has argued that the one utterly unambiguous result of a century of education research is that that quality education is necessarily a labour-intensive process which depends upon a low teacher-student ratio and significant interaction between the two parties. This is the essential problem for commodified models of virtual education. Commodified systems tend to be lean systems that strip away all those elements which are not strictly necessary. The end result tends to be an atomized model that focuses on individual students as consumers of knowledge. This means that activities in which teachers adjust to the needs of individual students, as well as group work, which develops social and interpersonal skills and fosters peer group learning, tend not to be designed in. In addition, commodified systems avoid spending money on social facilities, which promote peer interaction, on the grounds that they are not strictly necessary for learning.

Commodified virtual education is generally unable to provide active learning opportunities such as experimentation and real world and simulated problem solving.

The problems with this for organizations which are anxious to turn a profit from higher education is that such models are complex, unpredictable and expensive, and they often require a great deal of local knowledge and networks to set up and maintain. The process of feedback to students is also altered. Feedback is rolled up into formal assessment systems, in the worst cases reducing it to the results of computerized multiple choice tests. There may well be a role for such tests in certain subject areas as part of formative feedback on progress, but they are no substitute for the detailed, qualitative feedback required for high quality learning. Second, because of the close links between commodified systems and the view of students as consumers, the emphasis is placed on students producing feedback to staff on their teaching 'performance', rather than the reverse. Such an approach is very susceptible to surface as against deep processing (Marton & Säljö 1984, Biggs 1987, Ramsden 1998). Finally, if one accepts the argument that much learning develops by the process of supportive challenge of existing ideas, and the introduction of measured risk, then approaches which stress commodified education processes are unlikely to produce high quality, flexible graduates. The process of introducing measured risk into the learning process is a time consuming and skilled process and almost wholly resistant to the process of commodification, which tends to change the pedagogical dialectical relationship between teacher and student into one between producers and consumers of knowledge. In addition, risk is the antithesis of the safe, pre-packaged 'product' that is at the heart of the commodified exchange.

There is also a growing recognition that the virtual university presents some special quality assurance issues, because often there are a number of different components: the technology suppliers; the content suppliers; and the student support system. This raises questions even in large global ventures like Universitas 21. Ryan and Stedman (2002: 25) argue that "it is unclear how U21 pedagogica, the accrediting body of the U21 universities, can call on sufficiently wide expertise to validate proposed programmes without the deep expertise that a comprehensive university uses in its usual accrediting procedures, which proceed from departmental level, where the expertise resides, through the various academic bodies of the university."

One of the most striking pieces of evidence that casts doubt on the effectiveness of commodified education in its virtual form, is the actual or near collapse of many virtual learning ventures in higher education (Ryan & Stedman 2002, Levis 2003). The failures have included university ventures like Fathom, NYU Online, and eCornell; partnership ventures between private organizations and universities like Cardean, Pensare and Quisic; and partnerships between universities like Western Governors University. Although some of the problems might be attributable to the bursting of the 'dot com' bubble, most commentators believe the failures occurred because of more fundamental problems. Levis (2003) provides a good summary of the reasons for failure. Foremost among the reasons is a failure to grasp what is entailed in successful learning. By and large the failing institutions used a mechanistic model of learning predicated on the need, as they saw it, to deliver more information, more quickly and more cheaply to the students. They tended to go for scale rather than quality, and they made the fatal mistake in not understanding that people generally do not want to study alone. Levis even goes as far as to argue that "learning cannot be 'digitized', indeed it is an intensely human activity", and "eLearning is only really effective for certain kinds of well-motivated, self-disciplined adults" (Levis 2003: 1).

If this is the conclusion gained by looking at the evidence of unsuccessful ventures, we believe that the same conclusions can be drawn by looking at successful ventures into virtual learning in higher education. The two most quoted examples of success are the University of Phoenix in the USA, and the Open University which is based in the United Kingdom but which in fact has a presence in most European Union countries and in over 30 non-European Union countries. The Open University's success comes about partly by paying a great deal of attention to how students learn, not by being obsessed with the technology, but by creating successful communities of learners supported by a committed band of part-time tutors. The University of Phoenix has a very similar model. Although Phoenix makes good use of technology in the delivery of its programmes, its secret lies in its ability to blend eLearning with face-to-face instruction. A typical Phoenix student will in fact find themselves in a class from time to time where the staff-student ratio is less than 10:1.

The same conclusions are arrived at when one considers the most successful elements of virtual learning. Carnevale and Young (2001) argue that the most popular and successful forms of virtual learning are those which most closely approximate face to face learning: that is videoconferencing, television broadcasts and tele-conferencing. There is evidence that student attrition rates climb when the mode of instruction is wholly at a distance. Chen (2001) reports that attrition can be as high as 60 to 80 per cent in asynchronous non-award online generic programmes in IT and business. More generally, attrition rates tend to climb when programmes are dominated by generic teaching material that is delivered on-line.

Perhaps the unkindest cut of all is the evidence that even when students have graduated from such programmes some employers are reluctant to hire them, apparently believing that such students are unlikely to be as good as their face-to-face counterparts. Phillips (2001) reports a US survey by Vault.com that found that 37 per cent of human resource officials were reluctant to employ students with on-line graduate degrees.

Conclusion

In conclusion, we need to make clear that we are not reconstructing a mythical golden age of teaching and learning in higher education. Our argument is not that traditional higher education has all the positive qualities of effective learning that we have outlined, and the commodified education does not. We know enough about the traditional experience of higher education to know that the quality of what is offered varies enormously. In any case, the dichotomy between traditional and commodified higher education is too stark. It is also not inevitable that virtual education and commodification go hand in hand. On the contrary, we would argue that, carefully handled, the right blend of conventional and eLearning can produce a richer and more rewarding learning environment than either face-to-face or eLearning can by themselves. Some of the positive features are that eLearning does not have to be synchronous and it can produce learning materials in a multi-media format which can benefit learning. Devices like streaming video and animations can sometimes do things that are impossible in a lecture theatre or crowded laboratory. If students respond to assignments on-line and these, along with tutor feedback, are also available on-line, then it could well be argued that this significantly improves the quality of that student feedback so vital for effective learning. In addition, the use of web links and the internet opens up a very rich vein of learning resources for students. What we have argued is rather that commodification inevitably sets up certain pressures to force higher education along certain pathways, and these pathways are, in general, inimical to high quality learning in higher education. Our suggestion is that close inspection of the virtual dimension in higher education reveals that attempts to commodify education usually fail because the essence of high quality education cannot be easily commodified, at least not under the present set of conditions that hold in most parts of the world.

Acknowledgements

We thank Hugh Lauder and Phil Brown for helpful comments on an earlier draft.

References

Biggs, J.B. 1987. *Transformative Dimensions of Adults' Learning,* San Francisco: Jossey-Bass.

Biggs, J.B., 1996. "Enhancing Teaching through Constructive Alignment." *Higher Education* 32(3): 347-364.

Bourdieu, P. 1996. *The State Nobility.* Cambridge: Polity Press.

Brown, P., Green, A., & Lauder, H. 2001. *Globalisation, Competitiveness, and Skill Formation.* Oxford: Oxford University Press.

Brown, P. & Lauder, H. 2001. *Capitalism and Social Progress: The Future of Society in a Global Economy.* Basingstoke: Palgrave.

Carnevale, D. & Young, J. 2001. "Telecourses Change Channels". In *The Chronicle of Higher Education* (Online), July 13, 2001. http://chronicle.com/cgi2-bin/texis/chronicle/search.

Carnoy, M. 1994. "Universities, Technological Change and Training in the Information Age." In *Revitalising Higher Education* edited by J. Salmi & A. M. Verspoor. New York: Pergamon and IAU Press.

Castells, M. 2001. "Information Technology and Global Development." In *Challenges of Globalisation: South African Debates with Manuel Castells,* edited by J. Muller, N. Cloete & S. Badat. Cape Town: Maskew Miller/ Longman.

CVCP. 2000. *The Business of Borderless Higher Education: United Kingdom Perspectives.* London: Committee of Vice-Chancellors and Principals.

Chen, E. 2001. "Training Providers Adopt Live eLearning" *Eduventures Industry Report*, July 24. http://www.eduventures.com/.

Couturier, L.K. 2003. "The Global Challenge: Serving the Public's Needs in the Face of a Higher Education Market". Paper presented to Universities Challenged: New Strategies and Business Models Conference, London, December 4.

Crook, C. 2002. "The Virtual University: the Learner's Perspective." In *The Virtual University? Knowledge, Markets and Management,* edited by K. Roberts & F. Webster. Oxford: Oxford University Press.

Deem, R. 2001. "Globalisation, New Managerialism, Academic Capitalism and Entrepreneuralism in Universities: Is the Local Dimension Still Important?" *Comparative Education* 37(1): 7-20.

Dill, D.D. 1997. "Higher Education Markets and Public Policy." *Higher Education Policy* 10(3-4): 167-185.

Entwistle, N. 1990. "How Students Learn and Why They Fail". Paper presented to Conference of Professors of Engineering, London, January.

Entwistle, N. 1998. "Motivating and Approaches to Learning: Motivating and Conceptions of Teaching." In *Motivating Students* edited by S. Brown, S. Armstrong & G. Thompson. London: Kogan Page.

Entwistle, N. & Tate, H. 1989. "Approaches to Learning, Evaluations of Teaching, and Preferences for Contrasting Academic Environments." *Higher Education* 19(2): 169-194.

Fraser, B.J., Walberg, H.J., Welch, W.W. & Hattie, J.A. 1987. "Synthesis of Educational Productivity Research." *International Journal of Educational Research* 11(2): 145-252.

Fry, H. Ketteridge S. & Marshall, S. 1999. "Understanding Student Learning." In *A Handbook for Teaching and Learning in Higher Education,* edited by H. Fry, S. Ketteridge & S. Marshall. London: Kogan Page.

Garrett, R. 2003. "Towards a Map of the Education Industry, Parts 1 & 2." *Observatory on Borderless Higher Education,* Issue 9 January/February. Online http://www.obhe.ac.uk/products/briefings.html

Gibbs, G., Rust, C., Jenkins, A. & Jacques, D. 1994. *Developing Students' Transferable Skills,* Oxford: Oxford Centre for Staff Development, Oxford Brookes University.

Hall, M. 2001. "Education and the Margins of the Network Society." In *Challenges of Globalistion: South African Debates with Castelsl,* edited by J. Muller, N. Cloete, N and S. Badat. Cape Town: Maskew Miller/Longman.

Harris, M.H. 1998. "Is the Revolution Over, or Has It Just Begun? A Year of the Internet in Higher Education." *Internet in Higher Education* 1(4): 243-251.

Laurillard, D. 1993, *Rethinking University Teaching: A Framework for the effective Use of Educational Technology.* London: Routledge.

Lave, J. & Wenger, E. 1991. *Situated learning: Legitimate Peripheral Participation,* Cambridge: Cambridge University Press.

Levis, K. 2003. "Universities Online. The New Business Model?" Paper presented to Universities Challenged: New Strategies and Business Models Conference, London, December 4.

Marginson, S. & Considine, M. 2000. *The Enterprise University: Power, Governance and Reinvention in Australia.* Cambridge: Cambridge University Press.

Marton, F. & Säljö, R. 1984. "Approaches to Learning." In *The Experiences of Learning,* edited by F. Marton, D. Hounsell and N. Entwistle, Edinburgh: Scottish Academic Press.

Mezirow, J. 1991. *Transformative Dimensions of Adult Learning.* San Francisco: Jossey-Bass.

Moja, T. & Cloete, N. 2001. "Vanishing Borders and New Boundaries." In *Challenges of Globalisation: South African Debates with Manuel Castells,* edited by J. Muller, N. Cloete & S. Badat. Cape Town: Maskew Miller/ Longman

Naidoo, R. 2003a. "Repositioning Higher Education as a Global Commodity: Opportunities and Challenges for Future Sociology of Education Work." *British Journal of Sociology of Education* 24(2): 249-259.

Naidoo, R. 2003b. "A Comparative Survey of the Criteria and Process for the Use of the Title 'University' across Six Countries". Online. http://www.hepi.ac.uk/articles/docs/survey.doc

Naidoo, R. & Jamieson, I. 2002. "Consumerism in Higher Education and its Implications for a High Skills Society." Presented to the European Educational Research Association, Lisbon. September13.

Newotny, H, Gibbons, M. & Scott, P. 2001. *Re-thinking Science: Knowledge and the Public.* Cambridge: Polity Press.

Noble, D.F. 2002. "Rehearsal for the Revolution." In *The Virtual University,* edited by K. Robins & F. Webster. Oxford: Oxford University Press.

Phillips, V. 2001. "Elearning - The Other White Meat? Industry Wide Promotion Campaign Takes Shape." *The Virtual University Gazette,* October.

Raaheim, K. 1991. "From School to University." In *Helping Students to Learn,* edited by K. Raaheim, J. Wankowski & J. Radfrod. Buckingham: The Society for Research into Higher Education and Open University Press.

Ramsden, P. 1998. *Improving Learning: New Perspective.* London: Kogan Page.

Ryan, Y. & Stedman, L. 2002. *The Business of Borderless Education: 2001 Update.* Canberra: Department of Education, Science and Training, Evaluations and Investigations Programme.

Seltzer, K. & Bentley, T. 1999. *The Creative Age: Knowledge and Skills for the New Economy.* London: Demos.

Shulman, L.S. 1987. "Knowledge and Teaching: Foundations of the New Reform." *Harvard Education Review* 57(1): 1-22.

Slaughter, S. & Leslie, L. 1997. *Academic Capitalism: Politics, Policies, and the Entrepreneurial University* Baltimore and London: Johns Hopkins University Press.

Task Force On Higher Education in Developing Countries (convened by UNESCO and World Bank). 2000. Higher Education in Developing Countries: Peril and Promise. Online. http://www.tfhe.net/report/overview.htm.

3

How the West is Done: Simulating Western Pedagogy in a Curriculum for Asian International Students

Catherine Doherty and Parlo Singh

Introduction

This chapter builds from two premises: first that cultural processes under the conditions of accelerating globalization and 'new times', are no longer what they used to be; and second that the concept 'culture' cannot be used theoretically in the way that it used to be, that is, as an independent, inert, 'given' variable signified by a countable noun. Cultures are constituted through ongoing struggles. Thus, collective cultural identities are made and re-made relationally through contact with people socially and historically categorized as 'Other'. In this processual frame, an Australian university offering preparatory programs for international students can be understood to be engaged in cultural production, producing and enacting an account of 'how the West is done' pedagogically that positions the international student as outsider or Other. Thus, the Otherness of the international student is socially constructed in relation to the category of Western student. Moreover, the social and cultural differ-ence of the Other, in this case the international student, is typically constructed in negative or deficit terms and as potentially risky to the Western traditions of the university. However, the continuing and growing presence of international students in the globalizing Western university suggests that such a claim to a pure, authentic tradition is nostalgic, a simulation seeking to recreate an imagined purity which is no longer there, if it were ever so.

Our main aim in this chapter is to explore how one Australian university imagines and enacts a 'pure', 'authentic' Western pedagogy in the contact zone of foundation programs designed specifically for Asian international students. We argue that teachers employed in foundation programs invoke a past that is increasingly illusory and elusive, and teach it to Asian international students, the very category of student most likely to challenge and transform the Western academy by their increasing presence within the sector.

This chapter is presented in three sections. First, culture and cultural identities are theorized as processes of globalization, with pedagogy playing a more salient role in the constitution and maintenance of cultural scripts. Second, videotaped classroom activities in preparatory programs for international students at one Australian university are described to illustrate specific cultural scripts of 'how the West is done'. The section also deals with teachers' rationales for designing these particular cultural scripts or pedagogies for international students. Third, the chapter concludes by questioning the significance of simulations of notionally pure, authentic Western traditions in the Australian education export industry.

This chapter draws on a selection of data from a larger study funded by the Australian Research Council (Singh & Freebody 1997-2000). The larger study looked at questions of pedagogy, culture and knowledge in preparatory education programs offered by Australian providers to international students in on-shore and off-shore (Indonesia) campus settings. Such courses are typically referred to as 'Foundation', 'Bridging' and 'English for Academic Purposes (EAP)' programs. Teachers and students in university preparation programs offered in Indonesia and at an urban public university in Australia were interviewed, and a series of three to five class sessions for each of the nine teachers sampled in the on-shore programs was observed and videotaped. The interviews for these nine teachers included stimulated recall (Meade & McMeniman 1992, Keith 1988) pertaining to particular aspects of their observed practice. These questions probed the teacher's intentions, design and what they hoped the students would get from the selected activities.

The Changing Terrain of Australian Higher Education

Over the past fifty years, Australia has been a very successful exporter of higher education, in particular within its regional market of South East Asia. International education has been described as "Australia's seventh largest export earner" (Noonan 2003: 6) and a "5.2 billion (dollar) education export industry" (Illing 2003: 19). The top five source countries of full fee-paying international student enrolments are currently Singapore, Hong Kong, Malaysia, China and Indonesia (Noonan 2003: 6), with the vast majority being "ethnic Chinese" (Nesdale, Simkin, Sang, Burke & Frager 1995: 23; see also Maslen 2002: 2). International students may be enrolled at either on-shore campuses, off-shore campuses, and/or via on-line programs. The crucial point, however, is that international students now constitute a sizeable portion (21 per cent) of the total student enrolment of Australian universities (Department of Education, Science and Training 2003). Moreover, international student enrolments are typically clustered in certain disciplinary areas constituting 32.3 per cent of total enrolments in Information Technology fields of study, and 26.3 per cent in Management and Commerce fields (Department of Education, Science and Training 2003). At the same time, Asian international students are often at the centre of public controversies about the quality of higher education curricula (lowering of higher education standards) and the perceived declining exchange or market value of Australian academic credentials in the global market place. Recently, a number of cases of alleged plagiarism involving Asian international students, as well as claims of so-called 'soft marking' for this cohort of students, have received extensive media coverage (see Contractor 2003, Illing 2003, McWilliam, Singh & Taylor 2002).

We suggest that the accelerating (real and virtual) flow of international students, knowledge and symbolic resources, as well as struggles and contestations over these movements, are characteristic of new globalized times (Waters 2001). In this chapter, we ask how this increasing Asian presence within the Western university is negotiated and handled by teachers employed in front-line programs, such as foundation and bridging programs, designed specifically to induct Asian international students into the Western university.

Australian Universities as Global Cultural Contact Zones

In this chapter and others (e.g. Doherty 2001), we suggest that the well-worn regional circuits followed by international students to study with Australian universities constitute a fifty-year history of increasing cultural entanglement (Ang 2001, Clifford 1997). This increasingly "symbiotic" (Dalrymple 2002: xlvii) relationship renders the Australian university, and more generally the Western academy, a dynamic, evolving and generative contact zone (Pratt 1992, Kenway & Bullen 2003) as opposed to some pristine, impervious cultural site that can retain and reproduce some essential pre-contact authenticity in its scripts. These contact zones can never be neutral places (Smith 2001: 378). Rather, contact zones are places that have been historically constituted as sites of transculturation, where colonizers and colonized, travelers and travelees interact, co-exist, and engage in "interlocking understandings and practices, often with radically asymmetrical relations of power" (Pratt 1992: 7). Moreover, contact zones are fluid and changing places, constructed and re-constructed anew as people with disparate historical trajectories meet and struggle over issues of representation (i.e. who has the right to speak on behalf of who, how, and with what consequences). Thus contact zones are sites of cultural struggle where the "making and remaking of identities" takes place (Clifford 1997: 7).

A crucial tactic in these cultural struggles is the attempt by dominant groups to sanitize places of the historical legacy of unequal power relations. We argue that acts of purification or sanitization in contact zones, that is, attempts to construct pristine accounts of Western learning styles and pedagogy violently deny and repress the history of Western-Asian cultural entanglement (see Said 1995).

In this chapter we draw on video-taped lessons and stimulated recall interview data collected from nine teachers working on the onshore EAP and foundation programs at one Australian university, with a particular focus on the practice of two teachers. The size of the video-taped classes ranged from 12 to 26 students, with the vast majority of students from South East Asia (Hong Kong, Thailand, Taiwan, Malaysia, Singapore, East Timor, Indonesia). The age range of the students in these classes varied between 18 and 44, with all classes displaying a wide spread of ages.

Many students already had an undergraduate degree. In addition, all nine teachers who participated in the onshore component of the study had substantial teaching experience, ranging from seven to twenty-eight years across various education sectors. Five of the teachers had taught overseas, and seven of the teachers had postgraduate qualifications (see Singh & Doherty forthcoming).

The analysis of video-taped classes mapped the phases of different interactional practices (Lemke 1990), any shifts in thematic topics, and moments of interactive trouble in the pedagogy, such as student disruptions, challenges or failure to respond. The analysis of teacher interview data interrogated the categories of students constructed in their talk, and how these categories informed their operative models of Asian learner and Western teacher with which to regulate the choice of curricular content and pedagogic strategies. We focus on these two data sets because all the teachers talked about the Asian learner as passive, that is, not engaging in the desired forms of classroom talk or 'critical thinking', and therefore the need to explicitly teach or socialize students into these requisite skills.

The Impurity of Cultural Processes

There is growing recognition that 'cultures' have never been pure, stable and discrete - rather hybridity and change wrought through contact with Others is how cultural identity and cultural differences come into being, and then are sustained or reinvented over time (Friedman 1994, Trouillot 2002, Clifford 1988, 1997):

> The problem is not that cultures are suddenly changing: they have always been changing. Nor is it new that cultures are porous. Human groups have always been open, in various degrees, to new experiences, outside influences, borrowings, and impositions. The difference now is that the fiction of isolated cultures built by the nineteenth century on the assumptions of the Renaissance no longer fits the lived experiences ... (Trouillot 2002: 13).

The lived experience is different now because of the accelerating speed and quantities of global cultural exchange, and our growing consciousness of our place in the global order (Waters 2001). As Appadurai (1996: 10) has argued:

> The transformation of everyday subjectivities through electronic mediation and the work of the imagination is not only a cultural fact. It is deeply connected to politics, through the new ways in which individual attachments, interests, and aspirations increasingly crosscut those of the nation-state. The diasporic public spheres that such encounters create are no longer small, marginal, or exceptional. They are part of the cultural dynamic of urban life in most countries and continents, in which migration and mass mediation co-constitute a new sense of the global as modern and the modern as global.

In a globalized knowledge economy, Western higher education credentials are increasingly portrayed as the key or path to higher status, secure 'professional' employment. Thus *images* of the highly successful Western educated professional are relayed across the world via the web-pages of Western universities, other advertising media, including brochures, television advertisements, and personnel. Acquisition of Western higher education becomes the *imagined* gateway to upward social and economic mobility in an increasingly unequal global system. These *images* are appropriated in local contexts and used to launch individual and collective identities. Thus, for example, Perlez (2003) provides an account of 'study mothers' – women who travel from China to Singapore, take up menial work and live in cramped accommodation, in order to provide their children with what they *imagine* is the best education. Primary school education in Singapore is considered advantageous as instruction is in English, and English language competence enables Chinese children to apply for secondary school education programs in a Western country such as Australia or the United States. Thus, the *images* of Western education relayed across the globe, and the *imagined worlds* made accessible via Western education, provide a platform for *imagining* and launching individual and collective social actions such as the phenomena of 'study mothers' (see Appadurai 1996). The problem however, seems to be that many of the Chinese mothers who travel to Singapore, find it difficult to get jobs and struggle to make ends meet. Moreover, the children struggle to gain the necessary levels of English competency needed to apply for enrolment in Western secondary schools.

In this chapter, we are concerned with the pedagogic identities and practices imagined, constructed, and launched by Australian teachers for Asian international students. Moreover, we are concerned with analysing the struggles or politics over cultural identity enacted in the contact zones of Australian university foundation programs designed specifically for Asian international students.

Scripting How the West is Done

To report the observed classroom activities, we purposefully use the provocative term 'simulation' following Baudrillard (1988), to suggest that the versions of Western pedagogy constructed for international students are not simply a heuristic imitation or reflection of something that exists independently, but rather an act of masquerade that refers to a reality that is not in fact there. Baudrillard (1988: 167) defines simulation as:

> … no longer a question of imitation, nor of reduplication, nor even of parody. It is rather a question of substituting signs of the real for the real itself; that is, an operation to deter every real process by its operational double, a metastable, programmatic, perfect descriptive machine which provides all the signs of the real and short-circuits all its vicissitudes.

The illusory authority and purity of the pedagogic simulation create, we suggest, such an imagined, fictive and idealized script. Baudrillard (1988) deploys a metaphor of drama to describe the way in which social action creates or performs the 'scenodrama' of simulation. Similarly, we will describe the classroom staging of idealized Western pedagogic relations using the systematic metaphor of staging and scripting a theatrical production.

Two class activities observed in the on-shore preparatory programs in an Australian urban university have been selected as explicit exemplars of attempts firstly to invoke a notionally 'pure', authentic Western pedagogy, and secondly to explicitly socialize the students in this cultural script by simulating or enacting pedagogic roles. In addition, the rationale for these particular activities were discussed with the teachers in their interviews. Both class activities were designed to involve and immerse the Asian international students in a performance of Western student roles. The first example stages a class discussion, the second involves student oral presentations and the associated question time. Accomplishing or coaching in these two communicative orders constituted a common focus of the enacted curriculum observed across all nine class groups in the on-shore site. Our analysis of simulation/dissimulation asks:

- What model of Western tutorial is constructed in these lessons? What is the 'Other' of this model?
- How are 'international' students taught the skills and knowledge of Western tutorial?
- How is this mode of instruction different from that provided to 'Australian' students?

Activity A: Rehearsing a Group Discussion

In a weekly two hour class for a year long unit which uses Australian history content as a vehicle for 'study skills' instruction designed for international students, the second hour was devoted to watching a 25 minute video about Australia's changing immigration policies, and then to accomplishing a group discussion around these questions.

Teacher as director: Prior to taking a break after the first hour, the teacher suggested that students "Go off and have a break. Build up your energy so that you can be a bit more lively in your discussion than you are at the moment." In the ensuing class, students were provided with a set of questions that reflected the chronological order of ideas/themes in the video, and were encouraged to take notes as they watched the video. The instructions to the students highlighted the purpose of performing a group discussion, rather than the (secondary) purpose of engaging with the content of the video:

Teacher A: We'll watch the video and remember we're looking for answers to those questions so that at the end of the video you'll be able to contribute to a group discussion, and everybody will have to say something so if you want to sound intelligent, you'd better listen to the video.

Setting the stage: The 22 students initially sat at individual desks organized in rows across the room, facing the front in order to watch the video. At the end of the video recording, the video player was turned off and the teacher directed the physical reorganization of the furniture via a series of spoken directions and gestures, so that students were eventually seated in a circle facing each other, "so no-one has their back to anyone else". The teacher remained standing outside the circle, behind a student, thus excluding herself from the group.

Coaching the actors: Students were reminded, "when you're talking ... you aren't talking to me... so you want eye contact with the class". She then continued to outline the discussion modus operandi with reference to how it would proceed, and how it should ideally proceed: "I'll interrupt you but hopefully you'll be able to keep the discussion going yourselves".

Allocating roles: She then passed around a bag containing numbers from which students were expected to select one at random. By her account, this activity was designed to make sure that the students contributed to the staged classroom discussion. In other words, this activity was designed to randomly distribute student contributions across the time and space of the lesson to generate the theatrical effect of a spontaneously generated discussion. This preparatory 'stage-setting' episode lasted three minutes.

The rehearsal: The teacher then invited "Number 1" to start, then continued, "I'll get you started. The question was: why did the Australian government want more migrants?" The designated student did not immediately respond, so the teacher prompted her with: "I think ... I believe..." The student then offered a contribution. The teacher, from outside the circle, interjected after each student turn, moderating the discussion with comments such as, "Good. Number 3, anything to add?", and, "That's good. Number 4 can move on to Question 2." At this stage, the majority of students started to address their comments to the teacher, their eyes looking towards the teacher, and finishing with an upward inflection, thus seeking her confirmation. When this required the student seated directly in front of the teacher to turn her back on the student circle, the teacher reminded her to "turn around" to face the group again. Thus despite the considerable effort to reframe the communicative genre, the exchange fell back into the familiar initiation-response-evaluation chains of teacher-centred classroom discourse (Mehan 1979). Student contributions were usually a few sentences long, ranging from about three seconds to up to 30 seconds in length in a few cases. The teacher's contributions typically: (1) provided some evaluative feedback on the previous turn, (2) re-formulated the student's contribution, (3) developed the student's contribution to provide the desired instructional content focus, (4) restated the question, and then (5) called for the next turn. The teacher also alluded to previous students' comments, and invited the next speaker to respond to those ideas, thus modelling or scaffolding the process of cohesive backward referencing within the whole 'discussion' text.

Stage fright: Students often giggled or smiled in a self-conscious way before and after their turns. One student's contribution achieved a communal laugh when the teacher evaluated it as, "…good. It didn't actually answer the question, but it's interesting information. I mean, it's contributed."

Directorial feedback: When everyone had taken his or her allocated turn, the teacher started to close the activity, with an evaluation: "That's good. Everyone's said something." She was then interrupted by a student who offered another pertinent, unsolicited comment – the first spontaneous contribution as such. Following this, the teacher resumed her summary of the activity, indicating how the topic related to the next unit of work, and inviting students to self-evaluate their individual performances in the group discussion by referring to a self-evaluation guide in their textbook: "You might go through that criteria and think 'Did I do this? Did I do that?' You might be surprised." This book is a British publication (Cottrell 1999), and the relevant pages (pp. 98-99) outline a set of questions with which to evaluate one's own 'contributions' to seminars and group work, to invite other participants' evaluation of one's 'contribution', and to evaluate the group's 'overall working'.

Rehearsal closure: The class was then finally instructed to restore the desks and chairs back into the usual row layout.

This whole discussion 'scenario' lends itself to be understood as theatrical simulation, albeit a rehearsal, not the performance proper. The teacher acted as the director, coaching, prompting, stage-managing and giving feedback on the students' hesitant contribution and the comportment of their bodies, in order to fulfil a simple script of group discussion where talk is seen to be distributed randomly around the group, and 'everyone says something', while ideally looking each other in the eyes. The students displayed symptoms of stage fright before and after their performances. The spatial organization of furniture before and after provided clear cues of when the rehearsal started and when it finished. Though this might be what group discussion looks like and sounds like (*i.e.* randomized multivocality), this enactment was not the imagined 'real' tutorial genre in a number of ways. The students were acting through compulsion. They were expected to contribute something when their turn came up. They had little control over when they could contribute, what knowledge they could contribute, and how they would contribute to the tutorial. Rather, they were given explicit instructions of how to 'do tutorial talk', and thus were engaged in enacting this performance. Consequently, few of the students were actively occupied with the content of the Australian Studies lesson as such.

Teacher A: A Stimulated Recall Rationale

In her interview account of this activity's design, Teacher A constructed an idealized version of how Western tutorial discussion should be conducted as student-to-student interaction, requiring little teacher intervention. The teacher was cast as a background arbitrator. In her account, this was epitomized in the distribution of eye contact – peer to peer and not with the teacher – and operationalized in the time-consuming re-arrangement of seating to achieve this eye contact. Thus she constructed the idealized

Western student as an active, independent and confident co-constructor of classroom interaction and knowledge, in opposition to her account of the international students' tendency to be passive and non-interactive.

Moreover, this simulated rendition of the Western tutorial was constructed as 'not natural', which by inference equates the internalized Western genre and its constituent roles as 'natural'. In her commentary, Teacher A indicated that the exercise was designed to "try [and] to force them (international students) to do things that they should be doing all the time in the tutorial situation". Such an authoritarian/coercive construction of power relations seems at odds with the idealized democratic distribution of power in the imagined/fictionalized model of tutorial discussion constructed within the simulation.

By her selection of this instructional focus (how to do Western tutorial discussion) and her allocation of considerable time in this and subsequent sessions, Teacher A was producing cultural difference, namely, cultural difference between the students' domestic and Western learning environments that pivots around the valorization of oral participation. In the following segment of interview data, she made explicit the moral order behind this code:

> R: I suppose I'm asking why do you pursue participation? What's your rea-
> soning behind the idea that students should be participatory?
> **Teacher A**: Well, it's all based on our emphasis on critical and analytical
> thinking. If you don't participate then you're not contributing to whatever is
> developing and you're just relying on whatever the teacher is telling you. And
> they may be thinking about it as the teacher speaks but you don't know. So by
> having discussion you can have some sort of understanding about what they're
> thinking or how they're thinking…
> R: … you mean when they speak it's giving you information about how the
> teaching is going?
> **Teacher A**: Yes. How much they understand. And also because … otherwise
> they tend to lose concentration. I mean if I just talk, talk, talk for an hour they
> could go to sleep. I mean their eyes are open but they could still be asleep but I
> wouldn't know. So it's to keep them awake as well and keep them on target.

What are the students learning through this simulation of tutorial? Teacher A suggested that she provokes oral participation in order to encourage critical and analytical thinking. However, pedagogic strategies to elicit and develop critical and analytical thinking skills were not articulated. Rather, Teacher A went on to suggest that the pedagogic simulation of oral participation enhanced her control in classroom encounters. In other words, by encouraging students to talk, Teacher A could (1) gather information on what knowledge students had acquired and (2) ensure students stayed on task. The simulation of oral participation was thus explicitly tied to regulation of the international student. While regulation is a necessary feature of all classroom practices, by the higher education level students could be expected to be self-regulating and take responsibility for their own learning. As adult learners, students are expected to critically engage with the knowledge articulated by other class members in tutorial sessions. By contrast, the preceding account of a simulated Western tutorial infantilises the international student. The international student is constituted as a child who readily loses concentration, and needs supervised practice in 'doing tutorial'.

Activity B: Performing Oral Presentation and Question Time

As a major assessment item in a preparatory course on business communication, students were required to give a 15 minute oral presentation that described the communicative genre used by certain work roles in business. Students in the audience were also assessed on their participation in a question time following each presentation. Each student was required to ask a certain number of questions over the series of presentations. The following account details the first part of an hour long class that was devoted to a series of these oral presentations, in particular the preparation for the session, the oral presentation, and the question time following this particular presentation.

Setting the stage: The room was set up with individual desks and chairs joined into three straight rows, facing a raised platform in front of a whiteboard. There was a screen positioned in one corner of the front, angled towards the audience. An overhead projector was positioned towards the screen side of the raised podium, next to a large desk. There was a video unit against the wall in the middle of the podium. The teacher set himself up at a desk on the side of the middle row of desks. He had various papers on the desk, in readiness to record his evaluations and comments on the presentations. The ten or so students present were seated throughout the rows of desks. The teacher moved to the podium, and the murmur of chat subsided. He moved the video unit on the podium into a corner, thus setting the stage.

Master of ceremonies: The teacher sat on the edge of the desk and opened the proceedings with: "Good morning. Welcome to the first of our presentations". The teacher then gave some advice about deep breathing to relax, and explained that he would be sitting in the audience. He asked if any of the presenters had any problems with the "physical equipment" props, and then moved offstage to mark the roll. He then moved back to stand in the centre of the podium to make "a general comment" about the moral code pertaining to late arrivals in such sessions: "Please do *not* enter the room when someone is speaking. It makes it very difficult ... please wait outside. Sometimes, we can't help being late but we *can* help the person giving the talk by not interrupting." He pointed out the glass panel in the door, and suggested that students check what was happening before entering the room. This established a tightly insulated boundary around the space and the time devoted to these presentations, akin to closing the theatre doors just prior to a show starting.

Waiting for the call: The teacher returned to his seat in the body of the classroom, checked the class roll, established who would be the first presenter, then begged "just one moment" to prepare his assessment sheet. In the 17 seconds while he did this, the presenting student moved to the podium and waited, self consciously adjusting his clothing and hair. This student had noticeably dressed up for the day's presentation, wearing a collared shirt (as opposed to his usual t-shirt), and had pulled his long fringe back into a ponytail arrangement, so it was not falling over his face.

Let the show begin: With a cue from the teacher when ready, the student then commenced his presentation about the various communicative genres employed by a marketing manager in his/her work role, with the opening, "Good morning, my friends". The presentation proper lasted about seven minutes. The student had prepared props in the way of overhead projector slides, with concept maps, definitions and summary notes. As he spoke, he frequently cast his eyes to the roof, with some facial gestures of effort, suggesting he was trying to remember a memorized script. Through his presentation, the student remained standing, moving across the stage between the overhead projector, the screen side of the podium and the desk.

Audience participation: The student closed his presentation with the request, "If you have any questions please ask me". There was a 16 second hiatus, presumably while the teacher was completing his written comments on the assessment sheet. Finally, the teacher spoke from his seated position in the audience:

> I have a question, and whenever we ask a question, as part of the genre of the question period we always say our name first, so my name is … , and I have a question …

The question pertained to the student's interpretation of an important concept. Not satisfied with the student's first reply, the teacher then asked a more pointed question challenging the student's definition of advertising as a genre. The student conceded an error. A chain of questions with two students and answers followed. There was another marked silence of 10 seconds. No other students took the opportunity to ask questions.

End of the act and interval: The teacher then offered his thanks, and the class applauded the presenter, who moved back to resume his seat in the rows of desks. The teacher then asked for "a couple of moments" before the next presenter.

This class session essentially constituted a theatrical performance, with its stage setting, attention to costume, props, restricted entrance, ritual of applause, and the interval between presentations. Unlike the other data episode (Teacher A) on group discussion, this was not a rehearsal, but the actual performance. At the same time, however, the performance was a simulated version of a tutorial presentation that students might be expected to perform in their future, 'real' university courses. In the preceding data extract, the student had obviously rehearsed and memorized his script in detail. The teacher moved between being the stage-manager establishing the running order, the master of ceremonies announcing the proceedings as they unfurled, and the critic evaluating and documenting the quality of performance. The audience members had their role to play in performing question time.

In terms of the knowledge produced and transmitted in this activity, the meticulously detailed assessment instrument used to evaluate these presentations allocated 25 per cent of the score to the presentation content – half of this being a judgement of its 'quantity', and the other half a judgement of its 'quality'. The other 75 per cent of the score allocations addressed issues of manner, delivery, presentation, with penalties applied to poor time management. This imbalanced allocation of assessment criteria between the putative instructional discourse task (what the presentation was to be about) and the regulative discourse task (how to do Western oral presentation) demonstrates the effort to impart codified forms of knowledge about implicit Western pedagogic models in these curricula.

Teacher B: A Stimulated Recall Rationale

In his interview, the teacher explained the rationale behind the design and assessment of this oral presentation task. He justified the task in terms of its relevance to future work (in business) and study demands. As he explained the goals of the task, in terms of accomplishing nonverbal as well as verbal criteria, he referred to the student performance described above which he assessed as poor. The teacher outlined his belief that the speaker's bodily presentation is as much the performance as the content of the talk. He then mitigated his account of the assessment criteria with reference to the students' cultural differences and the supportive, bridging nature of the course. He called it a "test the water" type of situation. He thus drew a distinction between the criteria he had instructed the students in as applying to the mainstream university, and the softened, more accommodating assessment practices of this preparatory course.

By the teacher's account, these international students "will be expected to know" certain procedural and genre expectations, which extend to control and comportment of the body in oral presentations. For this teacher, these culturally specific rules included how one's hair should be styled when giving an oral presentation. "I think ... a lot of these [items] for us might be commonsense but I think their culture is specific", and he recounted making this explicit in his lead up to this task. This provided a rationale for instructional content pertaining to general grooming (criteria for styling hair) and deportment during oral presentations. So, for this teacher, the rules were present and enforced, but they were implicit 'common-sense' in the mainstream. The role of these bridging courses was to make the implicit explicit, that is, to codify and make transferable the tacit knowledge of socialization processes: "introducing them to things which they will be expected to know...just the whole box and dice of how to succeed as a student at this university". He outlined the curriculum leading up to the assessment of the oral presentation task as focussed on aspects of non-verbal communication and suggested that "in a different context what I'd be looking for there would be how much material was presented which is a function of the time". He was thus emptying the assessed curriculum of the instructional content (the 'what'), to focus on the regulative discourse (the 'how') of bodily and linguistic comportment, as evidenced by the assessment instrument.

In the interview, the teacher articulated his notion of what he could and could not expect of the international students, and used the metaphor of a bridge between presumably two mutually exclusive educational worlds. He referred to a hypothetical, unachievable, unrealistic "wish list" in which students reproduce the ideal desired

Western performance: "And I think we have to be careful because we have a "wish list" here that these students would do exactly what we want which is unrealistic. It's not realistic in life or at university but you do…" He characterized these courses devoted to the preparation of international students as a "secure environment" and "a special kind of unit", which constructs an unreality in terms of assessment practices, and a dilemma for the teachers: "you can't blame someone for something they don't know".

In his reflection on the design of the ritualized question time, he explained that it served a number of heuristic purposes. The involvement of the audience members demonstrated their understanding of the proceedings and secondly, fulfilled Western notions of active, argumentative participation, and exposed the international students to this expectation/practice. The ideal social order constructed here was of active, dialogic relationships between students, and teachers: "so I try to suggest to them that this involvement, the give and the take, the turn taking is part of what we do". In his version of the West, which he distinguished from other cultures, knowledge is tested and contested, even aggressively, in these relationships. So the question following a presentation was a contribution to the robustness of the academic enterprise: "Whereas, here, we go for the chink in the armour and we say, 'Well, now wait a minute, mate. What about that time? Why didn't it work then?'… and that's argumentative, the pros and cons". In his rationale, he valorized the quality of being active, his "active listener" being one that participated by asking questions. This invoked an implicit contrast with the passive, inscrutable Asian archetype. By his account, the action of asking a question also played a role in Western education of displaying understanding for assessment and classroom control: "because part of the whole thing is allowing someone to understand what you're thinking about. You could be sitting there and really concentrating but you could also be sitting there and be somewhere else".

The knowledge constructed within Teacher B's classroom lesson was an enactment of a set of principles, procedures or rules for selecting, combining, and realizing two separate discourses: a discourse of instruction and a discourse of moral regulation (Bernstein 2000). The latter discourse, namely regulative discourse, generates the arbitrary internal ordering of classroom knowledge. In other words, what is taught and how it is taught in terms of foundation/preparatory curricula are arbitrary constructions, generated by theories of instruction – "a model of the learner and of the teacher and of the relation" between teacher/learner (Bernstein 1996: 49). In the lesson discussed above, Teacher B prioritized a theory of instruction based on communicative genres, and a theory of the Asian international student as culturally different from the Australian university student. Moreover, the cultural difference of the Asian learner was constructed in terms of fashion codes (unaware of hair and dress codes for oral presentations) and learning codes (unfamiliar with the rules for oral presentations). Thus strong symbolic boundaries were constructed around the categories Australian and international student, and Asian and Western pedagogic practices. According to Teacher B, it was his pedagogic responsibility to create simulations of Western oral presentations in order to induct Asian international students into the ways of being and enacting Western/Australian student roles as a bridge/pathway into mainstream university courses.

Why Simulate a Pure, Authentic Tradition?

In previous work (Doherty & Singh 2002), we critiqued the simulations of Western pedagogy constructed in foundation/bridging programs, as well as the versions of academic knowledge made available to students in these programs. In that work, we theorized simulation as the 'concealment of the non-existence of something' (Kraidy 2002: 200). We suggested that simulacrums of Western pedagogy were displays of copies with no original. The Western pedagogy constructed in these international education programs, we argued, was a simulation of an imaginary or idealized pedagogy rather than actually enacted pedagogic practices. However, processes of simulation work in conjunction with processes of dissimulation. To dissimulate means to 'feign not to have what one has while to simulate is to feign to have what one has not (Baudrillard cited in Kraidy 2002: 200). Thus, to suggest that "chalk and talk" and "closed questioning" teaching strategies are no longer practised in the West is to engage in processes of dissimulation. Such processes of dissimulation deny that such traditional, as well as progressive and critical, pedagogic strategies continue to be deployed and enacted side-by-side in Australian educational systems (see Kubota 2001 regarding mixed practices in US settings).

In this chapter, we wish to go one step further and suggest that the pedagogic simulations serve also to produce and assert essentialized cultural differences, thus affirming a purity in 'how the West is done' despite the significant demographic changes taking place. In this way, Western identity is consolidated during a period of rapid cultural flux and instability, a period in which the 'Asian Other' is increasingly acquiring Western commodities, mimicking, indigenizing and hybridizing Western practices. It is through these processes of simulation and dissimulation that Western universities attempt to re-make and project legitimized institutional identities (see Castells 1997). In other words, fictionalized differences between Western and 'Other' pedagogues, or between Western and 'Other' education systems, are imagined, launched, and enacted as stabilizing devices or mechanisms during periods of intense cultural instability, fluidity, and complexification.

The crucial point we want to make here is that during these 'new times' of globalized modernity, a period marked by heightened flux, fluidity, contradiction, paradox, and anomalies, university teachers are likely to be positioned simultaneously and ambiguously by a complex inter-play and exchange between re-centring and de-centring discourses (see Kress, Jewitt & Tsatsarelis 2000, Tyler 1999). Indeed, these apparently oppositional discourses serve a complementary function. On the one hand, de-centring discourses need to orient the subject towards change and complexification (see Tyler 1999). For example, strategies are devised at the level of the state (policy positions, funding guidelines, regulatory mechanisms) and the institution (mission statements, organizational structures, teaching units) to orient university teachers to meet the changes wrought by increases in student numbers, diversity in the student body, reductions in public spending, and the exponential growth of knowledge internal and external to the university sector. On the other hand, re-centring discourses need to orient the subject towards stability. For example, retrospective discourses about the scholarly tradition of universities, the ideal scholar, and the professional ethic of care between academic-teacher and student-learner are evoked to ensure that external market-orientations are complemented by introspection. Tyler (1999: 282) goes on to argue that:

> In conditions of high turbulence, the tensions between these two opposing tendencies (complexification and stabilisation) will become quite intense and the overall state of the system of exchange quite 'unstable'. Under the extreme conditions of moral ambiguity, and the proliferating technical and legal innovations which accompany the excesses of consumerism, the contradictions at the heart of the functional model of regulation take on an unexpected centrality and importance.

In this context, re-centring retrospective discourses that project notions of pure, nostalgic, Western pedagogic and scholarly traditions serve as a counter-balance to de-centring prospective discourses aimed at internationalizing the Western university as it is increasingly populated by Asian international students. The work of the imagination, as collective fiction and invention, comes to play an increasingly important role in the construction of a politics of identity in these new times (see Appadurai 1996, Castells 1997, Clifford 1988). The "quotidian work" of imagination (Appadurai 1996: 5) can produce both an affirming essentialism from within the group and a repressive essentialism from without (Werbner 1997), to forge and articulate an identity in relation to, while distinct from, the imagined 'Other'. McCarthy and Dimitriades (2000: 193) draw on Nietzsche's concept of resentment to explain how a collective identity under stress:

> consolidates ... by a complete disavowal of the merits and existence of his social other. A sense of self, thus, is only possible through an annihilation or emptying out of the other, whether discursively or materially.

This strategy protects the self by imaginatively belittling the other. In other words, Western pedagogic identity is constituted through such "annihilation or emptying out" of the Asian other (Nietzsche, summarized in McCarthy & Dimitriades 2000: 193).

In the context of the internationalized Australian university, Bullen and Kenway (2003) demonstrate this containment by belittling, when they illustrate how university staff choose to construct 'imagined' third world women rather than deal with real, more complex, female postgraduate students from South East Asia. The script for the imagined women, they suggest, is drawn from generic culturalist assumptions that, in conjunction with the orientalist 'learning style' literature informing practices, diminish both the capacities and the needs of these students, resulting in "the infantilization of international students in general, and of international women students in particular" (Bullen & Kenway 2003: 43). A similar discourse was evident in the interview data above, where Teacher A justified oral participation on the grounds of keeping the international students awake, and Teacher B's insistence on aspects of grooming in the curriculum. In contrast, Rizvi (2000) identified a "global imagination" in the discourse of international students studying in Australian universities, who "are able to imagine the nation and its links to the outside world in radically new ways" (Rizvi 2000: 223). Similarly, Kenway and Bullen (2003), in their parallel study of the international postgraduate women's self-representations, demonstrate a heterogeneity in the students' own expressions of tactical and contingent identities. Our own teacher interview data collected in the offshore, Indonesian based component of the study reported in this chapter, suggested that students were keen to acquire a "global focus" via the acquisition of Western knowledge. Australian teachers working off-shore in Indonesia suggested that for many of the students in their classes, the "global focus", or focus on "globalization" meant acquisition of "English language and information technology literacy". Moreover, acquisition of knowledge to attain this "global focus" started early. Like the Chinese 'study mothers' reported earlier in this chapter, Indonesian 'study parents' often sent their children at an early age to other Asian countries such as Singapore or Malaysia for study purposes, and also ensured that their children had experience with the Australian secondary schooling system. Moreover, a few of the Indonesian 'study parents' owned property in Australia, and consequently were frequent visitors to the country (see Singh 2003).

This contrast between how teachers working in an Australian university (onshore campus) imagine Asian international students as culture-bound, and how the international students and Australian teachers working offshore imagine themselves and engage in transcultural practices, could not be starker. Another contrast is in how international students' educational outcomes are represented. Rizvi (2000: 223) suggests that international students are strategic and opportunistic, "chasing economic, social, educational and cultural opportunities", but do not consume Western education indiscriminately (see also Luke 2001). International students' mobility suggests more the purposive nomadic strategy of exploiting opportunities then moving on. Kraidy (2002: 205) suggests that the construction of hybrid cultural identities through such nomadic sampling processes is no simple add-on process, but a re-inscription, "an assertion of differences coupled with an enactment of identity, as a process which is simultaneously assimilationist and subversive, restrictive and liberating". This contrasts with the reliance on the discourse of cultural 'learning styles' that Bullen and Kenway (2003) reported amongst their sample of Australian university staff, and is further demonstrated in the essentializing accounts of the teachers profiled in this chapter. This discourse, evident in the empirical discussion above, works to polarize and exaggerate the way in which the Western learning style is constructed as a critical tradition and the Oriental as non-critical, implying the "behindness" and "outsideness" built into the modernization thesis (Pratt 2002: 29).

Education curricula are not disinterested conduits of such cultural scripts, but rather are active in the constitution and promotion of certain facts/fictions over others. The curriculum is an arena of competing alternatives wherein the more powerful will advantage their interests (Bernstein 1971). Thus curricula can work to legitimate certain social orders and relative advantages by mediating and resourcing the collective imaginary (London 2002).

This study looked at how the selling power of the Western academy shapes the curricula of preparatory programs for international students to privilege nostalgic versions of 'how the West is done' pedagogically. Such versions shore up the eroding facade of a notionally 'pure' Western tradition and deny the international student any constitutive "insideness" (Pratt 2002: 29). We are aware of the multiple, contradictory and competing discourses circulating within any one university: de-centring discourses that project notions of culturally inclusive curricula, an international university and so forth, as well as re-centring discourses that launch imagined nostalgic discourses of pure Western scholarly traditions and practices. In this chapter, we have been concerned with the workings of re-centring, retrospective discourses that imagine essentialized differences between the Western student and Asian 'Other'. By interrogating the curriculum enacted in the preparatory programs offered to international students we have demonstrated how retrospective discourses within a Western university work to resist any "negotiation of difference" (McConaghy cited in Bullen & Kenway 2003: 47). Rather, these retrospective discourses work to create/reassert a cultural script of an authentic, pure and essential pedagogical tradition, in active denial and suppression of any emerging hybridity, despite the escalating entanglement with 'Other' students.

We suggest that teachers employed in foundation education programs need to hear the complex, fluid, and changing voices of their students, and design education programs that meet the needs of this clientele. To continue to construct reified notions of the cultural 'Other' based on out-dated theories of fixed, static, cultural learning styles, is simply bad educational practice. Researching and designing innovative educational practices however, requires time, space and financial resources. All three conditions are often not available to preparatory studies teachers employed in the Australian university sector. Most of the teachers participating in the research study documented in this chapter were employed on a casual basis, and usually only paid for contact time, delivering pre-packaged curricular materials. These employment conditions must change if teachers are to meet the shifting educational needs of the large cohort of international students now attending Australian universities.

Following Boyer (cited in Zubrick, Reid & Rossiter 2000: 7) we argue that scholarship or scholarly activity should be part of every aspect of university work (including the work of preparatory studies teachers) and should be characterized by four features, namely that it: (1) emerges from enquiry and builds explicitly on existing knowledge; (2) is creative and progressive; (3) is generative and productive; and (4) its outcomes are public. Good teaching qualifies as scholarship or scholarly activity when:

1. teachers' lessons properly emerge from enquiry and build upon existing knowledge;
2. teachers' engagement with their subjects and their students is creative and progressive;
3. teachers' efforts are productive of learning and strategies for learning;
4. the results of techers' efforts are open to public evaluation; and
5. teachers' convey academic and disciplinary values and ways of thinking (Zubrick et al. 2000: 7).

The work of preparatory studies teachers is front-line, not peripheral, work in the new global knowledge economy and should be treated as serious, scholarly work. With the rigorous reflection, self-examination and scrutiny of practice such a charter entails, it will become increasingly untenable to unproblematically reproduce nostalgic versions of how the West is done.

Acknowledgements

Funding for the study reported in this chapter was provided by the Australian Research Council. This is a significantly revised version of the paper included in the 30th Annual Conference Proceedings of the Australian and New Zealand Comparative and International Education Society (Ninnes & Tamatea 2002).

References

Ang, I. 2001. *On Not Speaking Chinese: Living between Asia and the West*. London: Routledge.

Appadurai, A. 1996. *Modernity at Large: Cultural Dimensions of Globalisation*. Minneapolis: University of Minnesota Press.

Baudrillard, J. 1988. "Simulacra and Simulations." In *Jean Baudrillard: Selected Writings*, edited by M. Poster. Cambridge: Polity Press.

Bernstein, B. 1971. "On the Classification and Framing of Educational Knowledge." In *Knowledge and Control: New Directions for the Sociology of Education*, edited by M. Young. London: Collier MacMillan.

Bernstein, B. 1996. *Pedagogy, Symbolic Control, and Identity: Theory, Research, Critique.* London & Washington D.C.: Taylor & Francis.

Bernstein, B. 2000. *Pedagogy, Symbolic Control and Identity.* revised ed. Lanham: Rowman and Littlefield.

Bullen, E., & J. Kenway. 2003. "Real or Imagined Women? Staff Representations of International Women Postgraduate Students." *Discourse: Studies in the Cultural Politics of Education* 24(1): 36-50.

Castells, M. 1997. *The Power of Identity, The Information Age: Economy, Society and Culture.* Oxford: Blackwell.

Clifford, J. 1988. *The Predicament of Culture: Twentieth Century Ethnography, Literature, and*

Art. Cambridge, MA, & London: Harvard University Press.

Clifford, J. 1997. *Routes: Travel and Translation in the Late Twentieth Century.* Cambridge, MA: Harvard University Press.

Contractor, A. 2003. "Failing Grade for Uni's Overseas Courses." *The Sydney Morning Herald,* August 6.

Cottrell, S. 1999. *The Study Skills Handbook.* Basingstoke: Palgrave.

Department of Education, Science and Training (DEST). 2003. *Students 2002: Selected Higher Education Statistics.* Canberra: Commonwealth of Australia.

Dalrymple, W. 2002. *White Mughals: Love and Betrayal in Eighteenth-Century India.* London: Flamingo.

Doherty, C. 2001. "Internationalisation under Construction: Curricula and Pedagogy for International Students." In *Designing Educational Research: Theories, Methods and Practices,* edited by P. Singh & E. McWilliam. Flaxton, Qld.: Post Pressed.

Doherty, C., & P. Singh. 2002. "Simulating Western Pedagogy: A Case Study of Educational Programs for International Students." Paper presented at Internationalizing Education in the Asia-Pacific Region: Critical Reflections, Critical Times. 30th Annual Conference of the Australian and New Zealand Comparative and International Education Society, University of New England, Armidale, Australia, 6-8 December.

Friedman, J. 1994. *Cultural Identity and Global Process.* London: Sage.

Illing, D. 2003. "Compromised by Copying Allegations" *The Australian,* August 8.

Keith, M. 1988. "Stimulated Recall and Teachers' Thought Processes: A Critical Review of the Methodology and an Alternative Perspective." Paper presented at the 17th Annual Meeting of the Mid-South Educational Research Association, Louisville, KY, November 9-11.

Kenway, J., & E. Bullen. 2003. "Self-representations of International Women Postgraduate Students in the Global University 'Contact Zone'." *Gender and Education* 15 (1): 5-20.

Kraidy, M. 2002. "The Global, the Local, and the Hybrid: A Native Ethnography of Glocalization." In *Ethnographic Research. A Reader,* edited by S. Taylor. London: Sage Publications and The Open University Press.

Kress, G., Jewitt, C. & Tsatsarelis, C. 2000. "Knowledge, Identity, Pedagogy. Pedagogic Discourse and the Representational Environments of Education in Late Modernity. " *Linguistics and Education,* 11(1): 7-30.

Kubota, R. 2001. "Discursive Construction of the Images of U.S. Classrooms." *TESOL Quarterly* 35(1): 9-38.

Lemke, J. 1990. *Talking Science: Language, Learning and Values.* Norwood, NJ: Ablex.

London, N. 2002. "Curriculum and Pedagogy in the Development of Colonial Imagination: A Case Study." *Pedagogy, Culture and Society* 10(1): 95-122.

Luke, C. 2001. *Globalization and Women in Academia. North/West. South/East.* Mahwah, New Jersey: Lawrence Erlbaum Associates.

Maslen, G. 2002. "Asia Remains Our Largest Student Pool." *Campus Review,* September 11-17.

McCarthy, C., & Dimitriades, G. 2000. "Globalizing Pedagogies: Power, Resentment, and the Re-narration of Difference." In *Globalization and Education: Critical Perspectives,* edited by N. Burbules & C. Torres. London: Routledge.

McWilliam, E., Singh, P. & Taylor, P. 2002. "Doctoral Education, Danger and Risk Management." *Higher Education Research & Development* 21(2): 119-130.

Meade, P., & McMeniman, M. 1992. "Stimulated Recall – An Effective Methodology for Examining Successful Teaching in Science." *Australian Educational Researcher* 19 (3): 1-18.

Mehan, H. 1979. *Learning Lessons: Social Organization in the Classroom.* Cambridge: Harvard University Press.

Nesdale, D., Simkin, K., Sang, D., Burke, B. & Frager, S. 1995. *International Students and Immigration.* Canberra: AGPS.

Ninnes, P. & Tamatea, L. eds. 2002. *Internationalizing Education in the Asia-Pacific Region: Critical Reflections, Critical Times.* Proceedings of the 30th Annual Conference of the Australian and New Zealand Comparative and International Education Society (6-8 December). Armidale, NSW: School of Education and ANZCIES.

Noonan, G. 2003. "Overseas Student Numbers Surge 15%." *The Sydney Morning Herald,* July 2.

Perlez, J. 2003. "For Chinese Mothers With a Dream, Hard Knocks." *The New York Times,* September 23.

Pratt, M. L. 1992. *Imperial Eyes: Travel Writing and Transculturation.* New York: Routledge.

Pratt, M. L. 2002. "Modernity and Periphery: Toward a Global and Relational Analysis." In *Beyond Dichotomies: Histories, Identities, Cultures, and the Challenge of Globalization,* edited by E. Mudimbe-Boyi. New York: State University of New York Press.

Rizvi, F. 2000. "International Education and the Production of Global Imagination." In *Globalization and Education: Critical Perspectives,* edited by N. Burbules & C. Torres. London: Routledge.

Said, E. W. 1995. *Orientalism. Western Conceptions of the Orient.* London: Penguin.

Singh, P. & Freebody, P. 1997-2000. Australian Research Council funded project: *English Literacy in Off-shore Scientific and Technical Programs: A Case Study of Exporting Australian Education to Indonesia.*

Singh, P. 2003. "Offshore Australian Higher Education: A Case Study of Pedagogic Work in Indonesia." In *Disrupting Preconceptions: Postcolonialism and Education,* edited by A. Hickling-Hudson, J. Matthews & A. Woods. Flaxton, QLD: PostPressed.

Smith, Z. 2001. *White Teeth.* New York: Vintage International.

Trouillot, M-R. 2002. "The Perspective of the World: Globalization Then and Now." In *Beyond Dichotomies: Histories, Identities, Cultures, and the Challenge of Globalization,* edited by E. Mudimbe-Boyi. New York: State University of New York Press.

Tyler, W. 1999. "Pedagogic Identities and Educational Reform in the 1990s: The Cultural Dynamics of National Curricula." In *Pedagogy and the Shaping of Consciousness,* edited by F. Christie. London and New York: Continuum.

Waters, M. 2001. *Globalization.* 2nd ed. London: Routledge.

Werbner, P. 1997. "Essentialising Essentialism, Essentialising Silence: Ambivalence and Multiplicity in the Constructions of Racism and Ethnicity." In *Debating Cultural Hybridity: Multi-Cultural Identities and the Politics of Anti-Racism,* edited by P. Werbner & T. Modood. London: Zed Books.

Zubrick, A., I. Reid, & P. Rossiter. 2001. *Strengthening the Nexus Between Teaching and Research* (Evaluations and Investigations Programme Higher Education Division). Canberra: Department of Education, Training and Youth Affairs.

4

Hanging Together Even with Non-Native Speakers: The International Student Transition Experience

Anne Prescott and Meeri Hellstén

Introduction

In this chapter we seek to examine key issues for implementing successful teaching and learning methodologies for incoming on-shore international students (OIS) experiencing the transition from their home country to the Australian institutional, social and educational cultures. The chapter explores educational methodologies considered particularly from the student perspective. We claim that internationalization of teaching and learning is currently at a critical stage, which calls for systematic examination of our academic practices if we are to maintain our position as national providers of future international education offerings.

In this chapter we offer two central perspectives. First, we draw similarities between the OIS and mainstream students' transition experience into higher education (Levy, Osborn & Plunkett 2003) and we also identify aspects that may render the international student experience an increasingly cumbersome one. We hope to raise awareness about underlying social and cultural value systems constructed in and by the daily teaching and learning actions and decisions. Together these constitute Australian pedagogies and, as such affect individual self-perceptions.

While well documented in other parts of the world, there is relatively little Australian critical research reporting on the student perspective of the mechanisms involved in the international offerings in higher education, and their effects on the individual. This research is therefore exploratory in nature. However, in the latest account of the research on internationalization of higher education research in Australia, Harman (this volume) states that a considerable number of unpublished PhD and Master's research theses address areas such as student satisfaction, acculturation, learning autonomy and value, as well as differences in learning styles.

The current chapter is a contribution to this area, anchored in critical and systemic research outcomes.

The Mainstream Transition Experience

In the mainstream community, the transition process into tertiary education is well researched (see, for example, McInnes 2001). The notion of transition generally indicates the progression from the familiar to the unknown and involves the adoption of new cultural, social, and cognitive challenges. The transition period extends through the first year of tertiary study and widely acknowledged as being characterized by adjustment and other problems. Most academic failures can be traced back to problematic first year experiences (McInnes 2001, McInnes, James & Hartley 2000). McInnes (2001) further reports that the mainstream first year university experience research in Australian universities attributes cultural, pragmatic and discursive problems to differing assumptions and expectations held by the academic and the incoming student communities (Jepson, Turner & Calway 2002).

The acknowledgement of a positive first year experience as a function of success has resulted in the implementation of valuable program initiatives. For example, the work carried out in Australia and elsewhere reporting on the success of mentoring in university wide programs (Burns 1991, Dickson, Krause & Rudman 2002, Austin, Covalea & Weal 2002) have yielded similar results in terms of advocating the usefulness of systematic and deliberate assistance for students' academic integration. Among the examples cited by Dickson, Krause and Rudman (2002) are transition programs that enhance social integration, such as opportunities to meet with other students in semi-formal settings, facilitate the learning of new skills, such as library and information skills orientation, and familiarize students with the university environment.

The research field investigating the 'hidden curriculum' is another case in point (for an overview see Ramsden 2002). Ample evidence is now available in almost every discipline area on the impact on students' progression of sanctioned but covertly enacted disciplinary practices (Ivanic 1998, Krause & Barr 2002). Most of the problems occur very early in the first year of study. The research stemming from the academic reading and writing assistance area attests to the insufficiencies in mainstream first year students' knowledge about disciplinary cultures in the context of producing high quality academic work (see, for example, Barkhuizen 2003). The general conclusion from work in these areas is substantive in acknowledging the difficulties faced by members of the mainstream population in their transition into successful tertiary education environments (Austin, Covalea & Weal 2002, Dickson, Krause & Rudman 2002, Krause & Barr 2002).

We claim that foreign language issues and alienation from one's social and cultural comfort zone brought on by arrival in a foreign country exacerbate the international student transition experience. The most obvious issue is the language barrier that involves the learning of both verbal and non-verbal communication as well as pragmatic and literacy skills in a second or other language (Krashen 1987). Other challenges reported in the literature on the transition process experienced by OIS relate to both the students' self-concept and the effectiveness of teaching and learning (Ballard & Clanchy 1991, Biggs 1999, Hellstén 2002, Hellstén & Prescott 2002, Leask 2000, Volet & Ang 2000).

Language issues have been recognized as interfering with efficient learning among OIS. The field of TESOL widely reports on research attributing less than adequate levels of English language skills as the main variable preventing students from non-English speaking backgrounds (NESB) from learning effectively (Baynham 2002, Jones & Sim 2002, McKay 2002, San Miguel 1996). While it is acknowledged that language is a crucial component in the maintenance of internationalization globally (McKay 2002), we argue for further critical examination of the underlying social and cultural enactment of educational delivery. Such enactment mechanisms can be seen as constituting sometimes fruitless pedagogies for OIS. They can be manifest in attitudinal differences, assumptions and culturally important actions embedded in intercultural communication (Eglin & Hester 1992). This, in turn, creates double-edged challenges in perceptions of the international partnership as being effective or ineffective, meaningful or meaningless. Our argument is that the current cultural practices within the university reveal a poor fit between OIS expectations and the resulting on-shore experiences. Further, the poor fit can be the result of contrasts in culturally specific assumptions and stereotypical ways of enacting within and between the teaching and learning communities.

The philosophical and analytic underpinning for this chapter is based on the assumption that there is a set of reflexive relationships between identifications of appropriate behaviour (realisation), beliefs, value systems and their consequential actions (Hester & Eglin 1997b). This reflexivity involves understanding contexts and decision-making processes, and interpreting particular versions of 'reality' held by individuals. Reflexivity is a sense-making machinery in which language is the means through which communicative actions, and the subtleties of discourse and thus realisation, is made salient (Sacks 1996a, 1996b).

In our analytic context this framework is utilized as a tool for understanding the accomplishments of meaning making, and the identification of everyday matters and common sense know-how evident in interactions between individuals. This framework rejects *a priori* models for explaining behaviour and interaction. It is rather the reflexive relationship between belief and action that constitutes the context within which actions are manifest (Hester & Eglin 1997a). The contexts are made observable, for analytic purposes in, among other things, talk and discursive attributes between interactants. Individuals and their actions, statements and observable behaviours are inseparable parts of the whole that constructs 'reality' in interactive contexts such as the international student experience.

Cultural Clashes Attributed to Linguistic Factors

One of the founding ideologies of internationalization is its impetus for expansion of cultural understanding. However, research in the area of English language teaching provides findings to the contrary; cultural practices have been interpreted as obstructing the flow of understanding between lecturers and students (e.g. Levy, Osborn & Plunkett 2003, McKay 2002, McNamara & Harris 1996). Cultural clashes have been reported in the contexts of lecturers' marking and feedback on assignments (San Miguel 1996). For example, particular sets of cultural patterns in structuring an essay guide the subsequent composition of the text in culturally bound ways. Thus, when the structures of writing in a disciplinary culture (for example, Anglo-Australian) do not accord well with literary cultures in the international student's home background (for example, China), the result may see the OIS being penalized by low marks and confusing feedback on their written work. Some cited marker's comments found by San Miguel (1996: 32) were: "aspects do not flow logically", "your argument needs to be developed more fully and thoughtfully". Such comments are routinely found in marked essays (Lea & Stierer 1998). The difference is that while an Australian student may recognize the conventional writing errors referred to by the comments, they have little relevance to OIS from, say, Chinese writing cultures. In fact such comments are more likely to result in confusion and puzzlement in the case where a Chinese student has followed the conventions of Confucian heritage stylistics (Kelen 2002). There have been calls for more rigorous and linguistically descriptive academic literacy training for international students (Jepson, Turner & Calway 2002, San Miguel 1996). San Miguel (1996) also recommends professional development initiatives for lecturers to address the issue of commenting on written work. Since the time of her publication (San Miguel 1996), many such initiatives have been implemented. It is our experience however, that unless such programs are made compulsory, they seem to recruit only low numbers of academic participants.

Cultural actions are deeply ingrained and are enacted with little hesitation in everyday interactive encounters. Indeed it is very difficult to change our cultural subtleties. These include those literary composition styles into which we are indoctrinated through schooling. It is now widely recognized that the structures of composition in collectivist cultures such as China may differ greatly from writing structure in the West (Ballard & Clanchy 1991, Biggs 1999, Krause & O'Brien 2001, Leask 2000). For example, the focus on an explicit argument is often avoided in collectivist cultures. Rather, ample use of suggestions and surrounding information is used allowing for the reader to form their own opinion on the focus and argument of the composition.

Without explicit training in 'western' style academic writing, some OIS acculturated into Confucian heritage perspectives may unintentionally transfer their culturally learned writing practices onto their composition of university assignments in Australia. In this context international students from so-called 'Asian' backgrounds have been blamed for their inability to both write critically, and to form a coherent and strong argument (Biggs 1999, Volet & Ang 2000). The cultural academic writing transfer procedure is, in most cases, clearly accidental. Therefore, penalty for being uninformed about the 'preferred style' is highly unwarranted, and the possible outcome of this culturally 'ill-fitting' academic process is harsh. The OIS may find themselves in a negative spiral, wherein they are unaware of the writing errors that constituted their failure in achieving an acceptable grade for submitted work. The failure may pose further setbacks in terms of required resubmission of assignments and re-enrolment in study units, thus extending candidature.

Any extended duration imposed on their initial overseas candidature may impose further negative effects upon the financing and logistical effort of their overseas candidature. Further difficulties arise due to culturally specific politeness practices that prevent some OIS from approaching their Australian lecturers. When a taken-for-granted, cultural norm dictates that a student must not pass judgment on persons in higher positions of authority, the questioning of a marker's knowledge and marking style is an unavailable option (Biggs 1999, Volet & Ang 2000). It is likely that students will infer from such contextually confusing interactions that their understanding of the university 'system' and its incumbent disciplinary assessment practices are in some way erroneous, leaving them in an unreciprocated situation, where no help is available.

The key point in this scenario is that it demonstrates, and makes available for analytic purposes, the interpretative power of inference-making in human actions, interaction and normative behaviour. Note, that it is the *commentary* exemplified in the above scenario, that gives rise to the inferences made about individual's thought patterns and value systems, and the actions taken as a consequence, all of which have very real implications for the outcomes that are made possible in that particular and culturally constrained context.

We acknowledge the extensive work already published in the context of Confucian (Chinese) teaching and learning methodologies (see for example Kelen 2002, Ballard & Clanchy 1991, Biggs 1999, Hutchings, Jackson & McEllister 2002, Zhao & Guó 2002, Zou 2002). Such studies are principally concerned with the differences between the 'eastern' and 'western' teaching and learning paradigm (such as language issues). Our contribution to the current debate, however, derives from the intersection of the concept of international identity, the overall transition process, and the cultural practices which provide the context for the ways in which the OIS experience is constituted. This experience is not solely a function of language and interaction *per se*, but is evident in the mundane everyday discursive features that make up the learning environment. In this chapter we demonstrate that such discourse is determined by the meanings embedded into common sense understandings and expectations. For example, some naturally occurring mainstream academic assumptions can be interpreted in ways that lead to specific consequences for OIS. Analysing such discourse within this specific context is a powerful tool for gaining an understanding of the practices that constitute the quality of the teaching and learning.

Comments on Method

Our methods are data generative, as opposed to data gathered (Baker 1997). Thus, rather than being informed by *a priori* models or hypotheses we let the reflexive relationship between interactants provide the context for analysing the interview talk. This means that participants in the conversations are considered as culturally competent, rather than actors in an internalized world. This data driven framework considers as its measure of achievement the ability of the researcher to get the interview participants to make sense of, and to generate meaning about, both the intrinsic and external worlds they describe. Interview accounts are thus viewed as occasioned reproductions of past events. This renders the analysis of interview data as generative only of the situated context in which it occurs. The analysis can in this light at best generate versions of possible conclusions about possible outcomes and possible 'truths'. A situated view of 'truth value' then rejects the existence of one absolute truth. Like truth, knowledge is observable in practical action and is generated culturally so that its specific cultural features are indeed unavailable to outsiders of that culture (Heap 1984). Within this situated perspective of data analysis then, we do not claim absolutes, but accept that other and different analytic outcomes are also plausible.

The interviews consisted of one hour long semi-structured and open-ended questions relating to the international student's initial period upon arrival in Australia. This allowed for the interviews to adopt a natural conversational flow that put the interviewees at ease. Of central interest were identity issues of how the transitional experience may change participants as individuals, and the consequential effect upon their learning. The questions centred on the participants' social and cultural experiences of their arrival in Australia, their friendship patterns, peer relationships and their beliefs about how they were 'coping' in the new system. We sought comparative descriptions of 'typicality' in the context of national cultures. Each interview thus generated a series of perceptions about the practices constituting institutional and in some cases disciplinary cultures, the local and (inter-)national discourse patterns and their interactive infrastructures.

Participants were recruited from lectures across twelve discipline areas e.g. accounting, linguistics and anthropology. A total of forty-eight students from sixteen countries volunteered. These students ranged in age from 18 to 50 years, and were undertaking both undergraduate and postgraduate courses under the international university enrolment program. The sample is representative of a wide range of academic disciplines and countries, with the majority of participants from Asia.

The Analysis

The audio-recorded interviews were transcribed according to a method outlined in Gunn, Forrest, and Freebody (1995). On the whole the analytic process involved an interpretative method developed by Silverman (1997), whereby data materials are modified and re-modified into a coding scheme until all data and their incumbent discursive features are systematically accounted for. After this process the coded interviews were then listened to repeatedly in order to locate the main characteristics, themes and conversational features (such as cultural features) associated with descriptions about the OIS experience that emerged from the taped conversations. The discursive features were analysed for their representativeness of the issues most prominently emerging from all interviews.

Results and Discussion

The aim of the analysis and discussion is to showcase the mechanism through which the cultural 'ill-fit' is described in the interviews of the OIS experiences in the host university. Recall that it is the reflexive relationship between identifier and action that is taken to constitute the meaning of the international student experience. The OIS must move across a sequential process of actions in order to succeed in their transition into the Australian institutional environment.

When No Help Is At Hand

The initial culture shock inherent in the first months of the international student transition is well acknowledged (McInnes 2001). While recognizing initial teething problems with finding one's way around an alien system, we are more interested in the underlying practices that render the experience as either successful or unsuccessful for the interviewees. It is plausible that the new incoming overseas student assumes an ease of understanding of information and guidance that would speed up their transition into their new environment. One example about the way in which lecturers reciprocate assumptions about this information hunger can be found in the following statement made by a lecturer in response to an approach for help with study matters.

> I teach you and then like you have to learn it yourself. Well the ... lecturer before that he say that their duty is 'I teach you, you want to learn, you don't want to learn, that's up to you'. [Mary]

Here the initial statement carries an underlying assumption about the relationships between lecturer and student. The inference embedded in this statement is that of power and subordination of that relationship. The second inferential feature is that the student stands alone on their transition pathway. In 'western' cultures the statement can be clearly understood as promoting learner independence, even though it may invoke surprise because of its flippant nature. However, the cross-culturally salient problem with ambiguous assumptions and misconceptions available from statements such as this is that it is very possible the utterance may be interpreted contextually. The lecturer and the system that he represents are understood as 'not caring' about their (note plural) students' learning. The way in which this statement is constructed makes it possible to also interpret the contradiction in 'duties' of a teacher.

The outcome for students of such teacher-student reciprocity is the feeling of isolation and being lost in a new system. The feeling may be exacerbated by the sense that there really is nowhere a student can turn for help. Our data revealed many accounts to this effect. For example:

> You feel lost at the beginning, didn't know how, what to do in all your free time. You're supposed to read, but you are quite lost. [Diane]

We are interested in what practical actions and consequences these cultural misconceptions make obtainable for the newly arrived international student. The initial interpretation is a result of confusion and possibly mistrust. Indeed, we found many accounts of students' reluctance to approach lecturers after an initial 'embarrassing' encounter when seeking help.

> ... the thing is they know that I'm struggling because obviously I go to them for help. But in the way they answer my questions or in the way they put it, it just makes me feel like, oh I shouldn't ask them again. Because I mean like, in order for me to talk to someone I have to say: "OK they want to help me." But I don't feel that. And just the way they answer me and the way they situate the looks on their face, it's like, it's not inviting. Their look is not inviting. So basically, even if I am struggling I know I'm not going to go there again because I embarrassed myself one time and I don't want to embarrass myself again. [Lucy]

> So, after class: "-Teacher, may I ask you a question?", "-okay, okay" and at the same time the teacher holds the bag and goes quickly out. Maybe I lose my confidence to ask some question. [Peter]

The workings of the contextual conversational cues are self-evident in the above accounts. Lucy's convincing description of the subtleties inherent in the lecturer's demeanour reveals otherwise hidden value systems, and attests to the lecturer's seeming lack of 'duty of care'. The practical outcome of this descriptive account is that the student refrains from approaching someone when in need of help, leaving the student on an isolated transitional path. Also available for analysis in this talk are the ways in which cultural meanings are mediated. Note that it is not what the lecturer said but the ways in which utterances were made which are interpreted as rejecting the student's attempt at seeking help in this instance. In the cultural context of these utterances and inferences then, we see the justification for the interviewee's feelings that no help is at hand when in trouble.

Note that we are not suggesting the intentions of lecturers were discriminatory that they failed in their duties as members of the academic community. Our intention is rather to highlight the subtleties of contextualized talk by identifying inferential features otherwise considered hidden and unavailable for observation and scrutiny. We also demonstrate that these cultural readings of utterances make salient those features we argue are critical for implementing socially and culturally effective teaching and learning strategies for communication within the confines of international education.

Surviving the shock of cultural and contextual teething problems is very important for the students in this study. Once the concept of being independent is understood students begin to equate it with certain activities, such as extensive reading and visiting the library.

> I think I should work harder because once I don't know I just ask my tuition teacher to explain to me. But in uni I think you just have to be independent. We have to find, find ourself first, read a lot of book and go to library. [Jenny]

However, just what exactly is involved in independent learning seems to be still unclear to students at this initial stage of transition.

> You should learn by yourself … rather than asking some questions to your teacher. In other words, that you shouldn't rely very much on the teacher and (unclear) and also you can't rely on others. You should, um learn by yourself. You should research a lot of things by yourself. [Christine]

Thus, students' culture specific interpretations of the covert and overt workings of the host 'system' influence activities that are crucial in how students subsequently are able to cope with their transitions. In this context, survival is achieved by 'independent learning', which is constructed through a series of imposed actions such as: learning by one self; not relying on the teacher or peers for help; and not embarrassing oneself by making false assumptions about teacher support. The library has a central position in the construction of survival in this context. Many students made sense of the unanticipated expectation placed on them by spending large amounts of time in the library.

In sum, the transition process is depicted clearly by our interview participants as a progression from near or total sense of misplacement to the gradual realisation of the necessary course of action in the survival process. Personal characteristics such as attitudes and ways of thinking are often sacrificed in this progression. The accomplishment of these changes sometimes requires time and effort:

> It took me time to realise the difference between the Japanese way [of teaching] and Australian way and after I realised the difference, okay now I have to change the attitude, so it took me time as well. [Janet]

While many of these experiences resemble those of mainstream students, the cultural transition involved in the international transition experience seems to come at a price for the OIS. From our analysis of the interviews, it seems that OIS are unaware of the stakes before embarking upon their overseas study venture. While a case can be made that these experiences may be little different from those of non-OIS students, the realisation of the high cost to their personal integrity and identity may further complicate the ease of transition into the new educational environment. This leads to features of resistance (for example the previous quote from Lucy) toward the host 'system' and to its sanctioned cultural and social conventions.

The Cost of Time

Another prominent theme representative of the talk with international interview participants was the value afforded to time. Clearly, the international study candidature is both formally and financially confined to time. It seems, however, that the concept of time gains amplified cultural meaning in the context of the high stakes of the international experience. The interviewees gave us a sense that they are working against time, and that any delay is contrary to their expectations. Time management problems have resulted in repetition of study modules, failure to follow verbalized instructions, failure to produce acceptable levels of work, not to mention the immense increase in personal and monetary costs as a result of repeated study of units and the need to extend visas. Thus the concept of time carries enormous value for OIS in terms of learning efficacy, and access and participation in instructional sessions, and in terms of orientation during the transition period.

The issue of time produced extensive commentary. It seems to us that the international student learning experience is defined in terms of various time factors. In a cause and effect fashion then, time pressures are used as a rationale for accounting for various difficulties such as following conversations in class, comprehending written materials, and constructing personal traits such as confidence.

> At the beginning … I can't understand what the teacher said, but I can't stop the teacher, pardon, could you repeat again. So I just focus on my energy to understand, to pay more attention to understand. And little and little you just guess and try to understand and little and little you can understand what the teacher said. So, you just use your confidence, yeah, little and little. Anyway,

you know in the classroom, just … we have a few words the teacher must use and maybe according to the material, reading material, you can guess what the teacher said, yeah. So we can guess. Anyway, you can't stop the teacher, what do you say, pardon, can you repeat, yeah, just guess. [Peter]

Guesswork is used as a back up tool in conceptualisation of curriculum content and delivery. A large number of OIS reported using approximation to fill the gap between what is understood and what is not, and as we have established above, often without approaching academics for clarification. With no feedback system in place, the verification of 'truth' is left unreciprocated leading to further misunderstandings and communicative uncertainty. The ways in which these discursive cues are comprehended and put into practice by OIS mean that students are left to their own devices to draw conclusions as to the gist of the communicative content.

Efficacy of learning is weighed against time in a polarized way; the OIS compares their time demands with those of native members of the student population.

I have to spend at least 8 hours; actually I'm spending more than 8 hours on each unit. I think compared with Australian students who speak native English and I think only 6 or 5 hours is enough for them. [Paul]

The interesting analytic feature in this statement is the comparison with the assumed actions of native speakers. Whether or not the student knows the 'true' amount of hours spent by native speakers on study tasks, this excerpt shows that in order to make sense of their temporal study burden, the OIS need to assume comparisons with peers.

It takes me a long time to study. So say if it takes like my friend it takes an hour for her to study for her exam or whatever, it would, like, take me 2 hours, 3 hours. [Lucy]

There were many reasons given to explain time delays:

There's a big language issue, because it takes them double the time to read the assignments, the essays, you know, quotes and takes them double the time to write, yeah. Yeah, and then they tape record the lectures and things like that. [Sarah]

My first response to the native English speaker, I just translate their English into Chinese and then I will just translate Chinese into English, then I will speak out in English. [Christine]

Sometimes you want to say something or you want to interrupt, you want to

> say something, but you just can't find your words. Yeah, that's something that's really annoying. You open your mouth and you're about to say something and you go, oh, I lost it. [Anna]

The above statements are representative of early to medium stages of second language learning processes generally (Krashen 1987, International English Language Testing System [IELTS] Australia 2003). We raise the question of whether there is general knowledge within the academic community of the slower processing of languages among some international students. Our interviews support the need for further awareness-raising of second language users' actual language processes and the consequent changes to inter-language communication.

> In most cases ... lecturers are fine, but some of the tutors speak real fast and they've got an accent, you know, it's hard to understand and ... I hate to always say, I beg your pardon, all the time. You know, 2 or 3 times in the tutorial is enough for the tutor. If you are native speaker, you can response very quickly and you can think in English very quickly, but um, I don't know for other students, but in my case, when I think in English it takes me more time than in Japanese. [Janet]

Variations in communication styles are also experienced as problematic in the transition process. Individual English accents or accents from another language may produce comprehension difficulties between OIS and lecturers.

> I've met one ... tutor and he had a hard time even expressing himself and he's got an accent so bad I could hardly understand what he's talking about. So, finally I changed and went to another tutorial. [Peter]

Cultural politeness protocols may prohibit students from commenting on lecturer's individual speaking styles and pronunciation features. The action taken in this situation was to avoid confrontation and change tutorial groups rather than approach the program administrator for advice.

The inference available from the overall data analyses hint of a troublesome transition experience. We intend here to highlight the critical issues in the transition experience. The level at which the transition has been deemed successful is weighed against peer group criteria. We received many comments that were representative of the appreciation of the cultural exchange opportunities students receive outside their institutional learning environment.

> Um... ah... yeah. I like the way the people hang together. Australian people hang together (...).

I: What do you mean hang together?

P: Hang together in groups and go out and meet, have chats and go for a beer, and they are very, very friendly and welcoming. Ah, … even with you know, non-native speakers, foreign people. [Diane]

We found that evaluating the entire transition experience is based on interactions in the private domain of peer groups and social environments. Students ordinarily summed up these experiences based on the assumption of inherent difference between 'non-native speakers/foreign people' and Australians. There is a sense of surprise detectable in the last statement by Diane that signifies clearly an expectation to the contrary – she assumes a friendly and welcoming nature, even from non-native speakers. Hence, we detect a clear contrast in observable attitudinal and behavioural characteristics in the discourse between the academic community and student peer groups. Would we imagine an easier transition if they were the same?

In sum, the excerpts of talk portrayed here collectively elicit the reflexive constitution of meaning-making inherent in surviving the transition experience into a new international education environment. Through the reciprocal process of attributing meanings to actions, students make sense of their experiences. On the basis of the contextual descriptions provided by the interviewees and the ways in which the meaning and its related actions are interpreted we can draw some conclusions. For the students the Australian international experience may mean the following – each to a greater or lesser extent:

- Struggle and confusion
- Isolation (provides meaning for 'independence')
- No help is available from peers or the academic community
- Personal identity change, self-embarrassment and loss of confidence may be at stake
- Emphasis on time and its effects on learning, language processing and coping ability
- Learning is slow and arduous
- Participation in learning involves uncertainty and guessing of instructional content

Our in-depth analyses of the social and cultural enactment of teaching and learning in international contexts demonstrate a double edge challenge for the student body. A further interpretation is that the perceived attractiveness of the international education package means more than educational access to superior career pathways. Once on shore, the international students are confronted with the enactment of subtle and covertly enforced social and cultural contexts that provide a challenging transition path. Within these challenging transitional practices the stakes for success are high in terms of personal, temporal and financial investment.

Implication for Teaching and Learning in International Contexts

According to the theoretical underpinning of this study, the international student transition experience is constituted in and by actions that construct cultural practices. In this chapter we have demonstrated that educational practices are largely brought about by everyday discourse, values and their attributive actions.

Our findings have implications for three key aspects of academic work:

- the critical examination of academic teaching and learning
- social and cultural practices
- professional development initiatives.

We present these in terms of two key strategies we see as critical for the implementation of effective pedagogy. The first strategy recognizes the various transition practices experienced by the incoming students in Australian universities. We found very few differences in the literature between the transition experiences of incoming international students and mainstream first year students (see, for example, Levy, Osborn & Plunkett 2003). The smooth transition into successful learning environments is based on effective teaching and learning generally, including a transition into the wider geographical and social context. We draw on the implementation of inclusive practices in terms of communication and the integration of formal and informal learning environments in terms of teaching and learning.

We agree with Pearson and Beasley (1996) on the adoption of teaching methodologies that are developed with international students in mind but which are implemented for the general university student population. In this way, the principles of clear communication, making of explicit rules, and addressing discursive assumptions about processes and procedures will be of benefit to all students. An integration of informal introductory sessions and university orientation activities in which generic skills are taught and clear instructions on lecturers' expectations are provided should result in an optimal transition into the new learning environment. We believe that the latter process calls for a questioning of lecturers' and students' personal value systems and moral beliefs about the meaning of student achievement and the effects of individual diversity on sustaining learning success. It is these social and psychological constructs that constitute the cultural practices that evidently are taken to be the essence of the international experience by the incoming student population.

The second strategy relates to enhancing effective pedagogies and teaching methodologies among the teaching community. We have shown above that the discursive practices between lecturers and students have important consequences for the ways in which the international student experience is subsequently interpreted and acted upon. Inherent in these discursive practices are certain psychological and cultural assumptions (Freebody, Ludwig, & Gunn 1995) that need to be made explicit in the international teaching and learning context. For example, professional development initiatives could address the embeddedness of cultural and other assumptions in intercultural communication. More importantly, they could explore at a deeper level the psychological consequences that certain (albeit often well-meaning) discursive practices and actions impose on international students. Not only should such programs be run by expert organisational and cross-cultural psychologists, they also need to be made attractive to the academic community by being decentralized and integrated into the everyday workplace culture at local levels. It is our contention that such programs should be made available not only in those departments with high international student enrolments, but should cater for the general academic teaching community and thus bring about consolidated international, inter-cultural and organisational transformation.

Part and parcel of the university transition experience is also the development of acceptable academic literacy practices. The research reported here shows many similarities between OIS and local students in the cognitive and linguistic processes involved, and the difficulties experienced in orientation into disciplinary writing and conventions (Krause & O'Brien 2001). While many effective programs are currently being administered in Australian higher education institutions, there is room for integrating further content into such programs that are inclusive of international students. The body of literature targeting non-English speaking students' reading and writing skills is valuable. In response to such initiatives, however, our experience of OIS conversation is that time constraints do not allow for additional reading of 'non-vernacular' materials. International students report spending extensive time on reading their subject literature and have little spare time for foraging for additional readings.

Implementation of such teaching and learning initiatives would involve an expansion of academic literacy programs across the tertiary education sector. These programs would specifically target international students and would be delivered by qualified personnel. For such programs to be effective however, cooperation between teaching staff and lecturers is required in communicating the hidden discursive and disciplinary assumptions inherent, for example, in typical essay questions. The efficacy of delivery is then greatly enhanced by cooperative learning settings in consolidation with subject lecturers. The sessions must make available the exploration of cultural issues around particular learning contexts. Advocating the explicit use of language and communication for the delivery of culturally sensitive teaching modes is crucial for continuing success. Teaching academic literacy is the responsibility of both subject lecturers and learning support staff, not just the latter.

In the international transition context, mentoring programs (Austin, Covalea & Weal 2002) and support classes and workshops (Pearson & Beasley 1996) have been trialled with pleasing results. For example, Pearson and Beasley (1996) instituted support classes and workshops with materials and activities specifically designed for international students but open to all students. This framework proved useful in providing much needed cultural change in institutional practices made relevant and culturally meaningful to both international and Australian students.

Such frameworks provide opportunities for developing educational practices that are inclusive of both local and international student needs. For example, making the curriculum and its discourses explicit and unassuming is a starting point offered by Leask (2000). Provision of obvious and workable program and assessment guidelines that are sensitive to individual variation and diversity are also listed among her recommendations. The teaching and learning guidelines should explicitly state the learning objectives (for example, clarifying the meaning of a 'satisfactory' assessment work, clarifying expectations, providing reliable access for students including visiting hours, and alternate ways of communicating with lecturers). In other words, the teaching and learning practices of a culturally sensitive curriculum amounts to increased accountability of pedagogy generally.

International study skills texts such as those presented by Lewis and Reinders (2003) are a source of valuable information for how to survive transition into 'a new institutional system'. While the above publication particularly targets international student readers, there are important directives available also for lecturers. Procedural culturally-based know-how such as "how to address your lecturer", "how to explain yourself clearly", "when to ask questions in a lecture", and "who decides when a consultation is over" given by Lewis and Reinders (2003: 174-176) alert lecturers to potential cross cultural communication issues. In the context of the interaction with OIS these conversational rules can be made an explicit part of the teaching discourse and thereby miscommunication can be avoided.

It is our general consensus that many of the issues raised by OIS in the interviews are not much different from those encountered by newly enrolled local university students. Most universities today meet the needs of first year students by effective mentoring and transition programs. The further development of these existing programs would benefit significantly from consolidating with OIS transition areas. Such initiatives are relatively effortless to implement. Some suggestions include mentoring programs introducing contact between established and newly-arrived international students. A 24-hour call centre operation is also beneficial for OIS who may feel they have no one to turn to if an emergency takes place after official office hours. Austin, Covalea & Weal (2002) report favourably on one such trial. In that case the mentors were responsible for managing a mobile telephone service on a rostered basis.

Another cost effective strategy for integrating international students into existing transition programs is an online facility of general information about the institution, the local geographic area, study skills and management. The online facility could house a number of lecturers scheduled to answer questions about course work, particularly from the point of view of cultural and disciplinary assumptions. The effectiveness of such initiatives hinges on sound cultural awareness among the lecturers involved. To this effect, we suggest professional training and development in cultural communication skills as criteria for acting in such positions.

Reflective Teaching Practice

The adoption of reflective teaching and learning practices provides many advantages for the effectiveness of teaching pedagogy and practice. The continuous critical evaluation of one's teaching practices, followed by implementation and modification of teaching strategies is not merely limited to the context of teaching international students, but is of equal benefit to teaching generally. Effective teaching must involve critical perspective taking, self-critique and assessment of personal teaching methods. Such constitutive reflective practices yield effective teaching and learning environments.

Reflective teaching practices may involve clarifying one's personal assumptions, values and beliefs on issues that constitute difference in our society. Exploration of one's attitudes towards and belief systems about, for example, indigenes, refugees, homosexuals, spoken dialects, foreign accents, and politeness discourses provides a starting point that can be systematically addressed in a professional development environment. The exercises must be made accountable however, by following up on issues with effective implementation that reveal the consequences of actions taken as a result of certain beliefs.

Above all, there has to be recognition by academics that the enactment of culture is subtle but significant. Reflective practices allow for academics to see students as active members in the constitution of international education, and support the reflexive constitution of practice and action in the educational partnership.

Conclusion

Our critical examination of current social and cultural practices in and around teaching international students in Australia has revealed the continued need for evaluating and reviewing the subtleties inherent in cultural interaction. Our review of literature on the first year experience and our analyses of international student talk in the context of their initial encounters with a new educational system and culture reveal a double edged sword of challenges. The inferential message of the student talk in our interviews showcases a less than amicable transition into the Australian academic environment.

The conclusion available from our interviews reveals high expectations placed on incoming international students to Australia. These expectations are embedded with requirements of skills in orientation and navigation in a foreign country, language and culture. Conflicting with these transition skills requirements are the cultural navigation needs imposed upon the international student, and the unconstructive impact of reasoning misconceptions on the effectiveness of finding your way in the foreign cultural maze of institutional, disciplinary, interpersonal, geographical, general social and pragmatic discourses sanctioned by the host culture.

Recognition is due of the dexterity with which OIS have managed this double impact transition to date. In many sites they have managed with less than amicable institutional or other support and at a high financial and personal cost.

The collective student voice exemplified in this chapter therefore, provides valuable feedback to the teaching community about the social and cultural discourses and educational enactment inherent within but subtly visible to the incoming international student. We have in this chapter drawn together some common themes leading to implications for adopting strategies for addressing effective teaching and learning for international contexts.

The main implication of our discussion is that regardless of extensive and active discussions advocating the recognition of cultural diversity in the Australian higher educational setting, its everyday interactions and discursive practices do not confirm evidence of its accomplishment. This generates further implications for continued professional development incentives on culturally sensitive curriculum delivery, which critically includes inventiveness afforded to broad cultural change among the incumbent members of the international education partnership.

Acknowledgement

Meeri Hellstén and Anne Prescott thank the Macquarie University Early Career Grant Scheme for funding this project.

References

Austin, J., Covalea, L. & Weal, S. 2002. "Going the Extra Mile – Swinburne, Lilydale's Mentor Program." Paper presented at the 16th Australian International Education Conference, Hobart, 30 September - 4 October.

Baker, C. 1997. "Membership Categorisation and Membership Accounts." In *Qualitative Analysis: Issues of Theory and Method*, edited by D. Silverman. London: Sage.

Ballard, B. & Clanchy, J. 1991. *Teaching Students from Overseas: A Brief Guide for Lecturers and Supervisors*. Melbourne: Longman Cheshire.

Barkhuizen, G. 2003. "The Quest for an Approach to Guide Critical Reading and Writing." *Prospect* 17: 3.

Baynham, M. 2002. "Academic Writing in the New University." In *Integrating Theory with Practice in Second Language Teaching*, edited by A. Furness, G. Wong and L. Wu. Hong Kong: Language Centre, The Hong Kong University of Science and Technology.

Biggs, J. 1999. *Teaching for Quality Learning at University*. Buckingham: Society for Research into Higher Education and Open University Press.

Burns, R. 1991. "Study and Stress among First Year Overseas Students in an Australian University." *Higher Education Research and Development* 10(1): 61-77.

Dickson, J., Krause, K. & Rudman, S. 2002. "Making the Transition to University: An Evaluation of Academic Orientation." Paper presented at the Sixth Pacific Rim Conference: First Year in Higher Education – Changing Agendas, Christchurch, New Zealand, 8-10 July.

Eglin, P. & Hester, S. 1992. "Category, Predicate and Task: Pragmatics of Practical Action. Review Article." *Semiotica* 88(3/4): 243-268.

Freebody, P., Ludwig, C., & Gunn, S. eds. 1995. *Everyday Literacy Practices in and out of Schools in Low Socio-economic Urban Communities.* Canberra: Commonwealth Department of Employment, Education and Training.

Gunn, S., Forrest, T. & Freebody, P. 1995. "Perspectives on Poverty, Schooling, and Literacy: The Overviews of the Participants." In *Everyday Literacy Practices in and out of Schools in Low Socio-economic Urban Communities*, edited by P. Freebody, C. Ludwig and S. Gunn. Canberra: Commonwealth Department of Employment, Education and Training.

Heap, J. 1984. "Ethnomethodology and Education: Possibilities." *Journal of Educational Thought* 18(3): 168-171.

Hellstén, M. 2002. "Internationalizing the Curriculum." Paper presented at Internationalizing Education in the Asia-Pacific Region: Critical Reflections, Critical Times. 30th Annual Conference of the Australian and New Zealand Comparative and International Education Society, Armidale, Australia, 6-8 December.

Hellstén, M. & Prescott, A. 2002. "Learning at Macquarie: The International Student Experience." Paper presented at Celebrating Teaching at Macquarie, Macquarie University, Sydney, 28-29 November.

Hester, S. & Eglin, P. 1997a. "Membership Categorisation Analysis: An Introduction." In *Culture in Action. Studies in Membership Categorisation Analysis*, edited by S. Hester and P. Eglin. Wahington, D.C.: International Institute for Ethnomethodology and Conversation Analysis and University Press of America.

Hester, S. & Eglin, P. 1997b. "The Reflexive Constitution of Category, Predicate and Context in Two Settings." In *Culture in Action. Studies in Membership Categorisation Analysis*, edited by S. Hester and P. Eglin. Washington, D.C.: International Institute for Ethnomethodology and Conversation Analysis and University Press of America.

Hutchings, K., Jackson, P. & McEllister, R. 2002. "Exploiting the Links between Theory and Practice: Developing Students' Cross-cultural Understanding through an International Study Tour of China." *Higher Education Research and Development* 21(1): 55-71.

International English Language Testing System (IELTS) Australia. "International English Language Testing System 2003." Accessed 18 December 2003. Available from http://www.ielts.org/index.htm.

Ivanic, R. 1998. *Writing and Identity: The Discoursal Construction of Identity in Academic Writing.* Amsterdam: Benjamins.

Jepson, M., Turner, T. & Calway, B. "The Transition of International Students into Post-graduate Study: An Incremental Approach 2002." Accessed 15 December 2003. Available from http://www.aare.edu.au/02pap/tur02193.htm.

Jones, A. & Sim, S. "Perceptions and Priorities of Diverse Groups of 1st Year Accounting Students with Regard to Generic Skills/Communication Skills 2002." Accessed 28 May 2003. Available from http://www.ecu.edu.au/conferences/herdsa/main/papers/nonref/pdf/AlanJones.pdf.

Kelen, C. 2002. "Language and Learning Orthodoxy in the English Classroom in China." *Educational Philosophy and Theory* 34(2): 223-237.

Krashen, S. 1987. *Principles and Practice in Second Language Acquisition.* London: Prentice-Hall International.

Krause, K. & Barr, J. 2002. "Connecting Students to Academic Writing Online." Paper presented at Sixth Pacific Rim Conference: First Year in Higher Education – Changing Agendas, Christchurch, New Zealand, 8-10 July.

Krause, K. & O'Brien, D. 2001. "Adolescent Second Language Writers in China: A Socio-cultural Analysis." In *Research on Sociocultural Influences on Motivation and Learning*, edited by D. McInerney and S. Van Etten. Greenwich, CT: Information Age Publishing.

Lea, M. R. & Stierer, B. 1998. *New Contexts for Student Writing in Higher Education.* Buckingham: Open University Press and the Society for Research into Higher Education.

Leask, B. 2000. "Online Delivery and Internationalisation: Implications for Students, the Curriculum and Staff Development." Paper presented at International distance education and open learning conference, Adelaide, 11-13 September.

Levy, S., Osborn, M. & Plunkett, M. "An Investigation of International Students' Academic and Social Transition Requirements 2003." Accessed 15 December 2003. Available from http://www.qut.edu.au/talss/fye/papers03/Refereed%20Papers/Full%20papers/Levy,Osborne&Plunkett_paper.doc.

Lewis, M. & Reinders, H. 2003. *Study Skills for Speakers of English as a Second Language.* New York: Palgrave MacMillan.

McInnes, C. 2001. "Researching the First Year Experience: Where to from here?" *Higher Education Research and Development* 20(2): 105-114.

McInnes, C., James, R. & Hartley, R. 2000. *Trends in the First Year Experience in Australian Universities.* Canberra: Australian Government Publishing Service.

McKay, S. 2002. *Teaching English as an International Language.* New York: Oxford University Press.

McNamara, D. & Harris, R. 1996. *Quality Higher Education for Overseas Students.* London: Routledge.

Pearson, C., & Beasley, C. J. 1996. "Reducing Learning Barriers amongst International Students: A Longitudinal Developmental Study." *Australian Educational Researcher* 23(2): 79-96.

Ramsden, P. 2002. *Learning to Teach in Higher Education.* London: RoutledgeFalmer.

Sacks, H. 1996a. *Lectures on Conversation*. Edited by G. Jefferson. Vol. 1. Oxford: Blackwell Publishers.

Sacks, H. 1996b. *Lectures on Conversation*. Edited by G. Jefferson. Vol. 2. Oxford: Blackwell Publishers.

San Miguel, C. 1996. "Cultural Influences on Academic Literacy: A Case Study." *Open Letter* 6(2): 31-43.

Silverman, D. ed. 1997. *Qualitative Research. Theory, Method and Practice*. London: Sage publications.

Volet, S. & Ang, G. 2000. *Fostering Social Cohesion in Universities: Bridging the Cultural Divide*. Canberra: Australian Education Foundation, Department of Education, Training and Youth Affairs.

Zhao, J., & Guo, J. 2002. "The Restructuring of China's Higher Education: An Experience for Market Economy and Knowledge Economy." *Educational Philosophy and Theory* 34(2): 207-221.

Zou, Y. 2002. "Multiple Identities of a Chinese Immigrant: A Story of Adaptation and Empowerment." *Qualitative Studies in Education* 15(3): 252-268.

5

Internationalizing Chinese Higher Education: A Case Study of a Major Comprehensive University

Rui Yang

Introduction

In the current era of globalization, the challenge of the market is the centre of attention. We are witnessing an intensification of a variety of important social, cultural, economic, and political developments that affect higher education. There has been a deepening of the shift from Keynesianism to neo-liberalism. Strong market forces and corporate management ideas have affected the way universities operate worldwide (Slaughter & Leslie 1997). It is not that universities must do the same with fewer resources; they must do different things and in different ways (Schugurensky 2003: 296).

At the same time, countries approach the international dimension of education differently. As a response to globalization, internationalization is changing the world of higher education, while its own process is being changed by globalization. It is closely tied to the specific history, culture, resources and priorities of the specific institutions of higher education (Yang 2002a). This chapter examines how Chinese universities are implementing internationalization in their cultural complexity and social contexts, using Zhongshan University (ZU) as an example.

This chapter therefore contributes to higher education internationalization literature where there is a shortage of empirical studies and a neglect of the links between the international and local environments (de Wit 1999). By demonstrating how internationalization is based on local circumstances within an international context and relies on this base to respond to external forces, this chapter aims to reveal how factors in particular situations shape the particular forms that globalization takes in specific institutions and provide the basis for resistance and countervailing tendencies. It is based on the researcher's longstanding personal working experience at a Chinese university, and on some primary as well as secondary sources of information about the current situation in China.

A case study approach is used to gain an in-depth understanding of internationalization from within an individual university in its unique settings. ZU has been chosen for its officially designated status within the Chinese higher education system (Cheng 1998), The administration of higher education institutions in China follows the vertical and horizontal patterns of general public administration in that country (Cheng 1998). There are institutions all over the country that are administered, in the vertical system, by ministries of the central government. Another system is the horizontal system in which institutions within a locality are administered by the local authorities, mainly the provincial governments. Institutions in the centrally administered system, including ZU, tend to be more influenced by internationalization than those in the local systems. A detailed discussion of ZU's practices, therefore, sheds light on the general current state of internationalization in the mainstream of China's higher education.

The main method of data collection was semi-structured interviews conducted by the researcher at ZU. All interviews were conducted in Chinese, since language is a tool for constructing reality (Spradley 1979), more than simply a means of communicating about reality. The length of the interviews was flexible. Most of the interviews were tape-recorded. Of those who hesitated or declined to be recorded, the researcher asked for permission to take notes.

Globalization, Internationalization and Academic Capitalism

Conceptually, this chapter deals with the relationship between globalization, internationalization and the university from the perspective of academic capitalism. These key terms are all complex and contested, and thus they are briefly explicated here.

Globalization

The concept of globalization is complex and contested. It usually refers to the greater interconnectedness of the world (Waters 2001). Two main approaches to the concept of globalization can be distinguished. The first, politically neutral, approach defines globalization as an empirical reality in terms of the compression of time and space or 'action at a distance,' particularly associated with instantaneous communications technology. The second approach identifies globalization as an economic discourse actively promulgating a market ideology (Yang 2003a).

The concept of globalization spans separate yet overlapping domains (Sklair 1998). It is ultimately a process spearheaded by multinational financial and industrial conglomerates (Burbach, Núñez & Kagarlitsky 1997). The widely discussed globalization phenomenon fundamentally results from the globalization of economic life, which is largely the universalization of capitalism (MacEwan 1994). Today's globalization is a market-induced process (Mittelman 1996), driven by market expansion (United Nations Development Programme 1999).

With a market mechanism at the core of globalization, one strand in the debate on globalization and higher education suggests that market regulation should reign supreme. These values, reflected in the neo-conservative and neo-liberal agendas, promote less state intervention and greater reliance on the free market, and more appeal to individual self-interest than to collective rights. Parallel with globalization is the shift from social to corporate welfare and commodification of cultural goods. Cultural and scientific endeavours become profitable activities, cultural goods become commercial products, the public is redefined as customers, the university becomes a provider, and the learner a purchaser of services (Schugurensky 2003: 294-295).

According to Scott (2000), globalization is the most fundamental challenge facing universities in their history. Most of the new changes are expressions of a greater influence of the market and the government over university affairs. Arguably the most significant is the worldwide drastic restructuring of higher education systems. At the core of these is a redefinition of the relationships among the university, the state, and the market, with a net result of a reduction of institutional autonomy (Schugurensky 2003: 293).

Internationalization

The definition of internationalization has been the subject of much discussion. While globalization is radically reshaping the face of the university worldwide through market competition (Kishun 1998), internationalization is entailed. According to Knight (2003: 2), "internationalization at the national, sector, and institutional levels is defined as the process of integrating an international, intercultural, or global dimension into the purpose, functions or delivery of postsecondary education." With the advancement of human understanding and the universality of knowledge as its fundamental focus, internationalization is principally different from globalization in that it refers to the reciprocal exchange of people, ideas, good and services between two or more nations and cultural identities (Yang 2002a).

In the Chinese case, while internationalization signifies an integration of the international community with China's higher education community, the Chinese government regards it instead as a strategy to strengthen national economic competitiveness. For institutions, internationalization means the awareness and operation of interactions within and between cultures through their teaching, research and services functions. In practice, however, individual institutions often care most about their research strength and international ranking (Yang 2002b).

Internationalization is also perceived differently by scholars from different fields of academic enquiry. Most contemporary Chinese academics in social sciences and humanities place their focus on international scholarly communications and emphasize the increasing participation of Chinese scholars into the world academic community. In contrast, scholars from science and technology often respond more specifically, with concrete emphases on international similarities of science and technology research paradigms and output (Yang 2003b). Despite the disparities, these views collectively demonstrate that in addition to concrete contents of courses, internationalization encompasses commitments, attitudes, global awareness and orientation.

Academic Capitalism

The term academic capitalism was proposed by Slaughter and Leslie (1997: 8). According to them,

> To maintain or expand resources, faculty had to compete increasingly for external dollars that were tied to market-related research, which was referred to variously as applied, commercial, strategic, and targeted research, whether these moneys were in the form of research grants and contracts, service contracts, partnerships with industry and governments, technology transfer, or the recruitment of more and higher fee-paying students. We call institutional and professional market or market-like efforts to secure external moneys *academic capitalism.*

The focus that has been placed by Slaughter and Leslie is on the political economy of the relationship between universities and external business firms. They are concerned with both the external environment and academic culture. Based on their empirical investigation, they argue that academic work has been fundamentally altered. The model of government-funded research has shifted from long-term programmes of 'pure' research under academic control to university-industry partnerships in which the direction of research is directly shaped by potential commercial applications. Universities are now more incorporated in industry, and their ethos shifts from the client welfare of their students to the economic bottom-line. The shift from full public funding to partial dependence on market sources of income undercuts the tacit social contract whereby universities have been treated as unique institutions (Marginson & Considine 2000).

Like Slaughter and Leslie (1997), Clark (1998: xvi) has produced work on where universities are heading. He maintains that universities have been pushed towards internal change because there is a deepening asymmetry between environmental demand and institutional capacity to respond. This 'imbalance' leads to 'institutional insufficiency.' Traditional ways become inadequate. In the new context, universities need to develop a capacity for selective and flexible response. Successful universities in this period are doing so.

As Marginson and Considine (2000) point out, institutional missions and structures have changed in the encounter between the world of the academy and the world of business and industry. It is the purpose of this chapter to examine, through an in-depth case study, how China's current practice mirrors what is happening in a range of other countries, and to draw on recent relevant literature to frame these issues.

A Brief History of ZU and its Early Internationalization

In 1924, Dr. Sun Yat-sen, leader of the Chinese bourgeois democratic revolution of 1911, decided to set up two institutions of higher learning, one military, Huangpu Military Academy, and one civil, Guangdong University (GU). On 4 February of that year, Sun Yat-sen appointed Zhou Lu to the position of the director of preparation committee for the setting up of GU.

GU was built up on the basis of the amalgamation of three colleges: a national teachers' college and two provincial colleges of law and agriculture. The preparatory committee to establish GU consisted of many important personages from politics and academia at that time, including seven professors, five members of the Executive Committee of the National Party, two Senators, two university presidents, the Foreign Minister, the Mayor of Guangzhou, and the advisor to President Sun Yat-sen (Huang 1988: 4-5). This membership shows the importance and hope that Sun Yat-sen placed on GU.

GU began to recruit students in the Summer of 1924. Among the 1,067 students enrolled, seventy percent were from Guangdong and Guangxi, showing its strong provincial character. It had six faculties (arts, law, agriculture, science, engineering and medicine) and one research school. GU was changed into Sun Yat-sen (*Zhongshan* in the Chinese phonetic alphabet, which is currently used in mainland China) University in memory of him, following his death in 1925.

Starting with its first President, ZU attached great importance to arts and humanities, and recruited the most respected scholars in their fields. Much was accomplished by various faculties in these early years. The Faculty of Law, for example, translated foreign works of law and economics, and contributed substantially to the early assimilation by China of Western learning. Its Geology department was the second oldest in China after Peking University. The department of Geography was the first built within a science faculty. A number of plant samples developed in the Biology department attracted worldwide attention (Guangdong Education Commission 1995).

ZU suffered great reverses during the national higher education reorganization in the early 1950s. This reorganization aimed to gear universities to the needs of national reconstruction (Ma 1950). During this period, ZU was effectively dismembered. Most of its faculties became independent professional colleges (Liang 1988: 89). It continued to experience frustrations caused by the combination of domestic and international politics of the Great Leap Forward from 1957, while further twists and turns during the Cultural Revolution meant it suffered calamitous, ruinous damage to its teaching and research functions.

ZU recovered rapidly in the 1980s, however. In October 2001, Sun Yat-sen Medical University merged with ZU. By April 2003, it was a multi-disciplinary university covering humanities, social science, natural and technology sciences, medicine and management, comprising 17 faculties and two colleges including 79 undergraduate, 166 Masters and 104 Doctoral programs, nine post-Doctoral centres, ten national and five provincial laboratories, and four (out of 103) national centres of excellences in humanities and social science. In 2003 it had 11,850 staff numbers, with a fulltime enrolment of 1,970 Doctoral, 5,440 Masters and 17,100 undergraduate students, and 450 overseas students (Zhongshan University n. d.). The presence of post-doctoral centres is of particular significance here, because they indicate the highest academic research level in the particular field in China, and their establishment requires approval by the Minister of Education. These centres began to emerge within Chinese campuses and discipline or research areas in 1985, to make use of talented holders of doctoral degrees. Requirements for the establishment of post-doctoral centres are accredited doctoral programs, with well recognized and nationally leading research activities, and even stronger research resources and personnel than required for doctoral programs (see Hayhoe 1989, Gu 1991).

ZU was, at its early stage, quite outward looking. The Faculty of Agriculture, for instance, studied plants in Guangdong comprehensively in the late 1920s and expanded its research to plants that could be exploited economically. It compiled a series of annals of various plants in South China, and exchanged its samples with other Chinese universities and research institutes, as well as with those in Hong Kong, Singapore, North America, and European countries. Such contributions were widely applauded.

ZU's early achievement in internationalization was reflected by the structure of its faculty in the 1920s and 1930s. Many key figures in various departments were returned students or foreign scholars. Taking the Geology department as an example, its first head, concurrently the President of ZU, was a returned student from Germany with a Ph.D. in Geology from the University of Berlin (now the Humboldt University of Berlin). Succeeding heads were Dr. Ott Jacheg and Dr. Arnold Heim. Some of the teaching staff were from overseas such as Professor K. Krejei-Glaf. These foreign (in the Geology case German) teachers were already well known in world academic circles before arriving at ZU. Textbooks were foreign with some modification based on China's situation, and the instructional language was English.

Another example is the Geography department, whose first and second heads were both from Germany. The foreign professors, textbooks, facilities and instructional languages (mainly English) meant the department gravitated strongly towards international practice, and helped to improve teaching and research standards toward international levels.

The Faculty of Medicine initially followed the American style because a significant number of its teaching staff returned from the United States. Similar to the experience of Japanese, and to some extent, American universities in much the same period, it turned to the German model of medical education. Starting from the 1926-7 academic year, the major scholars were recruited from Germany. In 1927 alone, ZU's Faculty of Medicine had seven German professors. Most of them were well-known scholars, and internationally recognized as first class scientists in their fields. They used German, sometimes English, as instructional languages, wrote out prescriptions and medical records in German, and adopted German textbooks. Even the facilities were German-styled. This echoed Tongji University, which Hayhoe (1984: 214) identifies as the earliest model of Chinese-German collaboration in higher education.

Campus-wide, among the 374 faculty from 1924 to 1937, 41 (11.0 percent) were foreign nationals. An overwhelming majority (71.0 percent) of their highest qualifications were earned from overseas. Of particular significance is the fact that the percentage of the American degrees (24.6 percent) was even higher than that of the Chinese (21.1 percent). It is also important to note that many of those overseas-earned qualifications were research higher degrees (Huang 1988: 168-170).

ZU's early internationalization was also demonstrated by its research work. In addition to the aforementioned international achievements in law, geology and medicine, its Research Institute of Education serves as another example. Founded in February 1928, the Institute had two divisions, focusing respectively on pedagogical and psychological studies. It had substantial research strengths in secondary and primary teaching, civic education, and educational administration and psychology, with a considerable record in comparative and international education studies. Many of its members had close links with the outside world. Thirteen of its 17 staff members were returned students (Editorial Committee of *The Annals of Guangdong Education* 1995: 116-117). These members were active in conducting international collaborative research projects with the American Moral Education Society, the International Bureau of Education in Switzerland, the International Association of Home Education in Belgium, and the International Federation for Adult Education in Britain, to name but a few. The Institute even hosted international students. One graduate from the University of Edinburgh, for instance, studied teacher education in English at the Institute in 1933.

The Institute and its members were also actively involved in academic activities organized by international professional associations and/or agencies, attended international conferences, and exchanged publications and information (Guangdong Education Commission 1995: 117). However, from the mid-1930s to the late 1970s, such international exchange and collaboration was thwarted repeatedly, due to the Japanese invasion (1937-45), the Chinese Civil War (1945-49), and the successive political turbulences of the Chinese Communist Party (1950s-70s).

Perceptions of Internationalization

It should not be a surprise to see that while internationalization is becoming more accepted and more central to the provision of higher education in China, people are using the same term with very different definitions. This echoes the international situation: despite many attempts to formulate a 'tight' definition the core idea remains conceptually elusive. There is no simple, unique, or all-encompassing definition of internationalization (Knight 2003).

Also echoing the international situation, most people at ZU understand internationalization in terms of categories or types of activities (Knight & de Wit 1997). These include academic and extra-curricular activities such as: curricular development and innovation; scholar, student and faculty exchange; area studies; technological assistance; intercultural training; education of international students; and joint research initiatives.

Indeed, as a result of the comprehensive changes in the contemporary world, internationalization could be interpreted from various perspectives. Nevertheless, my field study at ZU confirms the finding from my previous studies on higher education internationalization in various parts of China that understanding of internationalization relies heavily on the particular socio-cultural context (see, for example, Yang 2002b, 2003b).

My fieldwork at ZU shows that in theory most of its members accept that the concept of *Jiegui* equates with, or at least very much relates to, internationalization in the field of higher education. *Jiegui* was a catchword in the early 1990s when "China decided to adopt a market economy. It means linking up China's practices with mainstream international trends. Thus the central focus of *Jiegui* is to regulate Chinese practices according to international criteria.

In practice, however, people at ZU had very different interpretations of internationalization. The most striking difference lies between higher education researchers and the academic staff from other areas. Scholars of educational studies tend to see internationalization as an unavoidable part of higher education develop-ment. The rationale they provided was the 'inner logic' of global higher education development, which they expressed as the common ground of various higher education systems in different countries, that makes international communication necessary and possible, and transcends geographical boundaries and social systems. Thus specialists from higher education in different countries need to communicate with each other, and borrow from each other's experience. According to a professor of higher education at ZU, this is what internationalization of higher education is all about. With an evident international perspective based on his experience of com-parative higher education studies for many years, he said:

> Higher education has its own logic of development. Higher education systems in different countries with different social systems and ideologies share certain common ground. The shared part is international, and is indeed a heritage of the whole human society. (Interview ZU/1)

While such a view has its merits and is the most influential in effect within Chinese higher education, it is one-sided. Citing the contemporary higher education reforms as evidence, these scholars argue for the widespread use of the market model for higher education. It needs to be pointed out that such a notion should be put in the context that among Chinese comparative higher education scholars little attention has been paid to analysing such market models, unlike in major English-speaking countries (Hayhoe 1989: 128). The persistent commitment in many other, especially European, societies to higher education as a public good that should not be provided on the basis of an individual exchange agreement between a producer and a consumer has regrettably largely been ignored.

The above opinion, however, is not most popular among ZU administrative and academic staff, of whom a majority view internationalization as a synonym for enhancing academic strength by using international standards. As the Director of Academic Affairs Office remarked, the meaning of internationalization was firstly to attain the international academic levels, which ZU has targeted. A distinguished scholar himself, and one of the key figures in the policy-making at ZU, the Director argued:

> The reason for various understandings of internationalisation is that there are many universities of various sorts in the world: American, British, German, Japanese, and so forth. People have different opinions about which model should we link to. However, academic level is indisputable. Mathematics research, for example: for our University, a leading finding in China is almost meaningless, (it is) only when it is acknowledged as internationally pioneering that can it have real value, and our mathematics research is then truly internationalised. (Interview ZU/3)

While he also mentioned that internationalization of higher education should encompass some administration, management and the training of student with skills, as well as knowledge and perspectives of other societies and cultures, he strongly insisted that academic strength was the most important part. According to him, in order to develop scholarship, a university needs to have frequent exchanges with its counterparts in foreign countries. Also evident was that the 'international standards' he referred to were in fact American. Here again, an obvious inclination to the American model and looking to the United States as the 'gold standard' for higher education can be discerned (Altbach 1989: 19).

Another point at issue is the relationship between internationalization and institutional identity. In the present era of increased globalization, there is a constant threat to the healthy survival of national identities and cultures of smaller and/or developing nations, the homogenization or 'McDonaldization' of cultures. How to preserve and promote national culture is a common question faced by non-Western countries, which often consider internationalization as a way either to respect cultural diversity and counter-balance the perceived homogenizing effect of globalization, or to expand the influence of their traditional cultures.

The relationship has therefore long been a concern of scholars in international relations in education. Based on her longstanding observation, rich knowledge and actual experience of educational development within China and internationally, Ruth Hayhoe expressed her concern about whether Guangzhou universities would sacrifice their regular duties of serving the needs of local society to international activities, during an interview in which I consulted her *en route* to China to do my field study.

The relationship, however, has never been a question in today's China. As reported in other studies (see, for example, Yang 2002b, 2003b), Chinese scholars almost unanimously agree that there are no conflicts between internationalization and institutional relevance to local demands, despite the fact that there are very different understandings of what these characteristics are (Yang 1998). There is an evident perception of convergence in the relationship between university internationalization and the building of institutional capacity at national, local and institutional levels.

Such an attitude needs to be interpreted in a context that opening to the outside world has been officially designated as a national policy. The real issue is that few faculty or university administrators have made efforts to distinguish integration with the international (in practice, the Anglo-Saxon) practice from conformity to it, a task that becomes especially pressing against a backdrop of globalization.

As noted in other studies (Hayhoe 1989, Yang 1998), the Chinese are well aware that the Open Door policy adopted in 1978 continues to be crucial to China's higher education development. It is thus comprehensible that ZU has adopted its own open door policy to actively maintain contacts with the outside world. Furthermore, its leaders regard such a policy as of great benefit, enabling the institution to learn from others' strong points, in order to offset its own weaknesses. In their judgement, ZU will certainly lose if it is not integrated with international practice.

Meanwhile, others argue that higher education operations should be based only on the actuality of the national, local and institutional conditions. Xia Shu-zhang, the former deputy President, with his Doctorate from Harvard University in the 1940s, argues:

> Chinese characteristics are geared to the actual circumstances of Chinese society. Our memory of hardships experienced, due to the mechanical copying of foreign models, is still fresh. The Chinese characteristics of higher education are not at all in conflict with its integration with international trends. However, one question is spelled out: with which international trends does Chinese higher education have to be in line? ... Internationalization is not a simple term. Its meanings vary depending on the specific circumstances: aims, contents, effects, and results. In higher education, the principle is that internationalisation must lead to mutual understanding, friendship, and progress. The integration of China's higher education with world community is not a simply one-way phenomenon (Xia 1994: 18-19).

While none of the interviewees at ZU thought internationalization was in conflict with Chinese characteristics, their explanations of the relationship differed. Some had more concrete reasons in mind. As a university in Guangzhou in Southern China, ZU has many unique research topics and foci. As one interviewee explained, ZU naturally attached priorities to research issues relevant to South China (such as plants, environment, regional culture and the local economy). By exploiting these advantages, ZU could take a lead in certain academic fields of study in world scholarship. In this sense, it was argued that international activities and the unique local/ institutional characteristics strengthen rather than stifle each other.

Another interviewee also listed the unique plants, animals and climate that were closely linked to the region and helped ZU to establish special programs. He pointed out that while it was more difficult for subjects such as mathematics and physics to have certain South China features, some research characteristics in certain aspects of those subjects could still possibly be fostered in the process of regional development, and indeed be seen as special characteristics. An example cited was spectroscopy, particularly in the field of hypervelocity. Research on optics is extremely competitive in Guangzhou: in addition to ZU, South China University of Technology, Jinan University, and South China Normal University all had Doctoral programs in optics. Nevertheless, optics research at ZU had its own strong identity, which had resulted in the establishment of a national key optics laboratory. This proved that even in natural sciences, unique characteristics could still be developed.

The above example provides a case of how research strength at the international level is therefore a necessary accompaniment to the needs of local characteristics. In some cases, the more unique are local/institutional characteristics, the higher are the level of their academic standards. Such optimism, however, does not always have sufficient basis, as the management of the global and local could be extremely problematic in practice. This reminds us of the old story in the nineteenth century when China expressed blind confidence that it could contain 'evil influences' from outside in the face of substantial influence of the Western powers upon China. It also suggests that most Chinese academics are naïve about being able to prevent unintended effects of foreign influences, and are ignorant of the darker side of globalization. Thus, they are less prepared for managing the hegemonic neo-liberal policy discourse and its impacts on higher education.

Internationalization Achieved

Internationalization is high on the agendas of national governments, international bodies, and institutions of higher education (de Wit 1999). Correspondingly, ZU has placed greater emphasis on international co-operation and exchange in all areas, and developed its own strategies to internationalize research and teaching.

International Communications

In the overall history of international relations in China's higher education, ZU's impressive accomplishments began early. In the 55 years since the foundation of the People's Republic of China, international communication at ZU reached its peak after China adopted the Open Door policy in 1979. In Spring 1979, a delegation of ZU teachers visited the University of Hong Kong, Chinese University of Hong Kong, and Hong Kong Polytechnic, while another delegation from ZU visited the University of California system, Harvard University, and the University of Nebraska, thereby opening up new prospects, not only for ZU, but for many other Chinese universities.

This second delegation was the first Chinese academic delegation to the United States since the two countries established diplomatic relations in 1972.

An equally important chapter occurred in September 1980, when ZU received the first academic delegation from the United States – from the University of California system – since the formal establishment of Sino-American diplomatic relations. The two universities signed an educational exchange agreement that stipulated faculty and information exchange as well as joint research. One of the direct results of this collaboration between the two universities was the Guangzhou English Training Centre based at ZU, which provided those who were going abroad for further study, training or collaborative research, with functional English.

After establishing contact with the University of California, ZU adopted a dynamic attitude toward international communications. In the past two decades, it has, in succession, signed agreements with some one hundred universities and other educational institutes in more than 20 countries including Australia, Belgium, Canada, Finland, France, Germany, Japan, Philippines, Russia, South Korea, Spain, Sweden, Switzerland, Thailand, the Netherlands, the United Kingdom, the United States, Vietnam, and Yugoslavia (as well as Hong Kong, Taiwan and Macau), and has frequent exchange programs and activities with them. ZU became a member of the International Association of Universities in 1985 (Zhongshan University Office of the President 1998: 22). It now routinely invites scholars from overseas, has an increasing number of internationally collaborative research projects, and recruits both honorary and guest professors from overseas.

A significant part of ZU's international communications consists of sending its personnel abroad to study for degrees, give lectures, conduct collaborative research, attend conferences, and to discuss educational exchange issues. The extent of such activities has continued to increase. In 1986, ninety faculty were sent overseas for further study and training, 38 attended international conferences held abroad, three were invited abroad to teach, and 139 went overseas for short-term lectures and/or academic visits (Liang 1988: 97). In 1993, 409 faculty were sent overseas for academic conferences, training, visits, or to give lectures, and ZU hosted 92 scholars and 898 visitors from overseas (Zhongshan University 1995: 58).

Hosting international conferences has proven to be an effective way to enhance international communications. ZU is determined to continue this endeavour, in order to attract international scholars to ZU. Since 1979, themes of the conferences have covered various academic areas from Sun Yat-sen study and anthropology to personal computing and geography. Some of them were jointly hosted by ZU and other institutions of higher education overseas, particularly in Hong Kong.

These external contacts also provide ZU with international financial support, which was viewed as a 'real need' by most interviewees. The support has contributed significantly to improved teaching and research. In addition to assistance from international agencies, especially the World Bank and the UNESCO, due largely to its historical prominence, ZU has benefited greatly from overseas contributions, particularly from its alumni. International donations have resulted in modern buildings being established, with the latest equipment. Its graduates have also established foundations in Hong Kong, Macau, North America, Europe and Australia to support ZU in various ways.

Appraisals in Different Contexts

Despite this impressive list of achievements in international communications, ZU members reported a generally similar assessment: it is still far from adequate. Such consensus aside, however, people from various fields have different assessments of the achievement in their own specialities. These differences result from the different perspectives utilized to evaluate the achievement. No matter what the frame of reference is, however, an accurate overall assessment is, as one interviewee suggested, difficult. When compared to its development from the 1950s to the 1970s, ZU has obviously made remarkable progress in international communications. However, as another interviewee pointed out, overseas travel for faculty remains quite inadequate. Library collections of foreign language books and journals are far from sufficient, especially due to increasing prices and financially straitened circumstances. All these stifle the internationalization process at the University.

ZU respondents noted almost unanimously that the acknowledgement of an international dimension was clearly expressed in the ZU mission statement, and internationalization at ZU is well ahead of the majority of Guangzhou universities. This is largely due to the favourable conditions at ZU. First, it has a long history, and its former graduates have long occupied positions of influence both within and outside China, something that has helped ZU establish international links. Second, its location in Guangdong, a well-recognized southern gateway to China, with many foreigners coming and going (Yang & Welch 2001), has provided ZU with substantial educational exchange opportunities. Moreover, Guangzhou is next to Hong Kong, one of the world's most established centres of information and a well reputed bridge between the East and the West (Bray 1999: 2), providing ZU with more access to first class scholars and their academic work (Postiglione 1998, Yang 2003c)

ZU's superiority in this aspect was clearly expressed in an example given by an interviewee. He reported that, at the electronic forum based on ZU's homepage, an academic with a Doctorate complained of his inadequate housing at ZU. He subsequently received a letter from Guangxi, asking him to transfer to Guangxi University where he was offered a three-bedroom apartment. The teacher refused the offer because he appreciated the extent of internationalization at ZU, and was prepared to await a chance to travel abroad.

Internally, striking differences exist among various disciplines. The overall picture is that internationalization is much better implemented in the natural sciences and engineering than in arts, humanities, and some social sciences. In some science departments, international contacts have become, in one interviewee's words, "extremely popular." This is mainly because these departments are much more likely to be successful in winning external funds, and thus have more resources to attract a higher proportion of young faculty who have recently returned from overseas with higher degrees. Their personal contacts, fresh knowledge, and international links, coupled with newly purchased teaching and research equipment and laboratory facilities, particularly with the assistance of a World Bank loan (World Bank 1997), have enabled rapid internationalization in these departments.

A very different scene is presented in arts and humanities, and some social sciences. One interviewee reported that, because of the shortage of funds, ZU's library collection of books and journals was woefully inadequate, let alone chances to travel abroad. Because of the inherent connection of these subjects with prevailing political ideologies (Altbach 1998) and their seeming irrelevance to short-term economic benefits, and partly as a result of the lack of financial resources, people in these areas seemed much more reserved, indeed overcautious, in their pursuit of internationalization than their colleagues in sciences and engineering. Equally, ZU leaders are much less active in directly fostering internationalization activities in these areas. Taken together, these factors combine to reveal a dispirited picture of internationalization among arts, humanities and social sciences at ZU.

The Institute of Higher Education at ZU, for example, was founded in 1982. It had seven researchers in 1998, and its composition was weak compared to that in the 1920s and 1930s. In sharp contrast to the natural sciences and engineering fields, no one from the Institute had any overseas study or training experience. By the late 1990s, there were no personnel exchanges, no collaborative research, and no publications in international journals. Even attendance at overseas conferences was extremely limited. Only the former and current Directors had occasionally attended conferences in Hong Kong. This situation generally delineates the difficulty faced by most arts, humanities and some social sciences, which were, and have long been, one major part of ZU's strength. While several interviewees from engineering expressed their complacency with the contributions to improving their "working and living conditions" made by their external funds, respondents from basic research often felt helpless with less public money and with their less control over the little money they had received.

This demonstrates the impact of globalization on higher education: employing economic standards as benchmarks leads to a tendency to overemphasize the practical, technical value of higher education. University achievements have been increasingly simplified to be deemed equivalent to applied research outputs. Within a context in which it is much easier to find funding for research into a new dandruff shampoo than it is to try and develop a cure for malaria (Bloom 2002), there is a real danger of the erosion of important values and traditions such as the social mission of the university, its institutional autonomy and academic freedom, its pursuit of equity and accessibility, or its disinterested search for the truth (Schugurensky 2003: 308).

Such diversity among disciplines and the different perceptions of internationalization across disciplines echo international findings (Knight & de Wit 1997). The meaning of internationalization, the means to implement it, and the extent of internationalization policies all depend on the specific subject. The general situation is that 'hard' sciences usually attain higher levels of internationalization than the 'soft'. Hence developments in the 'hard' sciences like engineering tend to be much more emphasized, while humanities and social sciences, and to a lesser extent medicine, are very much under-represented in internationalization programs. This aspect has its impact on institutional, and in particular on departmental, policies and strategies for international education (de Wit & Callan 1995).

These disciplinary disparities have a direct effect on internationalization programs in various subjects. As shown by the ZU experiences, there are significant opportunities in science, engineering and technology for increasing present levels of collaboration between overseas universities and those in China that already have well-developed expertise in these fields. The extent of internationalization is much less in humanities, social sciences and education, due to the more varied ideologies, paradigms and discourses inherent in these fields, and higher dependency on language to convey their meanings (Yang 2003d). Opportunities to co-operate with international partners or win grants from external resources are much more limited (Zweig & Chen 1998).

Basic Research in Difficulty

With the central focus of internationalization on international understanding, a country's unique history, indigenous culture(s), resources, priorities, and so on shape its response to and relationships with other countries. National identity and culture is then key to internationalization. It is in this sense that basic research plays a crucial role in promoting internationalization. As a public good itself, basic research often needs substantial investment to deliver long term, but highly uncertain, benefits. The market, however, is not good at funding such research on its own (Bloom 2002: 6).

ZU, however, has focused on basic theoretical studies since its early days. The separation of its engineering, agriculture and medicine departments in the 1950s further strengthened the central role of basic research as its focus and advantage. It has made every endeavour to maintain strengths in basic research. One major task is to undertake key research projects. In recent years, ZU has undertaken some 100 national key projects including the National 863 High-Tech Development Plan and other national basic research projects, as well as 60 selected projects as priority to tackle scientific and technological problems during the Seventh (1983-87) and Eighth (1988-92) Five-Year Plans. From 1986-1992, science research at ZU won 434 prizes from the State Natural Science Foundation Committee, the then State Education Commission and Guangdong Province Government (Zhongshan University 1994: 6).

ZU has also increased its scientific publications substantially. In 1982, ZU ranked third among all Chinese higher education institutions, winning five first prizes from the then State Education Commission. From 1987 to 1992, 4,271 research articles from ZU were published in scientific journals, of which 783 were in internationally refereed journals published overseas, 132 research findings were selected for national prizes (one first prize, three second prizes, eight third prizes, and four fourth prizes), and ministerial/provincial prizes (one special prize, nine first prizes, forty-six second prizes, and sixty-one third prizes) (Zhongshan University 1995: 56-57).

Internationally, based on the statistics provided by the *Science Citation Index* (SCI) of the Institute for Scientific Information, by university affiliation of authors, 92 scientific articles produced at ZU were published in internationally recognized scholarly journals in 1996, 17 more than that in 1995 (an increase of 23 per cent), a feat which placed ZU the thirteenth among all Chinese universities. The number of articles that were both included and cited by SCI reached 87 (ranked 14th in China), while the *Engineering Index* included 63 articles by ZU staff (ranked 29th in China).

Obvious achievements have also been made in arts, humanities and social sciences, albeit to a much lesser extent, reflecting perhaps the great difficulties in publishing Chinese-based social science research overseas (Zhong 1998, Yang 2003d). From 1979 to 1993, 1,194 books were published including textbooks, reference materials, and translation works. The total number of research articles published reached 9,781 over this period. During the Eighth Five-Year Plan, ZU undertook 132 research projects (of which 28 were at national level), 40 projects were granted by the then State Education Commission, and 39 were at the provincial level, respectively 150, 143 and 156 per cent more than those in the Seventh Five-Year Plan (Zhongshan University 1995: 58). In order to take full advantage of Guangdong's favourable conditions (Vogel 1989), ZU established a number of research centres such as the Centre for Pearl River Delta Studies, the Institute of Hong Kong and Macau Studies, and the Centre for Township Governments in Guangdong.

However, educational quality is increasingly measured by economic standards (Neave 1988, Mok 2000). In the context of globalization, China's higher education is compelled to become increasingly responsive to economic needs, accountable for its financial resources, entrepreneurial and competitive (Min 1999, Postiglione & Jiang 1999). As such, ZU has readjusted its academic programs and research priorities and shifted a majority of its strength to applied and development research to extract maximum economic benefits. New practical programs have been established to promote dissemination and application of new technologies to meet market needs.

In techno-science and fields closely involved with markets, particularly international markets, research products expand beyond national boundaries and intellectual property rights are involved on a global basis. Researchers thus have to ensure their own research product is internationally recognized. Private sector enterprises are closely related to this research market, both through their own research activities and through their search for newly patented technologies. This provides a strong incentive to ZU researchers in these fields to rush the dissemination of their research products into a well-recognized international market

Although relevant and mutually reinforcing to some extent, basic research is different from applied studies, and belongs to a different type of academic inquiry. ZU's shift of academic focus towards more applied areas is a direct result of the existing pressures because many in government and in academic administration feel that much of the basic research and analysis reported in academic journals is not relevant to day-to-day problems. Decision-makers increasingly eye market needs, which are both changeable, and often misleading, particularly in China where the implementation of a free market economy itself has just begun (Guthrie 1999).

Therefore, some basic research in arts, humanities and some social sciences has been eroded. Taking philosophy as an example, ZU had traditionally been one of the best in China especially in the study of the history of Chinese philosophy, and had some nationally distinguished scholars. However, in response to financial constraints, many such faculty have busied themselves working for factories and companies to earn extra income, thus their teaching and research responsibilities in the Philosophy department have been weakened considerably.

The overemphasis on economic benchmarks to assess different specialities is problematic. Such a climate is more favourable to applied studies, while basic theoretical inquiry often suffers. Resources for basic research have not kept up with needs. Academic infrastructure, including libraries and laboratories, has been starved of funds. Research quality and academic morale have been affected. As governmental funds for basic research reduce substantially, the current situation is difficult for universities like ZU. Various interviewees reported that their conditions for teaching and research had deteriorated. If the situation continues in coming years, it is not hard to foresee that research in the basic natural sciences, arts, humanities, and social sciences, which comprise the traditional academic strengths of ZU, will be seriously compromised.

According to many respondents, both within and outside basic research, it appears that ZU is obligated to the extra-academic market. The current difficult situation of basic research demonstrates the decreasing degree to which China's higher education is beholden to the public good. It is not surprising to see that visions contending that the university should be the critical consciousness of society, the engine of new knowledge, and the guardian of the long-term interest of the community are being displaced (Schugurensky 2003: 308).

Concluding Remarks

ZU began its journey to internationalization early in its initial period. Indeed, compared to its achievements in the 1920s-1930s, it fails to measure up to its strength in the past, at least in some aspects of internationalization, including foreign faculty recruitment and the proportion of highest qualifications earned by its faculty. In some areas, particularly arts, humanities and social sciences, it is relatively more isolated from the international community than it was some 70 years ago.

The case of ZU parallels the national scenario in China that universities are increasingly required to be responsive to the market-oriented economy. By the late 1990s, through implementing a series of policies of decentralization and marketization, the Chinese government had initiated fundamental changes in the orientation, financing, curriculum, and management of higher education (Agelasto & Adamson 1998). As Mohrman (2003: 24) notes, while Chinese scholars were traditionally at the top of the status hierarchy and merchants near the bottom, today's Chinese scholars have become merchants in order to support the academic enterprise. The worry "is the risk of going too far in responding to market demands," and "traditional academic values are being marginalized in the relentless pursuit of money."

The practises at ZU also echo what is happening internationally (Clark 1998): a number of recent changes have affected the way universities work and the work that academics do (Slaughter & Leslie 1997). Universities worldwide are being urged to behave in more competitive and enterprising ways. Universities develop their responses to global practices forced upon them by globalizing politicians and bureaucrats (Currie & Newson 1998). Within these processes, forces of internationalization and globalization pull in different directions. It is increasingly difficult for universities to reconcile the competing agendas (Welch, 2003). This synergy of the global and the local is not necessarily always the case, and indeed, is often problematic in practice. Successes depend heavily on the specific institutional circumstances (Yang 2000), including institutional infrastructure, policy priorities, and faculty profile.

ZU's experience indicates possible negative effects caused by the introduction of business practices into universities and the potential threat to traditional university values. This is again in line with the situation in other parts of the world, where many academics believe that intellectual traditions are being forcibly displaced by market directives (Coady 1996), and a market approach to international collaboration and exchange has been a trend in higher education (Knight & de Wit 1997, 1999), ZU now has to compete globally for research that can be transformed into marketable goods and services. This leads to a notion that simply regards internationalization as attaining world-class academic strength, which, in reality, is again simplified as research, confined overwhelmingly to science and engineering, and measured against clearly defined global standards. Such an understanding inflicts particular damage upon some academic fields that cannot bring immediate economic benefits such as arts, humanities and some social sciences that have long constituted an integral part of ZU's prestige.

At sector level, internal differentiation among various disciplines is becoming strikingly evident. This aggravates the tension between basic theory researchers and those from technological sciences. It becomes an even more severe problem considering the fact that an overwhelming majority of institutional and ministerial leaders in China are from the latter, and traditionally show scant concern for the social sciences. Even within one institution, the internationalization of research is not the same in each faculty. In humanities, social sciences and education, domestic considerations are given more weight than in the faculty of natural sciences, technology and medical sciences, which placed a larger importance on the dissemination of research results beyond the national boundary. The internationalization of higher education is indeed regional within universities, just as within the country overall.

References

Agelasto, M. & Adamson, B. eds. 1998. *Higher Education in Post-Mao China.* Hong Kong: Hong Kong University Press.

Altbach, P.G. 1998. *Comparative Higher Education: Knowledge, the University and Development.* Hong Kong: Comparative Education Research Centre, University of Hong Kong.

Altbach, P.G. 1989. "Twisted Roots: The Western Impacts on Asian Higher Education." In *From Dependence to Autonomy: The Development of Asian Universities,* edited by P.G. Altbach & V. Selvaratnam. Dordrecht: Kluwer Academic Publishers.

Bloom, D.E. 2002. "Mastering Globalisation: From Ideas to Action on Higher Education Reform." Paper presented at *Globalisation: What Issues are at Stake for Universities?* University of Laval, Quebec, Canada, 18-21 September.

Bray, M. 1999. "Comparative Education Research in Hong Kong: A Decade of Development, and an Agenda for the Future." *CESHK Bulletin,* Comparative Education Society of Hong Kong, 3:2-7.

Burbach, R., Núñez. O. & Kagarlitsky, B. 1997. *Globalisation and Its Discontents: The Rise of Post-Modern Socialism.* London: Pluto.

Cheng, K.M. 1998. "Reforms in the Administration and Financing of Higher Education." In *Higher Education in Post-Mao China,* edited by M. Agelasto and B. Adamson. Hong Kong: Hong Kong University Press.

Clark, B. 1998. *Creating Entrepreneurial Universities: Organizational Pathways of Transformation.* Oxford and New York: Pergamon Press.

Coady, T. ed. 2000. *Why Universities Matter: A Conversation about Values, Means and Directions.* St Leonards: Allen & Unwin.

Currie, J. &Newson, J. eds. 1998. *Universities and Globalisation: Critical Perspectives.* Thousand Oaks: Sage.

De Wit, H. 1999. "Changing Rationales for the Internationalisation of Higher Education." *International Higher Education* 15 (Spring): 2-3.

De Wit, H. & Callan, H. 1995. "Internationalisation of Higher Education in Europe." In *Strategies for Internationalisation of Higher Education: A Comparative Study of Australia, Canada, Europe and the United States of America,* edited by H. de Wit. Amsterdam: The EAIE.

Editorial Committee of *The Annals of Guangdong Education.* ed. 1995. *The Annals of Guangdong Education.* Guangzhou: Guangdong People's Press. (In Chinese)

Gu, M. ed. 1991. *Encyclopaedia of Education.* Shanghai: Shanghai Education Press. (In Chinese)

Guangdong Education Commission. 1995. *History of Guangdong Education.* Guangzhou: Guangdong People's Press. (In Chinese)

Guthrie, D. 1999. *Dragon in a Three-Piece Suit: The Emergence of Capitalism in China.* Princeton: Princeton University Press.

Hayhoe, R. 1984. "Chinese-Western Scholarly Exchange: Implications for the Future of Chinese Education." In *Contemporary Chinese Education,* edited by R. Hayhoe. London: Croom Helm.

Hayhoe, R. 1989. *China's Universities and the Open Door.* New York: Sharpe.

Huang, F. 1988. *A Study of Modern Chinese Higher Education: National Sun Yat-sen University 1924-1937.* Taipei: Institute of Modern History, Academia Sinica. (In Chinese)

Kishun, R. 1998. "Internationalisation in South Africa." In *The Globalisation of Higher Education,* edited by P. Scott. Buckingham: Open University Press.

Knight, J. 2003. "Updating the Definition of Internationalisation." *International Higher Education* 33(Fall): 2-3.

Knight, J. & de Wit, H. eds. 1997. *Internationalisation of Higher Education in Asia Pacific Countries.* Amsterdam: The EAIE.

Knight, J. & de Wit, H. eds. 1999. *Quality and Internationalisation in Higher Education.* Paris: The OECD.

Liang, S. 1988. "Zhongshan University." In *Higher Education in Guangdong,* edited by X.-H. Li and H.-M. Zhou. Guangzhou: Guangdong Higher Education Press. (In Chinese)

Ma, X. 1950. "Speech at the Conference of Higher Education." *People's Daily* (June 14). (In Chinese)

MacEwan, A. 1994. "Notes on US Foreign Investment in Latin America." *Monthly Review* 45(8): 4-16.

Marginson, S. & Considine, M. 2000. *The Enterprise University: Power, Governance and Re-invention in Australia.* Cambridge and New York: Cambridge University Press.

Min, W. 1999. "Global Challenges and the Chinese Response." In. *Higher Education in the 21st Century: Global Challenge and National Response,* edited by P. G. Altbach and P. M. Peterson. Boston: Institute of International Education and Boston College Centre for International Higher Education.

Mittelman, J.H. ed. 1996. *Globalisation: Critical Reflections.* Boulder: Lynne Rienner.

Mohrman, K. 2003. "Centre and Periphery: Changes in the Relationship between Chinese Universities and the Central Government." *International Higher Education* 33(Fall): 24-25.

Mok, K. 2000. "Impact of Globalisation: A Study of Quality Assurance System of Higher Education in Hong Kong and Singapore." *Comparative Education Review* 44(2): 148-174.

Neave, G. 1988. "Education and Social Policy: Demise of an Ethic or Change of Values?" *Oxford Review of Education* 14(3): 273-283.

Postiglione, G.A. 1999. "Maintaining Global Engagement in the Face of National Integration in Hong Kong." *Comparative Education Review* 42(1): 30-45.

Postiglione, G.A. & Jiang, M. 1999. "Academic Culture in Shanghai's Universities." *International Higher Education* 17(Fall): 12-13.

Schugurensky, D. 2003. "Higher Education Restructuring in the Era of Globalisation." In: *Comparative Education: The Dialectic of the Global and the Local* (2nd edition), edited by R.F. Arnove and C.A. Torres. Lanham, Maryland: Rowman & Littlefield.

Scott, P. 2000. "A Tale of Three Revolutions? Science, Society and the University." In *Higher Education Re-Formed,* edited by P. Scott. London: Falmer Press.

Sklair, L. 1998. "Competing Conceptions of Globalisation." Paper presented at the World Congress of Sociology, Montreal, 26 July – 1 August 1998.

Slaughter, S. & Leslie, L. L. 1997. *Academic Capitalism: Politics, Policies, and the Entrepreneurial University.* Baltimore: John Hopkins University Press.

Spradley, J. 1979. *The Ethnographic Interview.* New York: Holt, Rinhart and Winston.

United Nations Development Programme. 1999. *Human Development Report 1999.* New York: Oxford University Press.

Vogel, E. 1989. *One Step Ahead In China: Guangdong Under Reform.* Cambridge: Harvard University Press.

Waters, M. 2001. *Globalisation.* London and New York: Routledge.

Welch, A. 2003. "Going Global? Internationalising Australian Universities in a Time of Global Crisis." *Comparative Education Review* 46(4): 433-472.

World Bank. 1997. *China: Higher Education Reform.* Washington D.C.: The World Bank.

Xia, S. 1994. "Reforms in Higher Education Administration Should Have Chinese Characteristics and Conform with International Conventions." *Studies in Higher Education* 3: 17-19. (In Chinese)

Yang, R. 1998. "A Higher Education System with Chinese Characteristics: Rhetoric or Reality?" *International Education* 28(1): 26-41.

Yang, R. 2000. "Tensions between the Global and the Local: A Comparative Illustration of the Reorganisation of China's Higher Education in the 1950s and 1990s." *Higher Education* 39(3): 319-337.

Yang, R. 2002a. "University Internationalisation: Its Meanings, Rationales and Implications." *Intercultural Education* 13(1): 81-96.

Yang, R. 2002b. *Third Delight: Internationalisation of Higher Education in China: A Study of Guangzhou.* New York and London: Routledge.

Yang, R. 2003a. "Globalisation as a Context of Inequality and Scarcity for Higher Education Development: A Critical Analysis." *International Review of Education* 49(3-4): 269-291.

Yang, R. 2003b. "Internationalised while Provincialised? A Case Study of South China Normal University." *Compare* 33(3): 287-300.

Yang, R. 2003c. "The China-Hong Kong Connection: A Key to Internationalising Chinese Universities." *Asia Pacific Journal of Education* 23(2): 121-133.

Yang, R. 2003d. "Contemporary Higher Education Studies in the People's Republic of China." *Asian Research Trends: A Humanities and Social Science Review* 13: 61-78.

Yang, R. & Welch, A. 2001. "Internationalising Chinese Universities: A Study of Guangzhou." *World Studies in Education* 2(1): 21-51.

Zhong, W. 1998. "Chinese Scholars and the World Community." In *Higher Education in Post-Mao China*, edited by M. Agelasto and B. Adamson. Hong Kong: Hong Kong University Press.

Zhongshan University. N.d. "About Us". Accessed 29 September 2003. Online http://www.zsu.edu.cn/Aboutus/xxjj.htm (In Chinese).

Zhongshan University. 1994. *An Introduction to Zhongshan University 1924-1994.* Guangzhou: Zhongshan University Press. (In Chinese)

Zhongshan University. 1995. "Subjects Building and Educational Quality Improvement." *Studies in Higher Education* 1: 54-8. (In Chinese)

Zhongshan University Office of the President. 1998. *Zhongshan University.* Guangzhou: Zhongshan University Press. (In Chinese)

Zweig, D., & Chen, C. 1998. "The Open Door Policy and Chinese Universities." *Journal of Higher Education* 3: 50-56. (In Chinese)

6

Internationalization of Australian Higher Education: A Critical Review of Literature and Research

Grant Harman

Introduction

This chapter critically reviews scholarly and professional literature produced since 1990 on the internationalization of Australian higher education. It considers not only journal articles and monographs but also research theses and publications produced by government departments and agencies, non-government higher education organizations and specialized companies providing higher education support services. The chapter discusses briefly the concept of internationalization, traces Australian developments in the internationalization of higher education since 1990 and then reviews a wide variety of literature under the broad headings of: the processes of internationalization of higher education; national policy and evaluation; export of higher education services; international students; and various other aspects of the internationalization of Australian higher education. A final section attempts an overall assessment, pointing to both strengths and gaps in the literature and the unfortunate lack of effective interaction between scholars with distinctively different theoretical orientations and interests.

Since about 1990, a large amount of material has been produced by Australian and visiting scholars on various aspects of the internationalization of higher education, particularly relating to developments in and with regard to Australia. By far the main topics of concentration reflect the major commitment of Australian higher education institutions and governments to the export of higher education services and to the rapid expansion in international student enrolments. In many respects it is reassuring that the dramatic expansion in Australian international higher education student enrolments has been supported by such an impressive amount of research effort, particularly related to the social and educational characteristics of overseas students, their learning and study experiences, English language competence and development, and student support.

This chapter is based on work completed for an extensive annotated bibliography on the internationalization of the Australian higher education sector (Harman & Nolan 2002) but it also takes into account more recent work. Material was identified mainly by library and web searches using a variety of general and specialist search engines.

Internationalization of Australian Higher Education

Internationalization of higher education can be defined simply as a process of integrating international or inter-cultural dimensions into the teaching, research and service functions of higher education institutions. It is a process by which higher education is developed in a more international direction. As Hamilton (1998: 1) has observed, internationalization in the current context "is much broader than the export of education services; it involves scholarship, research and management issues as well as staff, domestic student and curriculum issues". Across many countries, it is being increasingly recognized that internationalization is, or at least should be, an important mainstream element of higher education.

The term internationalization of higher education is frequently used today not only within universities and colleges but also by governments and international organizations, including UNESCO, the World Bank and various Non Government Organizations (NGOs). However, the term is used in a number of different senses in the literature, often without being defined in any precise way. As Knight (1999: 13) has observed, "it is clear that internationalization means different things to different people and as a result there is a great diversity of interpretations attributed to the concept". Further, within the literature, frequently no clear differentiation in meaning is made between the terms internationalization of higher education and globalization in relation to higher education. There is also often some measure of confusion or overlap in the literature with related terms such as regionalization, nationalization and de-nationalization.

In practice, internationalization of higher education usually refers to one or a combination of the following activities:

- The international movement of students between countries;
- The international movement of academic staff and researchers;
- Internationalization of higher education curricula in order to achieve better understandings about other people and cultures, and competence in foreign languages;
- International links between nation states through open learning programs and new technologies;

- Bi-lateral links between governments and higher education institutions in different countries for collaboration in research, curriculum development, student and staff exchange, and other international activities;
- Multi-national collaboration such as via international organizations or through consortia such as Universitas Global; and
- Export education where education services are offered on a commercial basis in other countries, with students studying either in their home country or in the country of the provider.

In this chapter, the term internationalization of higher education is used to cover all these various aspects.

One notable feature of the world-wide literature on internationalization is that scholarly contributions and debate tend to be influenced by the geographic location of contributors and by local circumstances and issues. Thus, in many continental European countries, there is considerable interest in debates in internationalization of higher education on the impact of the European Union (EU) on higher education and its effects on the role of the nation state, especially in terms of higher education policy and provision. There also has been considerable interest in EU initiated student mobility programs. In contrast, in countries such as Australia and New Zealand much of the literature is related to the export of education services, education markets and marketing, and the characteristics and learning styles of international students, particularly those from Asian countries. Still again in other parts of the world the internationalization debate is primarily about international power and dominion, and new forms of neo-colonialism and western cultural domination.

The terms internationalization of higher education and globalization are sometimes used as being synonymous. However, it is helpful to make a clear distinction between internationalization and globalization. For the purpose of this paper, the term globalization is used to refer to systems and relationships that are practised beyond the local and national dimensions at continental, meta-nation regional and world levels. These relationships can be technological, cultural, political and economic as well as educational. They can be expressed in flows of ideas, images, and people, or in terms of flows of money, goods and services. In a broader sense, globalization means simply becoming more global.

Over the past decade or so, Australian universities have made some important developments towards the goal of internationalization of higher education. With government encouragement, many universities have put efforts into internationalizing curricula and expanding the study of Asian languages in order to facilitate understanding of other cultures and to support further expansion of Australia's trade, although generally progress in these areas has been far less than hoped for. University research is now more closely linked internationally by close collaboration with research groups and networks in other countries. However, by far the most dramatic and, in many respects, important developments in the internationalization of higher education have been the expansion in enrolments of fee-paying international students (Harman & Nolan 2002).

Today Australia is the third largest exporter of higher education services internationally, coming in rank order after the United States and the United Kingdom. In 2002, Australian public higher education institutions enrolled 185,000 international students and these enrolments constituted over 21 per cent of the total student load. Twelve years earlier Australian universities had only 29,000 international students. About two thirds of current international higher education students are enrolled on university campuses in Australia while the remainder are enrolled 'offshore'. 'Offshore' enrolments refer to students enrolled with Australian universities but who study entirely or largely within their own countries. Such enrolments include students enrolled in overseas campuses operated by Australian universities, in joint programs with overseas partner institutions, in institutions that offer Australian courses on a franchised basis and as independent distance education students. In addition, approximately an additional 30,000 international students are enrolled as foreign 'study abroad' students in Australian universities and as students in private higher education institutions. Recent figures indicate that international higher education enrolments generate well over AUS$2 billion annually for Australian universities (Nelson 2002: 52-54) while in addition substantial amounts are spent by international students in living expenses and by their visiting families and friends.

The large-scale export of higher educational services is a relatively new and somewhat controversial aspect of the internationalization of higher education. In many countries, the export of educational services is not even considered as a legitimate aspect of internationalization while in some cases the idea of selling a public good such as higher education is seen as being undesirable and even offensive. On the other hand, the export of education services is one of the new realities of internationalization. Recently it has received increased attention with the General Agreement of Trade in Services (GATS), which aims to promote freer trade in services including education by removing many of the existing barriers. Even within the Asia and Pacific region, the GATS negotiations are controversial, dividing nations into supporters and opponents.

The Processes of Internationalization of Higher Education

Australian scholars have contributed significantly to the recent world-wide debate on internationalization and globalization and their impact on higher education, although in more recent years the bulk of the Australian research effort on higher education internationalization has been directed to specialized aspects related to the dramatic and important expansion in the export of higher education services, especially in the Asia Pacific region. To a large extent, especially in the early 1990s, Australian work addressing broader global issues largely mirrored other contributions to international literature, covering a wide variety of topics and ranging from being highly critical of aspects of internationalization to being strongly supportive. More recently, work has concentrated on the precise meanings of the two terms, globalization and internationalization, and how they are applied in different situations, the main drivers of internationalization and globalization, the effects of globalization on university organization and academics, and recent developments with regard to GATS and what the possible implications might be for different forms of higher education, and higher education in different countries. The Australian literature also includes discussion of the benefits and threats from globalization and internationalization, trade in higher education services, the application of new technologies to higher education delivery, the impact of internationalization on quality assurance and Australia's international links in scientific cooperation. Australian scholars also have shown increasing interest in the higher education systems of those countries that have become Australia's main markets for overseas students.

Issues related to internationalization and globalization have been discussed by a variety of Australian scholars and visiting overseas scholars who have researched aspects of Australian internationalization of higher education. For example, Jones (1998, 1999) has put forward conceptions of globalization and internationalism that are somewhat different to those of European scholars (e.g. Enders 2002, Teichler 2002) and Australian government agencies. Jones sees globalization:

> ... as economic integration, achieved in particular through the establishment of a global market-place marked by free trade and a minimum of regulation. In contrast, internationalism refers to the promotion of global peace and well-being through the development and application of international structures, primarily but not solely of an intergovernmental kind. Despite important conceptual difficulties in formulating the case for internationalism and despite the world's patchy record in putting its principles into effect, the essentially pro-democratic logic of internationalism stands in sharp contrast to the logic of globalization (Jones 1998: 143).

Jones attributes the term globalization as having come from the business world where it has been referred to as a "means of conducting business more efficiently, more profitably and more discreetly" (Jones 1998: 144). He comments:

> It will come as no surprise to claim that an integral part of this aim was the intention to open up the world's markets and minimise the supervisory role of public authorities within them. Much of this globalization process came to be dependent on the adoption of reduced roles for government, not only as regulator but also as a provider of public services funded in a large measure through taxation (Jones 1998: 144).

In contrast, the well-known overseas scholars Jane Knight and Hans de Wit (1997), who undertook project work for the International Development Program of Australian Universities (IDP Education Australia) and had a significant impact on thinking on Australian higher education, took a less ideological and more pragmatic view, a view that has considerably influenced Australian thinking on internationalization and globalization. In her contribution to an influential OECD conference, Knight explained the concept of globalization "as the flow of technology, economy and knowledge, people, values, ideas ... across borders", pointing out that globalization "affects each country in a different way due to a nation's individual history, traditions, culture and priorities" (Knight 1999: 14). Knight saw internationalization of higher education as being "one of the ways that a country responds to the impact of globalization yet, at the same time, respects the individuality of the nation" (Knight 1999: 14).

The positive and negative impacts of internationalization and globalization have been dealt with by many scholars, including Welch and Denman (1997), Yang and Welch (2001), Meek (2002), Pratt and Poole (1999/2000), McBurnie (2000a), and McBurnie and Pollock (2000). Combinations of Australian based and overseas scholars have produced valuable collections of essays dealing with various aspects of the impact of globalization and globalized economies on university organization and management, and the academic profession (Currie & Newson 1998, Currie, DeAngelis, de Boer, Huisman & Lacotte 2002, Currie, Thiele & Harris 2002). In a number of these works, globalization is seen as being closely linked to the spread of a more strongly managerial culture within universities and a loss of traditional autonomy by academics. The global market for education services is discussed in detail from a strategic and services marketing perspectives by Mazzoral and Soutar (2002) while global quality assurance issues and their impact on and implications for Australia are dealt with by Woodhouse (2001) and Vidovich (2002). McBurnie (2000b) provides a useful case study of a review organized by GATE (Global Alliance of Transnational Education) of offshore courses operated by Monash University. A number of scholars have emphasized that the costs and benefits of internationalization should not be seen merely in economic terms.

Some of the few Australian scholars to deal with recent developments with regard to GATS are Meek (2002) and McBurnie and Ziguras (2003) who provide detailed discussion of GATS and Australia's involvement to date. GATS is administered by the World Trade Organization and its purpose is to promote freer trade in services by removing many of the existing barriers. Not surprisingly, GATS is strongly dividing nations, with supporters highlighting benefits in terms of innovations through new providers and delivery modes, greater student access, and increased economic gains while critics focus on threats to the role of government in higher education, public good issues and threats to the maintenance of high quality provision. Already a number of countries including the United Kingdom, the United

States, New Zealand and Australia have made commitments in relation to education. Australia's position in 2002 was as follows:

> Australia currently enjoys the benefits of having a relatively open education and training regime. This openness is reflected in the significant number of commitments that Australia has entered in its current GATS schedule for the following education services: secondary education, higher education and other education services. Australia believes that all Members should, in the context of the current round, consider entering commitments on education services similar to those already entered by Australia. This particularly applies to those Members who have previously failed to enter any commitments in relation to education services (Australian Department of Foreign Affairs and Trade 2002).

While the Australian Government is playing a leading role in promoting trade liberalization, it is also pursuing a more diversified approach to trade promotion including building confidence in international quality assurance mechanisms and demonstrating the benefits of trade-driven internationalization to importing countries (McBurnie & Ziguras 2003).

Work by the 'borderless higher education team' in Queensland has dealt well with the development of for-profit higher education, e-universities, universities on line, and the application of new media, and has been well recognized (Cunningham, Tapsall, Ryan, Stedman, Bagdon & Flew 1998, Cunningham, Ryan, Stedman, Tapsall, Bagdon, Flew & Coaldrake 2000, Ryan 2001). This work shows that while there has been considerable 'hype' about the likely involvement of global media networks in higher education, to date such developments are relatively small and the greatest single involvement by corporations is via the corporate university model. Work by this team has usefully complemented other work undertaken in the UK.

Other Australian research has included discussion of the role of OECD (Henry, Lingard, Rizvi & Taylor 2000), UNESCO and the World Bank (Jones 1997, Jones 2001), the regulation of transnational higher education (McBurnie 2000b, McBurnie & Ziguras 2001) and conceptual work by Marginson and Rhoades (2002) who put forward the idea of a 'glonacal' agency heuristic with the intersecting planes, emphasizing the simultaneous significance of global, national and local dimensions.

National Policy and Evaluation

There is now an extensive literature dealing with the recent policies and efforts of Australian governments (especially the Commonwealth Government) on various aspects of internationalization. This includes material tracing substantial shifts in government policy, ministerial policy statements, the reports of committees of enquiry, evaluations of government programs, and material relating to links between internationalization and immigration, studies of population flows and the labour market, and material on international agreements on the recognition of professional quailfications, and international scientific collaboration.

Australia's development as a higher education exporter has been prompted by important shifts in Commonwealth Government policy since the mid-1980s with regard to foreign students, the funding of higher education and economic reform. Particularly important were decisions to actively recruit foreign students on a commercial basis, to actively encourage higher education institutions to raise more of their own revenue, and to restructure the economy encouraging a broadening of the formerly narrow export base to include specialized services. These changes have been well documented by various scholars, such as Harris and Jarrett (1990), Marshall (1993), Borsheim Stundal (1999) and Smart, Volet and Ang (2000), while two key government reports (Jackson 1984, Goldring 1984) provide important perspectives on factors which drove policy changes.

Australia's policy shift from aid to trade took place in the mid-1980s, driven partly by concerns about the effectiveness of the sponsored overseas student program but more particularly from recognition of the commercial possibilities in selling specialized services. From 1985 to the early 1990s, the policy focus was almost entirely on the commercial export of higher education services. However, in 1992, in response to criticisms and pressures from particular nearby Asian countries, the Commonwealth Government signalled a broader vision for international education that was expressed in detail by a Ministerial statement by Education Minister Beazley in 1992:

> The Government recognises that international education is an increasingly important part of Australia's international relations. It uniquely spans the cultural, economic and interpersonal dimensions of international relations. It assists cultural understanding of all parties involved. It enriches Australia's education and training systems and the wider Australian society with a more international outlook (Beazley 1992).

Various reviews and commentaries have attempted to evaluate the results and impact of different policy initiatives. Some of this is historical, going back to the beginning of the Colombo Plan scheme and beyond (Auletta 2000, Back 1994). Internationalization strategies employed by Australian higher education institutions have been well documented by Back, Davis and Olsen (1996), while Grigg (1996) has provided an in-depth evaluation of the Overseas Postgraduate Scholarship Scheme, Smith and Smith (1999) have considered the internationalization of Australian vocational education and training while Baker, Robertson, Taylor, Doube and Rhall (1996) have assessed the impact of the presence of overseas students on the demand for and supply of labour and the efficiency of the labour market. A large number of papers have been generated for annual IDP Education Australia conferences, with papers being made available in published form (eg Davis & Olsen 1998, Olsen 2001).

A recent review by the Victorian Auditor General points to the clear benefits of export education and demonstrates that increased international student enrolments have not impacted adversely on access to university by domestic students (Cameron 2000).

Various types of international comparisons between Australia and comparable other countries have been attempted, mainly with government funding for project work. For example, Anderson and Johnston (1998) explored university autonomy, while Bourke and Butler (1995) and Matthews and Johnston (2000) analysed international research links and trends in public support for research and development, and Harman and Meek (2000) and Anderson, Johnston and Milligan (2000) explored Australia's quality assurance issues from an international perspective.

Overall the strong messages that emerges from the literature on national policy and evaluation are that Australia has achieved considerable success with the expansion of export education and that this has produced various positive impacts but that achievements in the internationalization of courses and capturing the benefits of internationalization for domestic students have been more limited.

Export of Higher Education Services

An impressive and detailed literature has developed dealing with various aspects of the export of higher education services, including studies of comparative costs to students, economic benefits derived by institutions and nationally from export of higher education, overseas student markets relevant for Australia, and marketing and marketing strategies. Much of this has been developed with funding provided from government and university sources.

Since the mid-1990s, Australian Education International (a division of the Commonwealth Department of Education, Science and Training) in combination with IDP Education Australia have sponsored and carried out a series of valuable studies assessing comparative costs to international students of study in Australia, New Zealand, the United Kingdom, Canada and the United States. The first major study by Back, Davis and Olsen (1997) found that total costs, including living expenses, were consistently higher in the United States and the United Kingdom than in other countries. It also found that tuition fees in Australia were generally in the middle of the field and consistently lower than in the United Kingdom and American public universities. More recent updates of this study have confirmed Australia's continuing cost advantages for students (Australian Education International 2002a). Other work has considered additional benefits for both overseas students and the Australian community, including the impact of the presence of international students on the Australian labour market (Baker 1996).

The literature on overseas student markets and marketing deals with particular geographic markets, marketing and student recruitment strategies, how students make choices of the country and institution for study, and student satisfaction studies. For example, Hill, Romm and Paterson (1992) report on pre-purchase decision-making by overseas students prior to their arrival in Australia, while Lawley (1993) identifies factors affecting choice of destination by students from Hong Kong, and Mazzoral and Soutar (2002) suggest strategies for higher education institutions to use in order to maintain a competitive edge in a rapidly changing education market. Significantly, the Australian Education International (2002b) study reports a high degree of student satisfaction amongst international students who completed a course of study in 1999 in an Australian higher education institution. Ninety-one per cent of respondents said that they were 'satisfied' or 'very satisfied' with the quality of education in Australia, 88 per cent were 'satisfied' or very satisfied with the quality of the course in which they were enrolled, while 92 per cent said that the would either 'strongly recommend' or 'recommend' studying in Australia to other students in their home country.

International Students and Student Experience

As already noted, by far the largest amount of literature is on overseas students, including their social and educational characteristics, their learning styles, their mastery of English language, teaching methods and support services. It covers both full-fee and sponsored students. This literature has been generated largely by university academics and research students and demonstrates a strong commitment by academics and their departments to provide high quality and relevant education to both full-fee and sponsored students. Relatively little of the material on overseas students was the result of large-scale sponsored research projects while a high proportion was generated by academic staff and postgraduate research students. Some seventeen PhD and research masters theses were identified dealing with English language competence, teaching English to speakers of other languages (TESOL) and English language intensive courses for overseas students (ELICOS), while eight dealt with the characteristics and perceptions of overseas students.

Work on student characteristics and student perceptions covers a range of topics including students' aspirations, student experiences and perceptions of their courses and institutions, and the experience of particular groups of students such as women and students from particular countries. For example, Andressen (1997) reports on the characteristics of students from the major markets of Hong Kong, South Korea, Taiwan, Malaysia and Singapore, while Leong (1994) reports on the perceptions of Australian tertiary education by Hong Kong students studying at three universities in Melbourne, and Suen (1994) considers the adjustment experiences of mature age Hong Kong students studying in Australia.

The material on the study and learning experiences of overseas students is particularly rich and draws on substantial work carried out by scholars in Hong Kong, Britain and America as well as Australia. This literature covers topics such as the impact of culture and values on learning environments, learning autonomy, and styles of learning. Major issues that have attracted considerable attention are whether or not

Asian and Australian students adopt distinctively different study and learning approaches (eg Biggs 1997, Smith, Miller & Crassini 1998) and common stereotypes about the prior educational experiences of international students from Asian countries (Ninnes, Aitchison & Kalos 1999).

Intercultural and social relations between overseas and Australian students have been another major topic of interest. This literature has been particularly interested in how well overseas students adjust to the Australian social environment and cope with different kinds of problems, the impact of overseas students on Australian students, and social interactions between Australian and overseas students. In a major review of this literature and their research, Smart, Volet and Ang (2000) conclude that Australian and international students mix relatively uneasily and infrequently on Australian campuses. Their report:

> ...reveals a picture of two parallel streams of students proceeding through university – the Australian and the international - within close proximity but, in the majority of cases, with little or only superficial contact and interaction. A variety of exit and other surveys confirms this fairly common experience and record repeated expressions of disappointed expectations by international students who had hoped to meet and form close friendships with Australian students, visit Australian homes and experience local culture first hand (Smart, Volet & Ang 2000: 9).

What is not clear, however, is how seriously these failures in social interaction are viewed by international students themselves and to what extent this affects their course satisfaction. For example, Romm, Patterson and Hill (1991) concluded from in-depth interviews with international students that the lack of social interaction with domestic students was a major source of dissatisfaction for international students. International students reported great difficulty in communicating and/or establishing any meaningful relations with local students. On the other hand, the survey of international student graduates from 1999 (Australian Education International 2002a) reported that 62 per cent of respondents were 'very satisfied' or 'satisfied' with the quality of interaction with Australian students, although it must be admitted that the level of satisfaction here was considerably lower than that for other aspects of their experience as students in Australia (see also Prescott & Hellstén, this volume).

Teaching methods particularly suitable for overseas students have attracted considerable attention. These include material particularly designed to assist academics (e.g. Ballard & Clanchy 1996, Brick 1991) as well as specialist studies of such topics as dealing with racism (Lilley 2001), 'deep' and 'surface' methods of learning (McLaughlin 1995) and distance education delivery (Leask 1999, Sloper 1990). A number of papers deal with teaching of particular subjects including management (Sharma & Roy 1996) and visual arts (Leong, Power, Mason & Wright 1997).

Not surprisingly, issues about English language competence and strategies for teaching English as a second language have attracted a great deal of attention, particularly from serious researchers including a relatively large number of PhD and research masters students. A number of studies point to the combination of language and learning style problems (McLaughlin 1996, Cho 2002). Several universities have experimented with a variety of methodologies in developing English language skills, including the Reflective Practice Method and the use of computers. Serious work has also been carried out evaluating the utility of different methods of testing overseas student competence in English, including the International English Language Testing System (IELTS) and the Test of English as a Foreign Language (TOEFL) (Broadstock 1995). How Vietnamese culturally situated notions of politeness influence writing in academic English is explored by Phan (2003).

More limited work deals with postgraduate students, teaching strategies used for overseas students, the use of distance education and new technologies, and the role of libraries and support services. Some particularly important work has been carried out on particular problems relating to thesis supervision of overseas postgraduate students (Aspland 1999, Ingleton & Cadman 2002) and financial support for international PhD students and their career ambitions (Harman 2003).

Other Aspects of the Internationalization of Australian Higher Education

While both the Commonwealth Government and higher education institutions have emphasized the importance of internationalization of the curriculum and encouraging increased numbers of Australian students to study abroad, as already noted, achievements have been far less than hoped for. At the same time, there is a growing literature on topics such as curriculum internationalization and there is evidence that particular universities are making impressive developments in internationalization of curricula. Literature on the institutional internationalization covers such topics as study abroad and student exchange by Australian domestic students and their international orientations; internationalizing the university curriculum; international links of university staff; and staff orientations with respect to internationalization in higher education.

Detailed general discussions of the internationalization of Australian higher education within institutions are surprisingly limited. At least a small number of universities have made serious efforts to develop detailed internationalization strategies and are proceeding with their implementation. The University of Western Australia (1999), for example, circulated a detailed discussion paper outlining a strategy for internationalization and has appointed a Dean for International Relations as a senior management appointment. While there is some information on arrangements for student exchange programs in particular universities, there is relatively little up-to-date information about the overall picture on student exchange and study abroad, although work by Corbie, McBurnie and Siribumrungsukha (1995), Clyne and Rizvi (1998), and Dethlefs (1998) indicates that the experience of Australian undergraduates on student exchange is strongly positive. Specialist professional programs in business, agribusiness, engineering, science, and teaching in a number of universities have experimented with various kinds of overseas experience for their domestic students, including study tours, student exchange, international practicum and intensive periods of language study in a foreign country. Dethlefs (1998), for example, reports on a University of Wollongong course which has a compulsory in-country study program during the summer session in Japan for a period of 5-6 weeks. With this arrangement, the benefits are seen to extend further than simply to language and culture acquisition. An example is how groups of Tasmanian pre-service teachers deal with cultural differences during the school experience and rural homestay in Indonesia is provided by Harbon (2002).

From the literature it is difficult to assess the extent of internationalization of curricula for Australian students that has taken place across the sector. Back, Davis and Olsen (1997) reported that 30 of 36 universities had in place strategies for internationalization of the form and content of the teaching curriculum and 21 universities gave themselves at least a pass mark in assessing their achievements in implementing these strategies. All but one university reported a policy of internationalization in their mission statements and all included a policy of internationalization as part of their corporate plan. Twenty five universities reported an explicit commitment to quality assurance and international benchmarking for their international activities. However, there is little information on how deeply internationalization efforts at departmental and faculty levels in curriculum development have been implemented across the sector.

At the same time, there is evidence of important innovation at least in a small number of universities, all of which are leaders in terms of total numbers of international students enrolled. For example, such experiments at Curtin University include the areas of health promotion education, social work, mining, agribusiness, culture, science and pharmacy (eg Collins 1997, Graham & Govindarajalu 1997, Maynard, Saunders & Lawrance 1997). Another example is at the University of South Australia where the Flexible Learning Centre is providing support to academic staff and departments in internationalizing courses so that graduates will develop an international perspective, and in devising ways to assist both international and Australian students to work more effectively together (Leask 2001a, 2001b, 2002). The Flexible Learning Centre of the University of South Australia has available impressive resource materials to assist staff (University of South Australia 2002a, 2000b) while the Division of Business and Enterprise has completed an exemplar project on embedding graduate qualities (Page 2002).

In contrast, apart from information on overseas qualifications by Anderson, Arthur and Stokes (1997) and information of research collaboration, there is almost a complete absence of material on the active involvement of academics in internationalization, their perceptions of other cultures and people, the value they place on internationalization and their competence in speaking and reading other languages than English.

Assessment and Conclusions

The review and discussion demonstrates the considerable recent interest by researchers in the areas of internationalization of Australian higher education and
internationalization of higher education more generally. This has led to the development of a substantial and impressive literature that has proved to be of considerable
interest to academics and other professionals working with international students and
in international education endeavours in Australian universities, as well as to policy-
makers in government and commercial agencies. This literature also has attracted
considerable interest from abroad, not only from scholars and policy makers in other
nations involved in the export of education services but from much broader groups
including senior personnel in NGOs and in government agencies in countries which
provide Australia with large numbers of international students.

The most detailed work on the internationalization of Australian higher education has focused particularly on processes of internationalization, discussion and
evaluation of national policy and government initiatives, the export and marketing of
higher education services, the social and educational backgrounds of students, the
social and learning experiences of students, and the efforts of teachers and professionals to facilitate student learning and provide effective student support. Within
these various areas, there are a number of nodes of particular concentration, such as
evaluations of student experiences and satisfaction, costs and marketing studies,
reports on patterns of social interaction between international and domestic students,
learning and intercultural student experiences, and English language competence and
ELICOS teaching. Australian researchers have also contributed to the worldwide
literature on internationalization, with possibly the most substantial contributions
relating to what has become known as borderless education and issues related to cross
border trade in higher education services.

Somewhat surprisingly, apart from an officially commissioned review of the
Overseas Postgraduate Research Scholarship Scheme (Grigg 1996), there have been
comparatively few Australian Government commissioned evaluations of sponsored
student programs and relatively little written about the views and experiences of
NGOs, international agencies and home governments that support sponsored students.
Neither is there available much in the way of detailed information on the views of
particular Asian Governments about Australia's efforts in export education, or how
the poorest nations in the Asian Pacific region view Australia's internationalization
thrust or the impact of internationalization more broadly on their education systems.
Comparatively little is available in the way of longer-term follow-up studies of
international students' education in Australian universities.

The material on the internationalization of Australian higher education students,
curricula and staff is relatively limited. While it is clear that student experiences with
study abroad and exchange are largely positive, few detailed studies are available
about the numbers of students involved in study abroad, where they go and for how

long, what credits students earn towards formal qualifications in their home universities, and how such programs are arranged and sustained. Very little is known about the foreign language competence of domestic students, or about the extent to which Australian institutions require foreign language competence as a basis for admission to particular courses. Neither does there appear to be much in the way of studies that deal with global understandings by Australian domestic university students, or of international graduate attributes among international students in Australian universities. Apart from the studies of social interactions of Australian and overseas students, there is relatively little in the way of work that assesses to what extent the presence of overseas students on Australian campuses contributes to internationalization of Australian education and training. A number of universities clearly are experimenting with internationalizing the curriculum, but the literature gives no detailed and up-to-date census of how extensive these initiatives are, the number of universities involved and the degree of success achieved.

The research push that has generated the impressive range of material on internationalization has come from the influence of different drivers. Students of comparative education quite naturally have been drawn to study the forces of internationalization and globalization, and their effects on different societies and education systems. Some scholars have been attracted by funds available for sponsored projects from government agencies, IDP Education Australia, NGOs and individual universities, while others have been successful in attracting competitive research grants from their own universities or from the Australian Research Council. However, a substantial amount of work has been achieved by academics and research students with relatively modest resources. Such work has concentrated particularly on such topic areas as international student characteristics and student learning experiences, and the internationalization of curricula.

Scholars from many different perspectives and disciplines have been involved in the research effort, but their interests have diverged to a marked extent so that work on any particular theme and topic usually has come from a limited group of scholars with shared interests. For instance, most of the work on internationalization of the curriculum and particular teaching efforts has come mainly from academics in such fields as accounting and business studies, management and computer science, and from specialists in university teaching and learning centres, while discussions of the globalization and the overall impact of internationalization has drawn interest mainly from scholars in comparative education and sociology.

Unfortunately, in many cases the various groups of scholars have gone about their research efforts largely in isolation from other scholars with different interests in internationalization. In fact, a relatively simple analysis of reference lists in various publications suggests that generally scholars in particular specialties seldom read literature outside their own specialization. This is unfortunate since a high degree of interaction could well be beneficial to scholarship generally on internationalization topics.

Associated with this is an urgent need to bring together some of the main findings, especially the in-depth work of higher degree research students on international students, student learning and language issues in order that academics generally might benefit in enhancing their approaches to the teaching of international students and internationalizing the curriculum. Possibly the Australian Department of Education, Science and Training (DEST) or IDP Education Australia could perform an important service by sponsoring a series of studies reviewing detailed research on particular topics and facilitating dissemination to academics and institutional managers.

References

Anderson, D., Arthur, R. & Stokes, T. 1997. *Qualifications of Australian Academics, Sources and Levels, 1978-1996.* Canberra: Department of Employment, Education, Training and Youth Affairs.

Anderson, D. & Johnston, R. 1998. *University Autonomy in Twenty Countries.* Canberra: Department of Employment, Training and Youth Affairs.

Anderson, D., Johnston, R. & Milligan, B. 2000. *Quality Assurance and Accreditation in Australian Higher Education: An assessment of Australian and international practice.* Canberra: Department of Employment, Training and Youth Affairs.

Andressen, C. 1997. "The Location and Characteristics of Asia-born Overseas Students in Australia." In *Asians in Australia: patterns of migration and settlement,* edited by J.E. Coughlan & D. J. McNamara. South Melbourne: Macmillan Education Australia.

Aspland, T. 1999. Speaking about Supervision: A Study of Six Overseas Women Students Enrolled in Doctoral Programs in Three Australian Universities. St Lucia: PhD thesis, University of Queensland.

Auletta, A. 2000. "A Retrospective View of the Colombo Plan: Government Policy, Departmental Administration and Overseas Students." *Journal of Higher Education Policy and Management.* 22(1): 47-58.

Australian Education International 2002a. *Comparative Costs of Higher Education Courses for International Students in Australia, New Zealand, The United Kingdom, Canada and the United States.* Canberra: Australian Education International.

Australian Education International 2002b. *How International Students View their Australian Experience: A Survey of International Students who Finished a Course of Study in 1999.* Canberra: Australian Education International.

Australian Department of Foreign Affairs and Trade 2002. *International Trade Services: Communication from Australia: Negotiating Proposal for Education Services.* Canberra: Australian Department of Foreign Affairs and Trade. Online. http://www.dfat.gov.au/trade/negotiations/services/np_education.html.

Back, K. 1994. *Education in the Aid Programme: Retrospective on Australian Aid.* Canberra: Australian Development Studies Network.

Back, K., Davis, D. & Olsen, A. 1996. *Internationalisation and Higher Education: Goals and Strategies*. Canberra: Department of Employment, Education, Training and Youth Affairs.

Back, K., Davis, D. & Olsen, A. 1997. *Comparative Costs of Higher Education Courses for International Students in Australia, New Zealand, the United Kingdom, Canada and the United States*. Canberra: Australian Government Publishing Service.

Baker, M. 1996. *Financing and the Effects of Internationalisation in Higher Education*. Canberra: Department of Employment, Education, Training and Youth Affairs.

Baker, M., Robertson, F., Taylor, A., Doube, L. & Rhall, T. 1996. *The Labour Market Effects of Overseas Students*. Canberra: Australian Government Publishing Service.

Ballard, B. & Clanchy, J. 1996. *Study Abroad: A Manual for Asian Students*. Kuala Lumpur: Longman Malaysia.

Beazley, Hon. K. 1992. *International Education in Australia through the 1990s*. Canberra: Australian Government Publishing Service.

Biggs, J. 1997. "Teaching Across and Within Cultures: The Issue of International Students." In *Learning and Teaching in Higher Education: Advancing International Perspectives*: *Proceedings of the Higher Education Research and Development Society of Australasia Conference, 8-11 July 1997*. Canberra: Higher Education Research and Development Society of Australasia.

Borsheim Stundal, A. 1999. Internationalisation of Higher Education in Australia: Development and Implementation of Policy Change. Armidale: MEdAdmin thesis, University of New England.

Bourke, P. & Butler, L. 1995. *International Links in Higher Education Research*. Canberra: National Board of Employment, Education and Training.

Brick, J. 1991. *China: A Handbook in Intercultural Communication*. Sydney: Macquarie University National Centre for English Language Teaching and Research.

Broadstock, H. J. 1995. The Predictive Validity of the IELTS and TOEFL: A Comparison. Parkville: MA thesis, University of Melbourne.

Cameron, J. W. 2000. *International Students in Victorian Universities*. Melbourne: Victorian Auditor-General.

Cho, S. 2002. The Problems Encountered by Korean Overseas Students at the Wollongong English Language Centre. Wollongong: MEd (Hons) thesis, University of Wollongong.

Clyne, F. & Rizvi, F. 1998. "Outcomes of Student Exchange." In *Outcomes of International Education: Research Findings: A Set of Commissioned Research Papers Presented at the 12th Australian International Education Conference, Canberra, 1998*, edited by D. Davis & A. Olsen. Canberra: IDP Education Australia.

Collins, J. 1997. "Internationalisation of the Postgraduate Diploma in Health Education Promotion (distance learning program)." In *Quality in Practice: Internationalising the Curriculum and Classroom*, edited by A.V. Butorac. South Bentley: Curtin University of Technology.

Corbie, B., McBurnie, G. & Siribumrungsukha, B. 1995. "Cultural Difference in Experience of Exchange Students Thailand/Australia – Providing the Props. Some Preliminary Findings." In *The Fourth International Symposium on the Role of Universities in*

Developing Areas: at the Royal Melbourne Institute of Technology 124 La Trobe Street, Melbourne 3000, Australia from 11-14 July, 1995 Vol 1. Melbourne: University Office of International Programs, Royal Melbourne Institute of Technology.

Cunningham, S., Tapsall, S., Ryan, Y., Stedman, L., Bagdon, K. & Flew, T. 1998. *New Media and Borderless Education: A Review of the Convergence between Global Media Networks and Higher Education Provision.* Canberra: Department of Employment, Education, Training and Youth Affairs.

Cunningham, S., Ryan, Y., Stedman, L., Tapsall, S., Bagdon, K., Flew, T. & Coaldrake, P. 2000. *The Business of Borderless Education.* Canberra: Department of Education, Training and Youth Affairs

Currie, J. & Newson, J. Eds. 1998. *Universities and Globalisation: Critical Perspectives.* Thousand Oaks: Sage Publications.

Currie, J., DeAngelis, R., de Boer, H., Huisman, J. & Lacotte, C. Eds. 2002. *Globalising Practices and University Reponses.* Westport: Greenwood Press.

Currie, J., Thiele, B., & Harris, P. Eds. 2002. *Gendered Universities in Globalised Economies.* Lantham: Lexington Books.

Davis, D. & Olsen, A. 1998. *Outcomes of International Education: Research Findings.* Canberra: IDP Education Australia.

Dethlefs, N. 1998. "The Effectiveness of Short Term In-country Study/Work Programs." *Overview* 5(1): 1-3.

Enders, J. 2002. "Higher Education, Internationalisation, and the Nation-State: Recent Developments and Challenges to Governance Theory." Paper presented at the annual conference of the Consortium of Higher Education Researchers, Vienna, 5-7 September.

Goldring, J. (Chair) 1984. *Mutual Advantage: Report of the Committee of Review of Private Overseas Student Policy.* Canberra: Australian Government Publishing Service.

Graham, A. & Govindarajalu, S. 1997. "Internationalising Mining and Society 202." In *Quality in Practice: Internationalising the Curriculum and Classroom* edited by A. V. Butorac. South Bentley: Curtin University of Technology.

Grigg, L. 1996. *The Internationalization of Australian Higher Education: An Evaluation of the Contribution of the Overseas Postgraduate Research Scholarships Scheme.* Canberra: Australian Government Publishing Service.

Hamilton, S. 1998. Setting the Foundation for the Internationalization of Australian Higher Education. Paper presented at Education '98: The Industry Practitioner Forum, Canberra, 17-19 March.

Harbon, L.A. 2002. "Stories of Raw Green Chillies and Unlocked Cupboards: The Value of In-country Experiences for Language Teachers." *Babel* 36(3): 23-29.

Harman, G. 2003. "International PhD Students in Australian Universities: Financial Support, Course Experience and Career Plans." *International Journal of Educational Development* 23(3): 339-351.

Harman, G.S. & Meek, V.L. 2000. *Repositioning Quality Assurance and Accreditation in Australian Higher Education.* Canberra: Department of Education, Training and Youth Affairs.

Harman, G. & Nolan, P. 2002. *Internationalisation of the Higher Education Sector: Draft Annotated Bibliography and Report on Literature Review.* Armidale: unpublished report, Centre for Higher Education Management and Policy, University of New England.

Harris, G.T. & Jarrett, F.G. 1990. *Educating Overseas Students in Australia: Who Benefits?* Sydney: Allen & Unwin.

Henry, M., Lingard, B., Rizvi, F. & Taylor, S. 2000. *The OECD, Globalisation and Education Policy.* Amsterdam: Pergamon.

Hill, C., Romm, T. & Patterson, P. 1992. *The Pre-purchase Decision-making Process: A Qualitative, Retrospective Longitudinal Study of Overseas Students in Australia.* Wollongong: University of Wollongong Department of Management.

Ingleton, C. & Cadman, K. 2002. "Silent Issues for International Postgraduate Research Students: Emotion and Agency in Academic Success." *Australian Educational Researcher* 29(1): 93-113.

Jackson, R. (Chair) 1984. *Report of the Committee to Review the Australian Overseas Aid Program.* Canberra: Australian Government Publishing Service.

Jones, P. 1997. "The World Bank and the Literacy Question: Orthodoxy, Heresy and Ideology." *International Review of Education* 43(4): 367-375.

Jones, P. 1998. "Globalisation and Internationalism: Democratic Prospects for World Education." *Comparative Education* 34(2): 143-155.

Jones, P. 1999. "Globalisation and the UNESCO Mandate: Multilateral Prospects for Educational Development." *International Journal of Educational Development* 19(1): 17-25.

Jones, P. 2001. "Education, Multilateral Cooperation and Globalisation." *International Education Electronic Journal* (IE-ej), 5(2).

Knight, J. 1999. "Internationalisation of Higher Education." In Organisation for Economic Cooperation and Development, *Quality and Internationalisation in Higher Education.* Paris: OECD.

Knight, J. & de Wit, H. Eds. 1997. *Internationalisation of Higher Education in Asia Pacific Countries.* Amsterdam: European Association for international Education in cooperation with IDP Education Australia and the Programme on Institutional Management in Higher Education of OECD.

Lawley, M. 1993. Factors Influencing the Choice of Destination in International Education: The Case of Hong Kong. Toowoomba: MBus thesis, University of Southern Queensland.

Leask, B. 1999. *Online Delivery and Internationalisation: Implications for Students.* Adelaide: The Curriculum and Staff Development Australia.

Leask, B. 2001a. "Bridging the Gap – Internationalising University Curricula." *Journal of Studies in International Education* 5(2): 100-115.

Leask, B. 2001b "Internationalisation: Changing Contexts and their Implications for Teaching, Learning and Assessment. In L. Richardson & J. Lidstone (Eds), *Flexible Learning for a Flexible Society: Proceedings of the ASET/HERDSA 2000 Joint International Conference, 2-5 July 2000 Toowoomba.* Toowoomba: Australian Society for Educational Technology and Higher Education Research and Development Society of Australasia.

Leask, B. 2002. "Crossing the Bridge from Both Sides: Strategies to Assist International and Australian Students to Meet Each Other Half Way." Paper presented at the 17th National Liaison Committee conference, Launceston, 8 July.

Leong, G., Power, B., Mason, P. & Wright, B. 1997. *Towards Internationalising Visual Arts Curricula*. Canberra: Department of Education, Training and Youth Affairs.

Leong, J.S.L. 1994. Hong Kong students' Perception of Australian Tertiary Education. Footscray: MBA thesis, Victoria University of Technology.

Lilley, R. 2001. Teaching Elsewhere: Anthropological Pedagogy, Racism and Indifference in a Hong Kong Classroom. *The Australian Journal of Anthropology* 12(2): 127-154.

Marginson, S. & Rhoades, G. 2002. "Beyond National States, Markets, and Systems of Higher Education: A Glonacal Agency Heuristic." *Higher Education* 43(3): 281-309.

Marshall, A.C. 1993. Aid to Trade to Internationalisation: The Development of an Export Industry in Australian Higher Education, 1984-1992. Perth: MEd (Hons) thesis, Murdoch University.

Matthews, M. & Johnston, R. 2000. *International Trends in Public Sector Support for Research and Development: A Preliminary Analysis*. Canberra: Department of Education, Training and Youth Affairs.

Maynard, C., Saunders, N. & Lawrance, B. 1997. "Asian Language and Culture for Engineers." In *Quality in Practice: Internationalising the Curriculum and Classroom*, edited by A. V. Butorac. South Bentley: Curtin University of Technology.

Mazzoral, T. & Soutar, G. 2002. *The Global Market for Higher Education: Sustainable Competitive Strategies for the New Millennium*. London: Edward Elgar.

McBurnie, G. 2000a. "Pursuing Internationalisation as a Means to Advance the Academic Mission of the University: An Australian Case Study." *Higher Education in Europe* 25(1): 63-73.

McBurnie, G. 2000b. "Quality Matters in Transnational Education: Undergoing the GATE Review Process – An Australian-Asian Case Study." *Journal of Studies in International Education* 4(1): 23-38.

McBurnie, G. & Pollock, A. 2000. "Opportunity and Risk in Transnational Education – Issues in Planning for International Campus Development: An Australian Perspective." *Higher Education in Europe* 25(3): 333-343.

McBurnie, G. & Ziguras, C. 2001. "The Regulation of Transnational Higher Education in Southeast Asia: Case studies of Hong Kong, Malaysia and Australia." *Higher Education* 42(1): 85-105.

McBurnie, G. & Ziguras, C. 2003. "Remaking the World in Our Own Image: Australia's Efforts to Liberalised Trade in Educational Services." *Australian Journal of Education* 47(3): 217-234.

McLaughlin, D. 1995. "Teaching Overseas Students and Learning from Them: A Professional and Moral Dimension." *Education Research and Perspectives*. 22(1): 103-113.

McLaughlin, D. 1996. "The Medium is Not the Message: Improving Australian Educational Aid to Papua New Guinea Students." *Higher Education Research & Development* 15(1): 97-114.

Meek, V.L. 2002. *International Higher Education and the Role of Government in Educational Exports.* Armidale: Centre for Higher Education Management and Policy, University of New England.

Nelson, The Hon B. 2002. *Higher Education at the Crossroads: An Overview Paper.* Canberra: AusInfo.

Ninnes, P., Aitchison, C. & Kalos, S. 1999. "Challenges to Stereotypes of International Students' Prior Educational Experience: Undergraduate Education in India." *Higher Education Research and Development* 18(3): 323-342.

Olsen, A. 2001. "Developing Regional Capacity: Public Policy and Private Links in Tertiary Education in Asia." IDP Education Australia Annual Conference, Sydney, 25-28 September.

Page, G. 2002. "Embedding Graduate Quality 7: An International Perspective." Bachelor of Business (Property) Course material. Adelaide: University of South Australia. Online. http://www.unisanet.unisa.edu.au/gradquals/example/exemplar.htm

Phan L.H. 2001. "How Do Culturally Situated Notions of 'Polite' Forms Influence the Way Vietnamese Postgraduate Students Write Academic English in Australia?" *Australian Journal of Education* 45(3): 296-308.

Pratt, G. & Poole, D. 1999/2000. "Global Corporations 'R' Us? The Impacts of Globalisation on Australian Universities." *Australian Universities Review* 42(2)/43(1): 16-23.

Romm, T., Patterson, P. & Hill, C. 1991. *International Students in Australia: A Qualitative Exploration of Pre-purchase Expectations, and Post-purchase Satisfaction.* Wollongong: University of Wollongong.

Ryan, Y. 2001. "Higher Education as a Business: Lessons from the Corporate World." *Minerva* 39(1): 115-135.

Sloper, D.W. 1990. "Meeting the Needs of Overseas Postgraduate Women Students through Flexible Distance Education." *Distance Education* 11(2): 266-286.

Sharma, B. & Roy, J. A. 1996. "Aspects of Internationalization of Management Education." *Journal of Management Development* 15(1): 5-13.

Smart, D. Volet, S.E. & Ang, G 2000. *Fostering Social Cohesion in Universities: Bridging the Cultural Divide.* Canberra: Australian Education International.

Smith, P.J. & Smith, S. 1999. *The Internationalisation of Vocational Education and Training.* Leabrook: VCVER, Leabrook.

Smith, S.N., Miller, R.J. & Crassini, B. 1998. "Approaches to Studying of Australian and Chinese University Students." *Higher Education Research and Development* 17(3): 261-276.

Suen, D. 1994. International Education: Experience of Hong Kong Students in Australia. Kensington: MA thesis, University of New South Wales.

Teichler, U. 2002. "The Changing Debate on Internationalisation of Higher Education." Vienna: paper presented at the annual conference of the Consortium of Higher Education Researchers, 5-7 September.

University of South Australia 2002a. *Teaching NESB and International Students at the University of South Australia.* Adelaide: Flexible Learning Centre, University of South Australia.

University of South Australia 2002b. *Graduate Quality 7 – Developing International Perspectives: Structural Options and Pathways for Program Design.* Adelaide: Flexible Learning Centre, University of South Australia. (http://www.unisanet.unisa.edu.au/learningconnection/intl/strat.htm).

University of Western Australia 1999. *Developing an Internationalisation Strategy for The University of Western Australia in the 21ˢᵗ Century.* Nedlands: University of Western Australia.

Vidovich, L. 2002. "Quality Assurance in Australian Higher Education: Globalisation and Steering at a Distance." *Higher Education* 43(3): 391-408.

Yang, R. & Welch, A. 2001. "Internationalising Chinese Universities: A Study of Guangzhou." *World Studies in Education* 2(1): 21-51.

Welch, A. & Denman, B. 1997. "Internationalisation of Higher Education: Retrospect and Prospect." *Forum of Education* 52(1): 14-29.

Woodhouse, D. 2001. "Globalisation: Implications for Education and Quality." Rockhampton: paper presented to the annual conference of the Association for Institutional Research, 3-5 September.

7

Higher Education Engaging with the 'Developing' World: The Case of the Virtual Colombo Plan

Peter Ninnes

Introduction

Australian higher education institutions are becoming increasingly globalized, in that they are becoming more and more entangled in the processes of global exchanges of capital, knowledge, and cultural practices. Large metropolitan universities with long standing international ties are expanding and enhancing their global positions, while newer universities in metropolitan and rural areas are moving into a range of international projects such as off-shore programs, development consultancies, twinning arrangements and the like. One major recent internationalization initiative in which Australian higher education institutions have been invited to participate is the Virtual Colombo Plan (VCP). Fostered by the Australian Government's aid organization AusAID, in collaboration with the World Bank, the VCP purports to link Australian higher education institutions and technology companies with 'developing' countries so that the latter can overcome poverty by accessing knowledge through information communication technologies.

In this chapter I analyse the major official documents describing the VCP, especially in terms of the models of 'third world' development they employ. Development is not an unproblematic concept; it has come under sustained attack in various quarters for a wide range of reasons (see, for example, Rist 1997, Carmen 1996, Escobar 1995, Dichter 2003). It is important, therefore, for Australian higher education institutions to engage in a critical reading of the VCP by examining the VCP proposals, and the merits and potential problems of the way the VCP depicts 'developing' countries, higher education, teaching and learning, and Australia's relations with its neighbours. Such an analysis is also salutary for higher education institutions in other countries that are seeking to expand their offerings and activities beyond their own shores, because it brings to the surface a number of assumptions of and problems with particular approaches to the internationalization of higher education.

The VCP takes its name from the original Colombo Plan, which in part involved citizens of Commonwealth countries in South and South-East Asia taking up temporary residence in Australia in order to undertake university awards. Auletta (2000) points out that the Colombo Plan emerged from a meeting of Commonwealth foreign affairs ministers in Colombo, Sri Lanka (then Ceylon) in 1950, in a context in which the newly independent countries of India, Pakistan and Ceylon desired economic development and countries such as Australia, Canada, the UK and New Zealand, fearful of the rise of China and wary of the Soviet Union, desired to limit the spread of communism. The Colombo Plan had a capital works component focusing on agriculture, communications and power supplies, and a technical cooperation aspect, that emphasized training students in sponsor countries, and providing technical experts and equipment (Auletta 2000: 50).

Given that one of the rationales for the Colombo Plan was to stabilize and grow capitalist economies in the newly independent nations of South and South-East Asia, it was clearly posited, like many other such programs of the era, within the modernization school of development thinking. Apart from combating the spread of communism by aiding free-market economic development, the Colombo Plan, according to Auletta (2000), had other less explicit Australian and international political purposes, such as combating the perception that Australia's immigration policy was racist, providing a bargaining chip in trade negotiations, as a means of enhancing diplomatic relations, and as a way of enhancing Australia's international reputation. Auletta (2000) concludes by noting that whereas the Colombo Plan was essentially an aid program, later review of the Colombo Plan flagged the possibility of Australian higher education becoming a trade commodity, a shift that occurred in the 1980s. Thus one curious aspect of the VCP is that it reintroduces the discourse of higher education for aid and development at a time when the internationalization of Australian higher education is predominantly an exercise in trade and revenue raising.

Theoretical Framework

As noted above, the Colombo Plan appeared at a time when modernization theory dominated development thinking. As such it was a product of its time. However, modernization theory and its accomplice, human capital theory, have been the subject of sustained critique in the last two decades. In this chapter I use two theoretical lenses, both of which are critical of modernization theory, to explore the VCP. The first is the notion of development as freedom, advocated by Sen (1999). The second is the poststructural critique of development as a discourse with effects, promoted by Escobar (1995).

Sen (1999: 293) argues that human capital theory provides a limited perspective on development because it views humans simply as a means of increasing economic capacity. Human capital theory focuses on broad indicators of 'development' such as gross domestic product and levels of industrialization, whereas Sen argues that development should be much more broadly conceived. In particular, Sen advocates conceptualizing development in terms of five freedoms. These are:

- political freedoms ("political entitlements associated with democracies in the broadest sense", Sen 1999: 38);
- economic facilities ("the opportunities that individuals respectively enjoy to utilize economic resources for the purpose of consumption, or production, or exchange", Sen 1999: 38-39);
- social opportunities ("the arrangements that society makes for education, health care, and so on which influence the individual's substantive freedom to live better", Sen 1999: 39);
- transparency guarantees ("the freedom to deal with one another under guarantees of disclosure and lucidity", Sen 1999: 39); and
- protective security (freedom from deprivation, which involves "fixed institutional arrangements such as unemployment benefits and statutory income supplements ... as well as ad hoc arrangements such as famine relief...", Sen 1999: 40).

Many of these ideas overlap with those contained in some of the alternative to development, alternative development, and gender and development literature, such as Datta and Kornberg's (2002) multilevel approach to empowerment and dis-empowerment, and Peet and Harwick's (1999) ideas about participation and democratic and egalitarian social relations. The five freedoms are linked. According to Sen (1999: 11):

Political freedoms (in the form of free speech and elections) help to promote economic security. Social opportunities (in the form of education and health facilities) facilitate economic participation. Economic facilities (in the form of opportunities for participation in trade and production) can help to generate personal abundance as well as public resources for social facilities.

Sources of non-freedoms, on the other hand, include "poverty as well as tyranny, poor economic opportunities as well as systematic social deprivation, neglect of public facilities as well as intolerance or overactivity of repressive states" (Sen 1999: 3). They also include starvation and undernourishment, lack of access to health care, clean water and sanitation, unnecessary morbidity, premature mortality, lack of access to functional education, lack of worthwhile employment, lack of economic and social security, gender inequality, lack of political liberty and denial of civil rights (Sen 1999: 15). Sen argues that development should enhance human capabilities. This idea incorporates the economic development of human capital, but goes beyond it to include social and political development (Sen 1999: 296). The focus is on developing human beings' capacity to "achieve outcomes they value and have reason to value" (Sen 1999: 291).

Sen's important contribution to development thinking lies in his sustained effort to expand the arena of what constitutes 'development'. However, his approach says little about the relations of power that imbue processes of deciding what are the outcomes people value and have reason to value, the possibility that 'reason' may be contextual and potentially conflicting, and therefore that different groups may come up with entirely contradictory and conflicting ideas about valued outcomes. With this caveat in mind, I will employ Sen's ideas about freedoms to evaluate the VCP documents. In particular, I ask whether the five freedoms are advanced or have the potential to be advanced by the VCP, and whether particular non-freedoms are diminished, advanced, or ignored.

The second lens with which I explore the VCP is the poststructuralist post-development approach followed by Escobar (1995) and to some extent Rist (1997). Escobar argues that many concepts that we have come to take for granted have been discursively constituted by the West as a means of governing and intervening in the affairs of the non-west. Thus concepts such as 'underdeveloped', 'developing', 'poor', and 'modern' are inventions used by the west to represent the non-west. In particular, the non-west is represented as an apolitical but scientifically solvable problem or abnormality (e.g. 'under-developed') requiring the intervention of experts. Development, then, is a technology of governance (pace Foucault 1991), in which discourses mainly originating in the west discursively produce the objects of which they speak (Foucault 1972), namely the 'poor', 'under-developed', 'least developed', and 'developed' countries and societies. Furthermore, development has become institutionalized at particular sites in which knowledge and power combine (Escobar 1995). The World Bank is an obvious example: it produces documents that discursively construct ideas about the purposes, processes and outcomes of education (e.g. World Bank 1995), and uses these discourses to impose particular economic conditions on donee countries. And although counter discourses arise that challenge the dominant educational discourses of the World Bank (e.g. Samoff 1996, Lauglo 1996), the World Bank still carries a large amount of influence (Samoff 1996: 250).

Escobar's work has been criticized on a number of counts. First, Nederveen Pieterse (2000) argues that it overgeneralizes development and its effects, it tends to criticize the development 'industry' or big D development, but does not address small scale, local, grassroots development, and it offers no viable alternatives to 'development'. The VCP, however, is part of the Development industry, given that it was born from a union of AusAID and the World Bank. Second, Peet and Hartwick (1999) argue that Escobar does not give due credit to some of the positive achievements of 'development' in the last three or four decades, such as improved health care for many people. Nevertheless, Escobar's work is important because first it shows the ways in which discourses operate in the development field to prescribe and constrain particular national, group and individual identities, possibilities, lifeways and futures. Second, as Peet and Harwick (1999) point out, discourse works both ways or, following Foucault (1977), discourse is potentially productive. That is, understanding how ideas about development are discursively produced allows us to voice "new imaginaries of development" (Peet & Harwick 1999: 209) that resist and disrupt dominant and subjugating discourses. Thus in analysing the VCP documents using this lens, I look for the ways in which various nations, groups and individuals are discursively produced. I ask questions such as how do the documents represent Australia, Australian society, Australian knowledge, and Australian people. Who do the documents say is Australia's Other? What is this other like, in terms of knowledge, wealth, social and global positioning, and in comparison to Australia and Australians? What is the relationship between Australia and its Others? What is the role of higher education in this relationship? How is development represented, and who or what are its objects, subjects, purposes, desired outcomes, and modes of operation?

Methods

The methods for this work are implied in the use of the two theoretical lenses described above. Analysing the VCP documents through the 'development as free-dom' lens involves a content analysis of ideologies in which the ways in which development is conceptualized in the VCP documents are compared and contrasted with the ways in which Sen (1999) frames development in terms of the five freedoms. Analysing the VCP documents through Escobar's discursive lens, on the other hand, involves a discourse analysis (Luke 1999), which can be conceived as providing an alternative, critical reading of the document. I identified all statements in the documents that I judged as concerning Australia and it's Others, and below I identify and critique the various forms of language used in these statements. I then explore the potential or likely effects of these discourses, and suggest some alternative ways of conceptualizing Australian higher education and its relationship to its neighbours.

I analyse six documents in this chapter, which I parsimoniously call the Background Study (Australia. AusAID 2001a), the Activities Outline (Australia. AusAID 2001b), the Hot Topics document (Australia. AusAID 2001c), the BDD Media Release (Australia. Ministry of Foreign Affairs 2001a), the Downer Speech (Australia. Ministry of Foreign Affairs 2001b), and the AC Media Release (Australia. AusAID 2001d), full publication details of which are found in the reference list.

The VCP and Development as Freedom

In this section I explore how the six VCP documents address the five freedoms identified by Sen (1999): political freedoms; economic facilities; social opportunities; transparency guarantees; and protective security. I analyse each document in turn, presenting analyses of direct quotes that relate them to one of the five freedoms.

Social Opportunities

The advancement of social opportunities, particularly educational opportunities, is the most prevalent of Sen's five freedoms within the VCP documents. There are numerous examples in which access to information and communication technologies (ICTs) and knowledge through formal and informal education are espoused as the outcomes of the VCP. In arguing for policy reform, the Background Study argues that "good policies can assist to improve access [to ICTs]. Specific steps should be taken to ensure the widest possible community access to ICT facilities" (p. 4). As well as enhancing women's economic livelihoods (see below), the VCP emphasizes "improving access to relevant and appropriate information and shared experience, focusing specifically on IT [information technology] skills of female teachers, both for direct educational reasons and to provide effective role models for male and female students" (p. 6). The Background Study then states that while "much progress has been made in developing countries in terms of educational access and achievements" (p. 7), it then goes on to observe that there are still many children with no access to primary schooling, that there are lower retention and progression rates in "developing" countries compared to "developed" countries, that difficulties have arisen in meeting "new international development goals for universal global primary enrolments" (p. 8), and that there is a perceived poor quality of education in "developing" countries. Having constructed this view of education, the Background Study then provides a number of examples of the kinds of educational opportunities that the Australian Government already provides, including distance education programs for upgrading the skills of "under-qualified" educators (p. 9), enhancement of an education management database in Papua New Guinea (PNG) (p. 10), and training support for satellite technology for the University of the South Pacific (p. 11). In addition to formal education, the VCP Background Study argues that ICTs can enhance access to knowledge and information. It describes information management and exchange in finance and health ministries in a number of Pacific island countries (p. 12), sharing of medical imaging knowledge between Tonga, New Zealand and Australia (p. 12), and the provision of internet centres in Palestinian refugee camps, thus "linking refugee communities separated by international borders" and "providing women and children with basic computer and IT skills, [thus] increasing their employment opportunities" (p. 13). One of the major purposes of the VCP, then, is to combine Australia's "strong expertise in DE [distance education] and the provision of knowledge by various means, including through ICTs" with Australia's expertise in "supporting education in developing countries" (p. 14).

The Background Study document spells out the specific form that the VCP will take. It is essentially concerned with providing social opportunities by bridging " the knowledge divide between industrialised and developing nations" (p. 21). Its goal is to "use the opportunities presented by Information and Communication Technologies (ICTs) to improve education and access to knowledge in developing countries" (p. 21). In particular, the Background Study envisages three stages, each of which concerns enhancing educational provision. The first stage focuses on basic education, especially teacher training and ICT policy development. The second stage involves "delivering knowledge" (p. 21) via ICTs to, first, enhance policy makers' skills in areas such as "public financial management, human resource management, change processes and policy challenges" (p. 24), and second, "make the best of Australia's world class research and knowledge readily available to users in the developing world" on topics such as "agriculture, health and environmental management" (p. 24).

Substantially more detail about these education and knowledge delivery projects are found in the Activities Outline document. In stage one, they include the delivery of ICT based distance education programs for teachers (pp. 2, 6-11), assistance in the development of ICT policies (pp. 3, 12-19), expanding ICT infrastructure to enhance distance education in developing countries, including supporting the World Bank Global Development Learning Network (GDLN) and the African Virtual University (pp. 3, 20-24), and supporting "Australian and regional participation in the creation of the World Bank's Development Gateway as the primary internet site for quality information on development issues" (p. 4; pp. 25-28). In stage two the projects include providing "policy-oriented training for policy-makers in developing countries through ICT-supported distance education programs" (p. 4; pp. 29-32), and promoting "global access to Australian knowledge on development issues" (p. 5; pp. 33-36). Stage three involves improving "the quality of higher education by developing and delivering new ICT-based learning programs for teachers and students" (p. 5; pp. 37-39).

Similar kinds of ideas concerning education, knowledge and specific projects are found in the other VCP documents. For example, the Hot Topics document reiterates that the major aim of the VCP is to "improve education and access to knowledge in developing countries, through distance education support for policy development using ICTs" (paragraph 1). This document also states (paragraph 4) that the key findings of the background study were, among other things, that "access to knowledge has been severely limited in developing countries", that "education and access to knowledge are increasingly important building blocks for development in the age of the ICT revolution", and that "ICTs can improve the delivery of education in schools and broaden the range of options available for distance education". This document then goes on to summarize the activities detailed in the Background Study and Activities Outline documents.

Economic Facilities

Following its introductory remarks, the Background Study consists of a number of sections: "The new technological revolution", "Why focus on education and knowledge?", "Needs in developing countries", "What Australia can supply", "The technological and regulatory environment", and "What might we do?" Although the document does not state what its purpose is or who is its intended audience, it appears to be mainly directed at an Australian audience, especially potential partners in private industry or the higher education sector.

In terms of improving economic facility, the document argues that policy makers should "plan for their policies and activities to augment and strengthen the operative of effective private markets in the ICT sector" (p. 4). It argues that ICT can be used to "address women's development concerns", including "a focus on production and market issues which will benefit women's livelihoods" (p. 6). When discussing needs in developing countries, the document promotes distance education as a "cost effective way of training pre-service teachers" (p. 9) and the need to enhance management skills in school systems "to ensure better use of existing facilities" (p. 9). Furthermore, "the ICT revolution opens up new opportunities for making participation in the global economy a reality for people in developing countries" (p. 12). The document argues that there are "many constraints that hamper the operation of ICT markets in the developing world" (p. 18) and that the "aim of policy-makers in developing countries should be to identify opportunities to relax these constraints" while the "international donor community should ... assist them in this task" (p. 18). Finally the document identifies "several key principles" that will be important to "successfully delivering the Virtual Colombo Plan", including "allowing for technical, institutional and financial sustainability as critical considerations" (p. 25).

The Activities Outlines document says very little about enhancing economic facilities in "developing countries". It appears that the purpose of this document is to identify the Australian contribution to the VCP. As a result, it does indicate, with no sense of irony, how the economic welfare of Australia and Australian firms and institutions can be enhanced through the VCP. For example, when discussing one component of the VCP that involves assisting in the development of ICT policies, the document suggests, "local/multinational private sector may be interested to support pilot projects in order to achieve market exposure" (p. 16). Similarly, the component that involves expanding distance education infrastructure provides "opportunities for Australian universities and related institutions to promote Australian education/ training programs internationally" (p. 21), while "local and multinational private sector organizations will potentially be important clients" and "the private sector in Australia may be interested in developing and manufacturing equipment for second/third tier learning centres" (p. 22). Another component involves providing ICT based distance education training for public policy makers. According to the Activities Outlines document, these courses could be supplied by both local and Australian providers. The latter "have relevant experience" and includes "suppliers in both the public and private sectors" (p. 31). A further activity outlined in this document involves promoting and encouraging "the use of Australian knowledge on a wide range of development-related topics" (p. 33). One partner in this project could be "Australian private sector providers of skills and knowledge including private sector software providers" (p. 34). Finally, the document discusses development of the higher education sector, and suggests, "prospects for at least partial cost recovery appear to be significantly better than at other levels of the education sector. A large amount of content and of the provision of post-university (commercial training and lifelong learning) services is likely to be supplied on a commercial basis" (p. 39).

The Hot Topic document makes direct links between the VCP and the Colombo Plan. It argues that "The Virtual Colombo Plan builds on the concepts of the original Colombo Plan" which "focused on economic and social development" (paragraph 3). The Hot Topic document also mentions the benefits of the VCP for Australia, suggesting that "The VCP also provides a new platform for Australia's world-class education providers, research institutions and technology companies to share their knowledge and skills with our developing country partners" (paragraph 2). Furthermore, the Hot Topics document claims that the VCP will "enable Australian [education] providers to access global opportunities" (paragraph 16) and then goes on to list a number of contracts that have been awarded and upcoming tender opportunities.

Enhancement of economic facilities, particularly from a modernization perspective, is prominent. The document argues that "developing countries want to capture the opportunities offered by ICT to 'leap frog' in the development process" (paragraph 5), while "education and access to knowledge are increasingly important building blocks for development in the age of the ICT revolution" (paragraph 5). One project that the document flags involves linking "an Australian and an African University to increase capacity in delivering business studies in Africa" (paragraph 7). The focus on enhanced economic facility is essentially absent from the other three documents, with the exception of the Downer Speech, which at one point draws attention to the opportunities for "Australian's world-class technology companies, research institutions and education providers to share knowledge and skills" (paragraph 6).

Political Freedoms and Transparency Guarantees

Sen argues that political freedoms involve democratic political entitlements, broadly constituted, while transparency guarantees involve "the freedom to deal with one another under guarantees of disclosure and lucidity" (Sen 1999: 39). The VCP documents make almost no mention of this set of freedoms. The only reference is in the Background Study, which states that the internet is "being used for increased community and civil society participation in government, which helps improve transparency and grassroots pressure for improved government services and accountability" (p. 12).

Protective Security

According to Sen, protective security involves "fixed institutional arrangements such as unemployment benefits and statutory income supplements ... as well as ad hoc arrangements such as famine relief" (Sen 1999: 40). In this study, I interpret Sen's definition to incorporate programs explicitly designed to directly overcome poverty or prevent unnecessary mortality. The idea of poverty alleviation is a recurring refrain in the VCP documents. The introduction to the Background Study commences with an epigraph comprising a quote from a lecture Sen gave in Melbourne on 15 May 2001. The quote concerns the fact that the "economic predicament of the poor cannot be reversed by withholding from them the great advantage of contemporary technology" (p. 2). The document then continues by identifying a technological and digital divide between the "information-rich" and the "information-poor", which "in turn, reflects a growing gap in the capacity of poor people in developing countries to escape from poverty" (p. 2). The Hot Topic document states that the VCP "addresses the root causes of poverty through the use of information and communication technologies" (paragraph 1) and that ICTs are "potentially valuable tools that can assist in meeting Australia's aid objectives of poverty alleviation and sustainable development" (paragraph 9). The document then goes on to state that the VCP activities will "be funded through AusAID's country programs" because "this process is in line with the Government's priorities for Australia's official aid program – sustainable poverty reduction; a focus on partnerships with developing country governments; and greater targeting." (paragraph 11). The BDD Media Release and Downer Speech make similar claims, suggesting that "we need to focus on how the new technology can be used to help tackle world poverty" (Downer Speech, paragraph 8) and that "for the developing world to bridge the 'digital divide', new technology must be harnessed and adapted in order to be a useful and an effective tool and help combat poverty" (Downer Speech paragraph 9). The VCP, we are told, is a "$1.5 billion partnership to combat global poverty" (BDD media release, paragraph 1) while according to the President of the World Bank, James D. Wolfensohn, it is "an initiative that all Australians can be proud of in providing new opportunities to meet the poverty challenge" (BDD Media Release, paragraph 5) and "this is a fantastic leadership role for Australia to take in helping to overcome the global poverty challenge" (BDD Media Release, paragraph 11).

Critique

As the above analysis shows, the emphasis in the rhetoric used to justify the VCP is on poverty reduction, but in the actual proposed programs the emphasis is on enhancing educational and to a lesser extent health-related social opportunities, and enhancing economic facilities. However, in the latter case the VCP seems to be as much about improving the economic outcomes for Australian businesses and institutions as about improving the economic circumstances of 'developing' countries. There is an almost complete absence in the documents of any acknowledgement of the need to enhance political freedoms and transparency guarantees, except for one brief statement in the Background Study.

Yet Sen, upon whom the Background Study epigraphically relies, argues that political freedoms and enhancement of economic facilities and social opportunities are intertwined. Indeed, Sen (1999: 147-148) argues that political rights are pre-eminent for two major reasons. First, political rights help to ensure free and open public debate about the conceptualization of needs, including economic needs and social opportunities, Second, political freedoms enhance the flow of relevant and important information in meeting economic needs and creating social opportunities. Without political freedoms, economic needs and social opportunities are less likely to be conceptualized in ways that serve the interests of the poor. And without political freedoms, there may be life-threatening restrictions on the flow of relevant information, as was demonstrated in the recent outbreak of sudden acute respiratory syndrome (SARS) in China.

Thus if we apply Sen's (1999) rationales, the VCP's emphasis on economic facilities and social opportunities, accompanied by its relative silence on political freedoms and transparency guarantees, imperils the fulfilment of the program's objectives if applied to countries where political freedoms are limited. Yet in some ways the VCP's silence on political freedoms is not surprising, since the documents themselves tell us very little about the process of consultation that occurred in the conceptualization of the VCP. The Hot Topic document says, "In March 2001, Australia and the World Bank embarked on a joint study to assess the opportunities presented by ICT to improve education and access to knowledge in developing countries" (paragraph 3). The result was the Background Study, "which focuses on ways that Australia, working with the World Bank and other donor partners, might help bridge the digital divide in the education and knowledge sectors" (Background Study, p. 2). Yet in none of the documents are we told who was consulted during the background study, what methodology was used, the size and nature of the sample, or any other issues that allow an assessment of the validity of the claims made concerning the key findings of the study. In Sen's (1999) terms, we are not told who values the outcomes proposed in the VCP and for what reasons. This lack of transparency produces serious doubts about whose interests are being served by the VCP.

The VCP and the Discursive Production of Australia and its Others

The second lens through which I read the VCP documents is a poststructural one that, following Escobar (1995), examines the way that particular subjectivities are constituted through the discourses employed in those documents. I am interested here in how the VCP documents represent or portray Australia: What is Australia like, what are its strengths and weaknesses, and what role should it play in the world. Similarly, I am interested in how the VCP documents represent or portray other countries with whom Australia will interact as part of the VCP. What are they like, what are their strengths and weaknesses, and what role should they play in the world?

Representations of Australia

The VCP documents are quite clear and consistent in how they represent Australia. Australia is both a Utopia and an active Saviour. In the following extracts I italicize the particular words and phrases that construct these representations. Australia is

Utopia because it has "*experience* and *innovation*" (Background Study p. 2) and "*world-class* technology companies, research institutions and education providers" (Background Study p. 2). Australia "has *acknowledged international expertise* in providing *accredited* in-service courses and other types of training using a variety of delivery modes" (p. 13) and "has *strong expertise* in DE [distance education] and the provision of knowledge by various means" (p. 14). Australia has a "*comparative advantage* in the provision of international DE" (p. 15) and "Australian institutions have *high quality* curricula for DE at primary, secondary and tertiary levels" that have been "developed and maintained over *many years*, they have been *well tested*, and they enjoy *strong acceptance*" (p. 15). In the Activity Outlines, the use of Australian "DE experts" (p. 7) is promoted, since "Australia is on the *frontier* of DE and so *has much to offer* in the development and delivery of cost-effective DE programs" (Activities Outline, p. 9). The risks to aid donors can be reduced because "Australia and the World Bank have" in the area of production of teaching materials "*adjusted* where appropriate to local needs" (p. 10).

Australia is an active Saviour because of its capabilities and its willingness to help and share. There are many examples of discourses that construct Australia in this way, and it is beyond the scope of this chapter to present each one here. Some examples (with the key terms italicized) from the Background Study include: "Australia is *assisting* the PNG education sector" (p. 10), "Australia provides ongoing *assistance* ... for training for academic and technical staff" at the University of the South Pacific (p. 11), Australia has provided "*assistance*" to Pacific Island finance and health ministries (p. 12), Australia has *provided* Tonga with a digital camera for medical diagnostic imaging (p. 12), Australia is "*helping* bring internet access to Palestinian refugee camps" (p. 13) and "has a long record of *supporting* education in developing countries beginning with the Colombo Plan in the early 1950s" (p. 14). Australia can "*help provide* knowledge" (p. 16) and "relevant, *world-class* material" (p. 17) and "is also ready to *provide assistance* in ICT policy development" (p. 17). Australia will "*support* a 21st century Colombo Plan using ICTs" (p. 21) and support "improvements in the quality of basic education" (p. 21). The VCP will include a "knowledge dissemination project [that] will make the best of Australia's world class research and knowledge *readily available* to users in the developing world" (p. 24).

Examples from the Activity Outlines include: Components of the VCP are designed to "*assist* developing countries to prepare polices" (p. 3), "*expand* ICT infrastructure for distance education in developing counties" (p. 3), "*provide* specialised policy-oriented training for policy makers in developing countries" (p. 4), "*improve* the quality of higher education" (p. 5), "*build the capacity* of selected central and local educational authorities" (p. 8), "*provide* technical assistance", "*provide* virtual scholarships" (p. 8), provide "local in-country training of teachers" (p. 11), "*fund* technical assistance projects" (p. 11), "*upgrade* distance education programs for teachers" (p. 11), "*assist* developing countries to prepare policies" (p. 12), "*raise awareness* in developing countries" (p. 12), "*build knowledge* of issues relating to the use of ICTs" (p. 12), "*offer* short courses" (p. 12), "*generate* tailored discussion papers" (p. 12), "*assist* those developing countries that wish to develop a policy on the appropriate use of new ICTs in school systems" (p. 12), "*provide* technical assistance ... and some funding in support of the development of policy statements on ICTs in school systems" (p. 12), "*support* the implementation of pilot projects" (p. 13), "*support* the evaluation of ICT strategies and pilot projects" (p. 13), provide "*support* for integration of the University of the South Pacific Network (USPNet) into the GDLN [Global Development Learning Network]" (p. 20), "*contribute* to the establishment of domestic learning networks" (p. 20), "*support* the creation of Country Gateways for selected partner countries in the Asia/Pacific region" (p. 25) by providing "funding" and "relevant content" (p. 25), "*provide* seminars and short courses for policy-makers" (p. 29), "*provide* IT literacy training" (p. 37), and "*build the capacity* of central and local education authorities" (p. 37).

It appears that Australia lacks nothing, although at one point the Background Study says that "To introduce ICTs into TVET [Technical and Vocational Education and Training], however, requires great changes in instructor attitudes, culture and practices" (p. 15). Furthermore, "all providers will face challenges" (p. 17), such as sustainability, "cultural acceptance in recipient countries" (p. 17), competition from local education providers, and "language and cultural impediments" (p. 17). Most of these challenges, however, appear to be a consequence of the characteristics of the 'developing' countries' institutions and people (eg language and cultural impediments), rather than of the Australian ones. In addition, some Australian knowledge may not be "sufficiently relevant to the specific needs of users to be useful" (Activities Outline, p. 35) while "Australian institutions may need both financial and administrative assistance to adapt their knowledge resources so that the information available is useful for partners in developing countries" (Activities Outline, p. 34).

The representations of Australia in the VCP documents are of a Utopia which not only flows with milk and honey (with one or two exceptions, such as the lack of integration of ICTs in TVET), but which is also willing to help save its neighbours. Yet it is not only what is said about Australia that is relevant here, but also what is not said. There is very little sense that Australia is lacking in any way, or is deprived, or needs help. Certainly there is no sense that the relationship between Australia and its neighbours may be anything other than a one-way transfer of Australian expertise, knowledge and largesse. Apart from economic gain for Australian industries and education providers, there is no sense that Australia could gain anything of social or cultural value from its 'partnerships' with 'developing' countries. This is because those countries are predominantly constructed as lacking, deprived, passive and needy, as I show below.

Representations of the Other

The VCP documents represent Australia's 'other' as lacking by setting up a binary between Australia and its 'developing' neighbours. In many cases, the way Australia is represented as having expertise and being willing and able to help implies this binary, even when 'developing' countries are not specifically mentioned. In order for there to be experts, there must be those who lack expertise; in order for there to be helpers, there must be those who are helpless; in order for there to be 'developing' countries, there must be developed countries the emulation of which is the implied goal of the former. In addition, there are numerous examples of this binary in which Australia's 'other' is explicitly represented as lacking (I have added italics to indicate the key words and phrases). The Background Study quotes the Australian Foreign Minister, Alexander Downer, who argues that "The initiative will use the opportunities presented by information and communication technologies to *improve* education and access to knowledge in developing countries" (p. 2) using Australia's "*experience and innovation*" (p. 2). Here Australia's neighbours are represented as lacking quality education, access to knowledge, experience and innovation. This sentiment is echoed in the Hot Topic document (paragraph 1). The Background Study also argues, "'Knowledge *deprivation*' is widespread in developing countries. There are *great needs* for more effective access to knowledge. Areas of highest priority include knowledge about agricultural issues, health, government administration and finance, and environmental issues" (p. 13). Furthermore, "many developing countries *need assistance* with ICT policy development" (Background Study, p. 17), lack access to hardware, content, services and development assistance (Background Study, pp. 18, 24), lack adequate protection for intellectual property rights (Background Study, p. 19), lack coherent ICT policies (p. 20), lack appropriate trade laws (p. 20), have governments whose operations need improving (Activities Outline p. 33), and have "*problems*" (Activities Outline, p. 34). As well as the representation of "developing" countries as impoverished, which occurs through the discourse of poverty alleviation employed by the documents (see the section on Protective Security above), these countries are also represented as "needy". At times this is only implied. At other times it is specifically stated. For example, the BBD media release quotes FM Downer as saying that "The choice can no longer be between meeting basic needs and adopting advanced technology. Instead, developing countries *need and deserve* both" (paragraph 9).

At times, Australia is incorporated into an entity referred to as "the international community" (p. 4), but at the same time this entity exists as the Other to "developing countries" (p. 4). The international community, therefore, does not refer to all the countries of the world, but only those that are not "developing". That is, "international community" here is a euphemism for the "west", which resonates with Edwards and Usher's (2000: 20) critique of internationalization as "the spread of Western institutions, culture and practices". Indeed, the Background Study also argues there is a "great demand for access to many kinds of international training" (p. 10), and in the context of the VCP, this clearly means training in western educational institutions.

In a small number of instances the VCP documents disrupt their own discourse of Australia's others as lacking. In particular, the Activities Outline documents suggests that there should be consideration of "the use of local [ICT training] providers where appropriate" (p. 29). Furthermore, one of the strategies to improve teacher education is to "network with colleagues in Ministries of Education in other developing countries to assist in piloting and learning from the implementation of distance education programs" (Activities Outline p. 8). Finally, ICT policy development will involve generating "tailored discussion papers, including by drawing on local and other developing country experience" (Activities Outline, p. 12). Apart from these instances, the dominant representations in the documents are of Australia as expert and knowledgeable, and Australia's "developing" neighbours as lacking in relevant or useful knowledge, skills, policies, or practices. Binaries of this kind have been critiqued for a substantial period of time. In the literature this critique can at least be traced back to Edward Said's "Orientalism" (1978). Such binaries ignore, marginalize and devalue local cultures and knowledges, while privileging 'western' knowledges and cultures. Such binaries render invisible the social and cultural problems and lacks of 'western' countries such as Australia. They potentially cause psychological damage to peoples whose cultures and knowledges are ignored or devalued (see Fanon 1967). The construction of these kinds of binaries of valued and devalued knowledges is a long-standing colonial technique. Said (1983: 12), for example, quotes Thomas Macaulay's famous assertion made as part of the debate about the medium of instruction and curriculum content in colonial schools in British India that "all the historical information which has been collected in the Sanskrit language is less valuable than what may be found in the paltry abridgements used at preparatory schools in England." Furthermore the construction of such binaries is a mechanism for countries such as Australia to justify their interest in and intervention in 'developing' countries (Escobar 1995). Indeed, the Background Study states that "priorities vary from country to country" and therefore "*intervention* points will need to be identified on a country-by-country basis to ensure maximum effectiveness" (p. 13, emphasis added). By intervening in neighbouring countries, Australia can control the direction of a range of social policies in those countries. Just as the original Colombo Plan was about limiting the attractiveness of communism through attempting to facilitate economic development in the region (Auletta 2000), the VCP, despite the rhetoric of the documents, is about intervening in and controlling the social, economic, cultural and political directions of Australia's neighbours.

These binaries and their logic of the "developing" countries needing to catch up or indeed "leap frog" (Hot Topic paragraph 4) up to the standard of the "developed" countries are also characteristic of modernization theory. Apart from paying lip-service to the need to adapt information to local needs and make it culturally relevant, and apart from some empty rhetoric about partnerships and consultations, the VCP blithely ignores the long standing critiques of modernization theory, including its exclusionary, disempowering and unsustainable characteristics and the widening gap between rich and poor (see, for example, Carmen 1996, Escobar 1995, Rist 1997, Peet & Harwick 1999, Datta & Kornberg 2002). The Background Study claims to have been the result of consultations with various stakeholders, but nowhere are we told who was consulted. There is nothing in the documents to allay the suspicion that whatever consultations occurred were only with members of local elites.

Alternative Scenarios for Higher Education's Global Engagement

There are a number of possible responses that Australian higher education could make to the VCP. These scenarios differ little from the kinds of possibilities that face higher education institutions in their ongoing engagement with the wider world, and so this discussion is pertinent beyond the confines of Australian higher education and the VCP. First, Australian higher education could take the VCP on face value and uncritically engage with it. To do so, however, runs the risk of higher education institutions becoming in some contexts uncritical partners with oppressive and undemocratic governments, given that the VCP takes little cognisance of political freedoms. Furthermore, this approach would implicate higher education institutions in the ongoing and dehumanizing process of depicting our neighbours as almost entirely deficient, and in the delusional process of depicting Australia as utopian saviour. This is an approach that does not admit to the possibility, and thus excludes the opportunity, that Australia might be able to learn things of cultural, social, political, economic, educational, intellectual, philosophical or practical value from our neighbours.

Second, Australian higher education institutions could refuse to engage with the VCP, on the grounds that it has the problems identified above. While this position might be represented as the moral high ground, it disengages Australian higher education from an engagement with its neighbours that, if differently conceived, could be mutually enriching for all parties concerned. It also lessens Australian higher education institutions' constructive or positive influence in the region.

A middle path involves engaging with the VCP in a way that works to overcome its weaknesses and build on its strengths. For example, although the VCP emphasizes social opportunities and economic facility, the courses offered by higher education institutions and other providers through the VCP could contribute to enhancing political freedoms by being framed in terms of democratic teaching and policy development processes, and by modeling and teaching values such as openness, transparency and accountability. Similarly, courses could involve representations of Australia and its neighbours that disrupt the oppositional binary of utopian saviour Australia and deficient neighbours that bedevil the VCP. One way of disrupting this binary is by inverting it, and valorizing Australia's neighbours while pointing out the deficiencies of Australian society and culture. However, such an inverted binary is just as problematic as the original, since it omits any weaknesses in Australia's neighbours that should be addressed, while ignoring Australia's strengths. A more balanced alternative involves providing content and learning opportunities that allow students to critically reflect on the strengths and weaknesses of both Australia and its neighbours in a range of areas, including culture, society, economics, politics, intellectual life and so on. In this way students can be encouraged to neither uncritically accept Australia (and other 'western' countries) as utopia and the source of all solutions to problems, nor accept that their own culture and society has little of value to offer or cannot contribute in some way to the creation of endogenous solutions to local problems. Furthermore, a more balanced alternative would not only critically reflect on representations of Australia and its neighbours, but also address a major silence in the VCP, which concerns the ways in which global networks of power and influence work to provide economic facilities and social opportunities for some people while excluding or minimizing the opportunities afforded to others. As Escobar (1995: 213) suggests in reference to reading development data, we can engage our students in analysing contemporary practices in terms of "political consequences, … the crafting of subjectivities, the shaping of culture, and the construction of social power – including [the] surplus material and symbolic consumption in those parts of the world that think of themselves as developed".

References

Auletta, A. 2000. "A Retrospective View of the Colombo Plan: Government Policy, Departmental Administration and Overseas Students." *Journal of Higher Education Policy and Management* 22(1): 47-58.

Australia. AusAID, 2001a. *Virtual Colombo Plan Joint Australian-World Bank Background Study: Bridging the Digital Divide*. Canberra, ACT: AusAID.

Australia. AusAID, 2001b. *Virtual Colombo Plan: Activity Outlines – The Australian Contribution*. Canberra, ACT: AusAID..

Australia. AusAID 2001c. Virtual Colombo Plan. Updated 7 April 2003. Online. http://www.ausaid.gov.au/hottopics/topic.cfm?Id=326_3216_5474_6437_2910 Accessed 8 May 2003.

Australia. AusAID. 2001d. Virtual Colombo Plan: Australia's Contribution. Media release. Canberra, ACT: AusAID.

Australia. Ministry of Foreign Affairs and Trade. 2001a. Virtual Colombo Plan – Bridging the Digital Divide. Media Release. 2 August 2001. Online. http://www.ausaid.gov.au/media/release.cfm?BC=Media&Id=7100_3867_2762_5309_1373. Accessed 8 May 2003.

Australia. Ministry of Foreign Affairs and Trade. 2001b. Virtual Colombo Plan – Bridging the Digital Divide. Speech by the Hon. Alexander Downer, MP, Minister for Foreign Affairs, 2 August, 2001. Online http://www.ausaid.gov.au/media/release.cfm?BC=Speech&Id=5514_6625_545_6903_2234 Accessed 8 May 2003.

Carmen, R. 1996. *Autonomous Development: Humanizing the Landscape. An Excursion into Radical Thinking and Practice*. London: Zed Books.

Datta, R. & Kornberg, J. eds. 2002. *Women in Developing Countries: Assessing Strategies for Empowerment*. Boulder, CO: Lynne Rienner Publishers.

Dichter, T. W. 2003. *Despite Good Intentions: Why Development Assistance to the Third World Has Failed*. Amherst, MA: University of Massachusetts Press.

Edwards, R. & Usher, R. 2000. *Globalisation and Pedagogy: Space, Place and Identity*. London: Routledge.

Escobar, A. 1995. *Encountering Development: The Making and Unmaking of the Third World*. Princeton, NJ: Princeton University Press.

Fanon, F. 1967. *Black Skin, White Masks*. New York: Grove Press.

Foucault, M. 1972. *The Archaeology of Knowledge*. London: Tavistock.

Foucault, M. 1977. *Discipline and Punish: The Birth of the Prison.* Harmondsworth: Penguin.

Foucault, M. 1991. "Governmentality." In *The Foucault Effect,* edited by G. Burchell, C. Gordon & P. Miller. Chicago: University of Chicago Press.

Lauglo, J. 1996. "Banking on Education and the Uses of Research: A Critique of World Bank Priorities and Strategies for Education." *International Journal of Educational Development* 16(3): 221-233.

Luke, A. 1999. "Critical Discourse Analysis." In *Issues in Educational Research* edited by J. P. Keeves & G. Lakomski. Amsterdam: Pergamon.

Nederveen Pieterse, J. 2000. "After Post-Development." *Third World Quarterly* 21(2): 175-191.

Peet, R. & Harwick, E. 1999. *Theories of Development.* New York: The Guildford Press.

Rist, G. 1997. *The History of Development: From Western Origins to Global Faith.* London: Zed Books.

Said, E. 1978. *Orientalism: Western Conceptions of the Orient.* Harmondsworth: Penguin.

Said, E. 1983. *The World, the Text and the Critic.* Cambridge, MA: Harvard University Press.

Samoff, J. 1996. "Which Priorities and Strategies for Education?" *International Journal of Educational Development* 16(3): 249-271.

Sen, A. 1999. *Development as Freedom.* Oxford: Oxford University Press.

World Bank. 1995. *Priorities and Strategies for Education.* Washington, DC: World Bank.

8

The Viability of Aid Scholarship-Funded Study in Australian Universities: The Case of Indonesia

Pam Nilan

Introduction

This chapter considers the viability of aid scholarship-funded study in Australian universities through an examination of some of the major discourses and tensions around the scheme as it operates in Indonesia. Some examples of prevailing discourse are drawn from focus group interviews with Indonesians aged 19-26, conducted by the author in 1999 and 2002 on their experiences of social change and their visions for the future. These groups involved 18 young Hindu Balinese in Singaraja, North Bali, and 28 young Muslims and Christians in Makassar, South Sulawesi. Interviewees were purposively selected for tertiary education, community group membership, public speaking skills and strength of religious convictions – all qualities deemed indicative of future Indonesian political and community leaders in the provinces (Nilan 2003). One focus group question asked for discussion about moving away to take up an educational opportunity. It was evident that the question aroused both excitement and apprehension in the young people interviewed. Many of them talked about overseas study. Some of their responses are used to illustrate points in the argument advanced in this chapter. Pseudonyms are used throughout.

Presenting the *Simons Report* to parliament in 1997, the Minister for Foreign Affairs, Alexander Downer, stated that the overall objectives of AusAID (Australian Agency for International Development) were "to advance Australia's national interest by assisting developing countries to *reduce poverty* and *achieve sustainable development*" (Downer 1997: 3, emphasis added). The minister stressed that even though giving aid to poorer countries in the region matched Australia's altruistic "identity" (Downer 1997: 5), our long-term interests lay in ensuring political stability in the countries closest to us, and enhancing their capacity for Australian trade (Downer 1997: 8). Echoing this, the 2003 AusAID Annual Report begins with a quote from AusAID Director-General Bruce Davis:

> Aiming for peace and stability is very much at the forefront of our work. We live in a region that is threatened with the possible challenge of *failed states* and Australia has taken a *key leadership role* (AusAID 2003: 11, emphasis added).

As Everingham (2002: 3) points out, "there is more here than just meeting the basic survival needs of the poor". The Australian Development Scholarship (ADS) scheme sits within the aid objectives articulated above by Downer (1997), which remain as core. However the latest report adds five further "guiding themes" within the two basic objectives of reducing poverty and enhancing development (AusAID 2001a). These are: good governance, accessing the benefits of globalization, effective basic service delivery for stability, promoting regional security and meeting trans-boundary challenges, and sustainable resource management (AusAID 2003: 12). The penultimate theme clearly addresses Australia's sense of security "threat" (see Davis quote above). Accordingly, as a single country Indonesia receives the highest per-centage of Australian aid. In 2002-2003 this was A$130.7 million – 27 percent of all overseas aid given (AusAID 2003: 50). Specific aid objectives for Indonesia are: improving economic management, strengthening democracy, enhancing security and stability, delivering quality social services, and basic education (AusAID 2003: 12). Of the total Australian aid budget for education, scholarships represent 44 percent (AusAID 2003: 31) and basic education (delivered in-country) only 27 percent.

In 2002-2003 about 1100 ADS-funded students commenced studying in Australia, most from Asia-Pacific countries (AusAID 2003: 80). In 2004 approxi-mately 360 Indonesian ADS awardees will arrive. Their arrival to take up post-graduate study fulfils the dominant thesis of Australian aid for education since the Colombo Plan – to take promising candidates from 'developing' countries and place them in Australian universities (Auletta 2000, Back 1994: 21). The prevailing logic is always that they will return and assist the development of their nations toward economic progress through reducing poverty and contributing to sustainable development. This paper maintains that there is not much evidence that this occurs in any direct way. In fact, elsewhere it has been strongly argued that the very opposite effect is achieved:

> Scholarships for study in Australia in Australia are a repressive anti-poor aid mechanism because they amount to a subsidy of rich Australian universities at the expense of poor developing country ones and the funds could be better used to increase student access (Guthrie 2002: 325).

This chapter takes the claim advanced by Guthrie and examines it critically. While the arguments advanced here bear out the above claim to some degree, it is concluded that there is some value in scholarship schemes, so it may well be a question of balance and lateral thinking rather than abandonment. Perhaps the most serious issue for critical concern is the lack of evidence that the current scheme actually fulfils its central aims. The knowledge, skills and qualifications that ADS awardees take back to Indonesia, while culturally valuable for other reasons, may have no direct impact on reducing poverty or achieving sustainable development. The logic of the aid scholarship scheme is best understood as the neo-liberal discourse of a 'trickle-down' effect (Stieglitz 2002: 80). It is imagined that the mere presence of these knowledge-enhanced individuals will somehow produce all kinds of benefits, including outcomes such as better governance, more political stability and a superior climate for globally-driven economic investment. Guthrie dismisses the ADS scheme as purely political – 'the use of scholarships as a diplomatic tool' (Guthrie 2002: 329; see also the Davis quote above). While the aims of the scheme remain highly abstract and idealized it is easy to dismiss it this way. Certainly the logic of international scholarship aid implies a theoretical rather than empirically verified link between forms of capital. The rhetoric constructs the idea that aid scholarships build human capital (see Patrick 1999: 70) through enhancing cultural capital (privileged knowledge/ skills; see Bourdieu 1984, Bourdieu & Passeron 1990) via a western education. The expertise and influence of overseas-educated graduates (Livingstone 1999: 173) then build up the economic capital (Apple 2001: 410) of their countries (but see Raffer and Singer 1996). It is further assumed that this kind of aid also builds positive social capital (Coleman 1988, Putnam 1993, Putnam 2000, Woolcock 1998, World Bank 2001, Everingham 2002).

However, we actually know very little about the impact on social capital, or indeed any other kind of capital, of scholarship-funded Indonesian graduates returning home from Australian universities. As economic and security tensions in the region deepen post September 11th 2001, and after the anti-western bombings in Bali in 2002 and the Indonesian capital, Jakarta in 2003, we must try to find out whether developing Asia-Pacific countries such as Indonesia are actually being assisted toward economic sustainability and political stability through ADS awards. As regional inter-ethnic and religious conflicts intensify, we should also question whether the in-country selection of candidates implicitly favours the interests of particular ethnic and other elite groups. Using Indonesia as an example, this chapter argues that firstly, returning graduates may not have much effect on the economic/political profile of their country, and secondly, the selection of scholarship awardees may implicitly favour certain kinds of candidates over others. Finally it is argued that aid for education in Indonesia should not necessarily be discontinued, but that Australian aid should contribute more effectively to productive capacity building though education in Indonesia, and thereby better address the issue of economic prosperity fostering regional harmony.

Australian Development Scholarships and Indonesia

ADS awards form a significant component of Australia's educational aid budget for Indonesia. However, it is not direct aid. ADS awards are provided for return travel, tuition fees and a stipend in Australia, which may include allowance for accompanying family members. Thereby, most of the funds allocated for ADS awards in Indonesia get paid back into Australian universities and businesses (see Guthrie 2002). The idea is that Indonesia gets back a pool of skilled graduates who can build development capacity:

> Australian Development Scholarship graduates return home and significantly contribute to the development of their countries, many attaining positions of responsibility and influence. Indonesian ministers for Health, Finance and the Environment as well as the Chancellors of several prestigious Indonesian universities such as *Universitas Gadjah Mada* and *Institut Pertanian Bogor,* all held Australian Development Scholarships (AusAID 2003: 30).

As Patrick points out, "the political dimension of aid cannot be underestimated" (1999: 77). Since some key Indonesian government and academic posts are now held by ADS graduates it is imagined they are well disposed toward Australia and her interests, as one recent Indonesian Ambassador to Australia observed:

> In the next century, there will be a whole generation of Indonesians in the leadership of various professions and fields of endeavour who not only understand their immediate neighbour to the south but who also nurture an abiding affection for it (Wiryono 1998: 49).

Given the history of political tension between the two countries we can perhaps see how the ADS scheme might contribute to "promoting regional security and meeting trans-boundary challenges" (AusAID 2002: 3), although the outcomes of poverty alleviation and sustainable development are still hard to glimpse.

Indonesia is the fourth most populous nation in the world, with a population of 203,456,000 according to the 2000 Census (Hull 2001: 104). It is the nation in the world with the largest Islamic population. Over eighty per cent of the population is Muslim (Hassan 2002: 23). It has a relatively young population, and the number of young adults (20-24) is predicted to increase from 20.7 million in 2000 to 23.1 million in 2005 (Hull 2001: 109). Indonesia's economy grew at an average annual rate of 7.1 percent between 1985 and 1995. Between 1970 and 1996, the proportion of the population living below the official poverty line declined from 60 percent to an estimated 11 percent or about 28 million people (World Bank 1999). However, the Asian currency crash in 1997 crippled the economy, which has recovered only very slowly. In the second quarter of 2002, GDP grew by 3.51%, higher than for the first quarter, and inflation fell at the same time (Ikhsan 2002). However, one in ten

Indonesians still lives in poverty. This particularly affects people in the eastern islands, and women. AusAID sets aside a special quota of ADS awards for female candidates and for those from the much poorer eastern islands and provinces (East Kalimantan, Sulawesi, the Moluccas, Lombok, Flores, Sumba, Sumbawa, West Timor, and West Papua).

Australia has had an uneasy relationship with Indonesia since President Sukarno took power in 1950 (Sulaiman & Sofyan 1998: 2). The newly independent Republic of Indonesia was included in the Australian Colombo Plan aid program during the 1950s. After the failed Communist coup in 1965 Australian aid to Indonesia increased greatly, and by 1973 Indonesia was the largest recipient of aid under the Colombo Plan (Ziegler 1973: 587). Australia maintained an ambiguous stand on the question of East Timor until 1999 when tensions flared between Australia and Indonesia after the independence vote. Subsequently, diplomatic ties between the two countries came under pressure over the issue of refugees. Indonesia has been one of the countries suspected by the USA and its allies of harbouring active Muslim terrorist groups. The 2002 bomb attacks in Bali and at the Marriott Hotel in Jakarta in 2003 heightened some of the pre-existing tensions. Yet throughout all these crises, Australia has continued its aid to Indonesia and even increased it to the 2004 level of A$130.7 million.

Since the fall of President Suharto in 1998 the country has been chaotic and prone to fragmentation as it struggles toward democracy and tries to move beyond crippling economic crisis and debt (Kingsbury & Aveling 2002). The government of President Megawati Sukarnoputri has been making efforts to reform both the economy and civil infrastructure. One of the most significant structural reforms is the decentralization of limited financial and civil authority to the regions, a process targeted at local autonomy and self-management *(otonomi daerah)*. However, despite some improvements, a recent report on Indonesia finds that although the country is now more democratic, it remains at 110th position on the human development index (HDI), the same as in 1995 (UNDP 2002). Indonesia is one of the countries noted in the United Nations 2002 Human Development Report as a nation where public spending of all kinds is most often skewed in favour of rich people (*The Jakarta Post* 2002). This is very much so in the case of education, which varies greatly in quality between regions (Fox 2002: 300, see also Welch 2002: 36). In the tertiary sector, as Bayhaqi (2000: 241) shows, prestigious public universities in Indonesia (nearly all in Java) show a skewed distribution of students from rich families. For many of the ADS applicants, who usually do not come from wealthy families, obtaining a university qualification from Australia may be more likely than gaining entry to the most prestigious universities in their own country.

Advantages for Recipients of ADS Awards

The broad objective of the ADS scheme is the social and economic advancement of target countries through 'helping' selected individuals so that, on return, the increased knowledge and skill capacities of key figures in the public and private sectors will directly contribute to economic development (see above). However, it is far easier to point to the immediate career and financial advantages for individuals and families than to tangible evidence of 'trickle-down' (or perhaps 'trickle-up') macro-level benefits. For example, Tiedeman (2002) reports that one Indonesian ADS awardee maintained that the scholarships were sought by public servants "so they can get a promotion and a pay rise" (Tiedeman 2002: 6). Hellstén (2002: 359-360) quotes an international student (non-ADS) as saying: "If I go to Australia I will get a really good degree that is valued in my country and so you can get a good job and make a lot of money". The personal goals of ADS awardees are unlikely to differ greatly from those of other ambitious Indonesians seeking overseas study. Other research confirms that personal and career advantages for ADS awardees include:

- Acquisition of specific technical and professional skills (Smith, Morey & Teece 2002: 38)
- Acquisition of superior English language competence (see May & Bartlett 1995, Welch 2002: 17)
- Development of a regional consciousness (see Robison & Goodman 1996)
- Improved social and professional mobility opportunities (see Daroesman & Daroesman 1992, Tin Hta Nu 1995)
- Greater awareness of the political, economic and social context of Australia (see Phillips & Stahl 2001).

These advantages multiply when ADS awardees bring their families with them, as both spouses and children gain some of these enhanced capacities. Yet the logical weaknesses of the scheme remain. The study by Daroesman and Daroesman (1992) identified problems in allocation of scholarships, selection of candidates, placement of candidates in disciplines, and appropriate thesis supervision. They concluded that the major weakness was lack of follow-up by the Australian government, but since then not much has changed. Despite some invited input from bodies such as the Australian Alumni Association in Indonesia, the problems inherent in an "altruistic, perhaps paternalistic approach" (Back 1994: 29) remain, even while the number of ADS awards to Indonesia has increased in the last five years. Few independent evaluations of success in relation to its key objectives have taken place.

If we look at relevance of qualifications, the first possible problem emerges. When candidates in Indonesia apply for ADS scholarships from the public sector, they must nominate one of the stated priority areas and explain how their chosen area and field of study in Australia will bring benefit to Indonesia. However, they often do this without a very clear understanding of the knowledge base of the selected study program. For example, many of the postgraduate degree programs offered in Australia in the broad field of social sciences deal specifically with Australian policy and practice, and even assume some knowledge of these things. Fields such as biotechnology, business law and agribusiness are also examples of this mismatch. So it may be that in some cases the foreign skills and knowledge newly acquired will not be directly transferable to local Indonesian contexts (Welch 2002). The graduate may return to performing his or her original set of tasks with little opportunity for new knowledge input (Butcher 2002: 360). Nurhadi (1998: 183) bemoans the fact that so many students study social science and humanities programs in Australia rather than engineering and agriculture, which he maintains are most needed. One reason for this is that candidates in science and allied disciplines are much less likely to meet English Language requirements, since they do not have the same opportunities in their degrees.

The fourth benefit listed above identifies improved social and professional mobility. Certainly, whether the study abroad is relevant or not, returning graduates enjoy high social and career status. However, their considerably enhanced social status and upward mobility potential may serve primarily to strengthen the existing privileged position of elite groups (see Adams & Chapman 1998: 583, also Robison 1996, Pinches 1996). Accordingly then, in any appraisal of the effectiveness of the ADS scheme for Indonesian development, we first need to grasp assumptions about what kind of formal 'knowledge' acquisition the scheme logically implies. We need to evaluate whether the acquired 'knowledge' (formal or informal) is really likely to have any effect on the economic progress of Indonesia.

Knowledge For What?

While one might agree that the intense and rapid development of human capital for economic progress relies on substantial expansion and extension of higher education (Welch 2002), this does not tell us what kinds of knowledges are most useful for a sustainable economy and polity. Upgrading of skills has been identified as strategic for economic and social advancement (Phillips & Stahl 2001). Yet this may be better done at a local level. Capacity building around the process of decentralization is new in Indonesia, a country which has always operated as a centralist state in both the public service and in business. Surakhmad (2002: 23) argues that in contemporary Indonesia, capacity building should be "defined as an educational strategy to uplift the professional competence of every member of society within the framework of decentralization". According to a variety of Indonesian and international commentators, capacity building must include: skills of political debate (Antlov 2002), local public service provision and accountability, balancing fiscal inequalities (Rasyid 2002a), drafting laws to deal with significant local environmental threats (Lay 2002), budgeting for economic sustainability (Colongan 2002) and even dealing with regional separatist and militia movements (Malley 2002). One can see that not all of this capacity-building can be handled under a study abroad scholarship scheme. For example, Malley's claim might be addressed by training exercises with the Australian Defence Force, or better still retraining the local military as peace-keepers. Given significant differences in legal systems (Sulaiman & Smith 1998: 305), Lay's point above would certainly be best met by in-country training. In fact, it can be argued that nearly all these emerging human resource needs are best met by forms of in-country training, yet Australia devotes almost half of its educational aid budget to scholarships for study in Australia.

Further specific capacities toward successful decentralization include: small-scale local management of government finance and personnel, community-based planning, entrepreneurship for small-to-medium enterprises, urban planning and skills in information technology. It should be noted that the economic survival of poor and lower-class people in Indonesia during the post 1997 crisis was due to the strength of the informal sector, local trade and entrepreneurship and small-to-medium enterprises (Mietzner 2002). Obviously, professional expertise in engineering, science, health, education, sustainable agriculture and manufacturing appropriate to each province and region will also be necessary. Most of these skills already exist in the labour force, but are in need of refinement and specialization. This process may be best achieved either in-country, or in neighbouring countries which have faced similar challenges, rather than in an English-speaking western country such as Australia which faces an entirely different set of economic, political and legal circumstances. Furthermore, graduates from disciplines most crucial for economic rebuilding frequently lack the English language competence necessary to obtain an ADS award.

Indonesia itself has at least seven universities theoretically capable of delivering world-class education and training (in the national language) in fields relevant to rapid modernization and decentralization. Yet they are all in desperate need of financial assistance. Three of these (*Universitas Indonesia, Institut Teknologi Bandung* and *Institut Pertanian Bogor* – all headed by overseas educated academics) planned to introduce expanded places for full-fee-paying students from 2004 in order to cope with demand and to improve their extremely sparse educational resources. *Universitas Gadjah Mada* is expected to follow suit soon. Like many other developing countries, the higher education sector in Indonesia suffered in the past from prevailing World Bank/UNESCO imperatives that universities and higher education should not receive development funding – probably a legacy of Cold War thinking (Heyneman 2003: 322).

Rasyid (2002b), the Indonesian Minister of State for Regional Autonomy from 1991 – 2001, names local economic management, human resource management and technical expertise as three areas in which public servants should take Masters coursework degrees to facilitate the process of decentralization in Indonesia. These degrees are all readily available in Indonesia, and probably their content is more directly relevant to capacity-building for regional autonomy. However, while the academic quality and resources of Indonesian universities remain so low, the prestige of a western tertiary qualification remains strongly attractive. In 2002, there were 18,000 Indonesians studying in Australia, predominantly at postgraduate level (Jalil 2002), most of them privately funded, and enrolled in business, management and information technology programs.

The Hegemony of Western Knowledge and Qualifications

The basic ideological premise which drives Indonesian students to head overseas for western education is the same as it has always been. We can see this in the history of Australia and elsewhere in the British Commonwealth. Even up to the early part of the twentieth century, upper-class Australian males were sent to Britain to get a 'superior' education with which they returned to enlighten the intellectually and culturally impoverished local inhabitants. The ideological assumption is that a western (or mother country) education is implicitly superior to anything one might get at home:

> I have always had a great ambition to study outside Bali, or even abroad, such as in Australia and the United States of America, as their educational quality is excellent. Australia and America's educational quality is better than ours since they are developed countries (Dewa Ayu Eka, prospective ADS awardee, Bali, 1999, author's translation).

> Of course if I was given a scholarship to study abroad, in England or Australia for post graduate studies, I would go and study there. The reasons are obvious! Firstly, the quality of education in Sulawesi is different from education in England, Australia or America. Of course the quality is higher and better there (Sili-Suli, prospective ADS awardee, Sulawesi, 2002 author's translation).

These comments confirm that the canon of western scientific and intellectual tradition (Aronowitz and Giroux 1991: 41) still holds considerable symbolic status (see Bourdieu 1985) in non-western countries. Yet we must question whether the enthusiasm of prospective ADS candidates is justified in terms of knowledge content. Anecdotal evidence from returning ADS awardees indicates that some find the courses they undertook at Masters postgraduate level in Australia rather irrelevant to the work situations to which they return (Tiedeman 2002). Admittedly this is not just their problem. Many Australian students completing postgraduate coursework might make the same claim. Universities everywhere are struggling with increasingly limited resources to ensure that the knowledge sets which comprise their professional and applied degree curricula keep pace with work force needs. As Schapper and Mayson (2002: 168) point out, curricula are now supposed to meet both the needs of domestic students and those of a highly diverse cohort of international students at exactly the same time (see also Rizvi & Walsh 1998).

While the symbolic capital of privileged western knowledge remains attractive, in an increasingly globalized world economy and culture (Appadurai 2001), the very nature of knowledge itself has changed, even in western countries. In trying to grasp the international context of contemporary education, we should avoid imagining Bourdieu's notion of privileged knowledge sets and genres, that is, cultural capital (Bourdieu & Passeron 1990), as a fixed entity. Cultural capital in late modernity is best conceptualized as fluid and dynamic. The status and sophistication of a fixed set of qualifications in relation to types of work is contested and fragile. Castells (1996: 17-18) maintains that it is no longer the acquisition of knowledge, but the pursuit of knowledge and information that characterizes the informational age. Moreover, possessing cultural capital probably now indicates the stylish and confident capacity to identify what a certain body of knowledge or skills is turning into, or is about to change into. Rapid learning and refining of new skills amounts to more than flexibility in a given contemporary labour force; it amounts to constantly shifting definitions of task, and approach, as well as ever-changing constitutions of self in relation to those things.

So what does this mean for ADS awardees who return home with a set of new skills and capacities acquired from postgraduate coursework at an Australian University? In the first place it may not be clear that there is any relationship at all between what they have studied and the demands of their job in the new context of a decentralizing Indonesian state. Second, it may be some time before they get to apply any aspects of their new knowledge in the workplace, as they rarely return to instant promotions. The field of international knowledge may have already moved on by the time they attain the necessary promotional rank to make changes. Third, they may try to apply their knowledge, skills and capacities to situations where they are not appropriate, or they may find considerable local and/or cultural resistance to new, western-derived ideas. This is particularly likely to occur where the returning ADS awardee is a woman, since traditionally women do not occupy high status managerial positions in the workforce. Gender should be a significant factor in any appraisal of the transformative potential of returning ADS awardees (World Bank 2001: 89). For example, even though the selection procedure in Indonesia insists on gender equity, statistically fewer females than males take up public sector ADS awards (AusAID 2002: 3). More women than men drop out of programs, and male awardees report more rapid promotion on return to their public service jobs. "This is a reflection of the male dominance of public sector organizations" in Indonesia (AusAID 2002: 5).

Personal Gain and Upward Mobility

It is claimed that in the UK, overseas "students are not buying degrees; they are buying the benefits that a degree can provide in terms of employment, status, lifestyle etc." (Binsardi & Ekwulugo 2003: 319). If this is so, then what are Indonesian ADS awardees getting from their funded study in Australia? Anecdotal evidence suggests that specific skills and capacities directly related to their work are way down in the list of benefits. Instead they talk about improved English skills, information technology skills and the cultural experience of living and studying in Australia. Once back home, they seem mainly concerned with the social and economic advancement of themselves and their families, made possible by the symbolic value of the study-abroad experience itself, which has a long history in Indonesia dating back to the Dutch. The history of Indonesians studying in countries like Holland (for example Djelantik 1997) and accruing symbolic capital for their families by assumed familiarity with the canon of western intellectual/scientific tradition (Aronowitz & Giroux 1991: 41) has imbued the experience with particular and lasting cultural meanings which encode a myriad of social mobility possibilities. For example, a tangible sign of the value (either symbolic or actual) of study abroad is the association of high quality Indonesian tertiary education with universities where the majority of senior academics have completed doctoral study overseas, especially in English-speaking countries. The topics of their actual doctoral research theses usually matter less, it would seem, than the symbolic value of the foreign location and language in which they were completed.

So if we examine the list above of individual advantages for public servants who study in Australia under ADS awards, then it is really the acquisition of superior English language competence (see May & Bartlett 1995), and improved social and professional mobility opportunities (see Daroesman & Daroesman 1992, Tin Hta Nu 1995) which are the most tangible outcomes for individuals. One might also add computer and information technology competence to this list. In Indonesia, English language competence and computer skills constitute the new cultural capital that leads to social and professional mobility. In the experience of the author of this chapter it is the highly competent demonstration of these two generic capacities that are considered by employers and policy-makers to point iconically to the overseas graduate possessing a range of more specific capacities and knowledge sets. These two skills in particular are equated in the popular imagination with enhanced human capital.

Human Capital and Overseas Qualifications

Human capital theory is a neo-liberal discourse (Apple 2001: 410) that theorizes people's learned capacities as comparable to other natural resources involved in the modern industrialized production process. Thus, "when the resource is effectively exploited the results are profitable both for the enterprise and for society as a whole" (Livingstone 1999: 173). In the context of a developing nation, human capital theory equates workers' knowledge levels with the measure of their formal education. The economic 'return' of different levels and kinds of education can then be calculated quantitatively to show relative advantage of education to the development and nation-building project (Livingstone 1999: 173, but see also Heyneman 2003). However, these calculations are usually performed internally on national systems of education. It is difficult to find any reports which attempt to calculate the benefits to a nation of externally-funded overseas tertiary study. Accordingly, the human capital benefits to a developing country from international aid scholarships cannot be calculated or measured using the usual empirical tools. The claim that ADS awards build human capital in Indonesia therefore exists at the level of rhetoric around regional strategic relations (Guthrie 2002) rather than fact.

So we return to inspecting the logic of the ADS awards scheme. If the objective is to reduce poverty and achieve sustainable development in the target countries

(AusAID 2001b: 1), then according to the arguments I have presented so far, there is little evidence available that this actually occurs in any measurable way. Knowledge, skills and qualifications acquired in Australia may not prove relevant or valuable even though the actual study opportunity has strong symbolic cultural value. Even if some returning ADS awardees can see the relevance of their study in Australia and do try to apply it, then we need to consider how much impact a tiny number of public servants and others can have on reducing poverty or achieving sustainable development at either the national or the local level. In short, the logical link between the ADS scheme and its larger foreign aid objectives cannot be understood except as a neo-liberal discourse of 'trickle-down' human capital effect where the mere presence of these culturally enhanced individuals will somehow make for better governance, more political stability and a superior climate for economic investment. The already dubious probability of this effect is further diminished by processes of preliminary award selection which implicitly favour certain elites.

Award Selection and Elites

In any country, if no scholarships of any kind were available for tertiary study abroad, then those students who did travel overseas to complete postgraduate coursework and research programs of study would inevitably come from the privileged elite, the really wealthy strata of society, since a great deal of money is involved. However, where a range of scholarships for tertiary study abroad is available, this theoretically provides an open opportunity for academically excellent students from poorer, lower status backgrounds to complete postgraduate education overseas. Quotas are in place to ensure that less privileged candidates are equitably represented in ADS award selection. Yet there are subtle mechanisms prior to the formal selection process which favour the interests of privileged groups over less privileged groups. The first group is men. Each year, fewer women than men get awards. Women often seem to lack the confidence or ambition to apply. Fewer women apply, and more drop out after selection because of family reasons. In 2001, females (n=117) were over-represented in the open category (academic excellence only) compared to males (n=70). Females (n=219) were under-represented in the public sector (government employees) compared to males (n=304) (AusAID 2002: 23). Those in the open category were younger, so we can see a skewing of age and gender in the scheme toward preservation of the dominance of older males in the Indonesian public sector. More males are selected to complete doctoral research degrees (n=23), which carry much higher status than a coursework Masters. In developing countries, elitist tertiary education (even if acquired overseas) tends to perpetuate and legitimate gender, social and wealth divisions (Adams & Chapman 1998: 583).

A second effect in the informal process which precedes selection has to do with certain kinds of candidates routinely failing to make applications, failing to meet English language standards, or failing to meet academic criteria. This has to do with the quality of some universities in Indonesia, with the high cost of English language training and testing, and with issues of patronage and support. As Bayhaqi (2000: 241) shows, prestigious public universities in Indonesia show a skewed distribution of students from rich families. Regional, and private universities (usually Islamic), on the other hand, show a skewed distribution of students from poorer families. Raysid (2002b) maintains that since 1998, in all but the best Indonesian universities, the quality of education has become progressively worse (see also Fox 2002: 300) due to disorganization and resource scarcity. So it is applicants from the most prestigious, high quality universities who are most likely to present the winning combination of: (a) a competitive undergraduate grade point average, (b) better English language skills, (c) specific information about the field priorities and mechanisms of the scholarship scheme, and (d) information about Australian universities. To get accurate information, potential candidates need to be competent in information technology search and retrieval skills. This is another capacity, which less privileged applicants may not possess to any great extent.

ADS Scholarship Selection at Hasanuddin University

As an example of the scholarship selection process, consider the case of Universitas Hasanuddin in Makassar, South Sulawesi. The observations referred to below derive from fieldwork conducted at intervals in Makassar between June 1999 and January 2002, by the author. Universitas Hasanuddin is the only university in the eastern islands region with a fully-functioning postgraduate program and an international reputation. Consequently, most of the scholarships awarded to eastern province candidates go to open category candidates from this university, and to public category candidates from this city (most of whom are directly connected with this university). Makassar has an ethnically and religiously diverse student and worker population. Although the local Buginese ethnic majority dominates (Antweiler 2001: 17), students and minor public servants come from all parts of Sulawesi. Others come from Irian Jaya, the Moluccas, Ambon, Kalimantan and Flores. Many of these candidates are Christian and/or Melanesian. There are also many Indonesian Chinese living in the city. Ethnic Chinese in Indonesia are rarely found in the public service. Although often wealthy as a result of family business ventures, they suffer from racial prejudice (Mackie 1999, Kian Wie 2001). According to Nesdale, Simkin, Sang, Burke and Frager (1995), up until the mid 1990s in Australian universities, the vast majority of self-funding overseas students were ethnic Chinese from Malaysia, Singapore, Hong Kong and Indonesia. Ethnic Chinese in Indonesia are oriented to privately-funded overseas study, often accompanied by a desire to emigrate. Although they often have good English language skills, they do not tend to apply for ADS awards, possibly because the conditions mandate return, and possibly because the priority areas of scholarship study do not match their ambitions.

Christian and Muslim communities have long co-existed in the eastern islands, but violent religious conflict has been a feature of the past ten years. The result has been a turning inward, an inclusionary process in Sulawesi which has seen Universitas Hasanuddin in the south become identified as the favoured major public university for Muslims on the island, while Universitas Sam Ratulanggi in Manado in the north has become identified as the favoured major Christian university. However, only Universitas Hasanuddin has a comprehensive postgraduate program. Historically, Universitas Hasanuddin, like many other public institutions in South Sulawesi and Makassar, has been dominated by the Buginese. As a result, it is rare to find a successful ADS award candidate from Universitas Hasanuddin who is not Muslim and is not from a Bugis ethnic background. One Christian alumnus from Ambon described his experience of religious bias as follows:

> When I finished my education at the university, I was given a choice of working either in Makassar or Java. I chose Java because I had been in Makassar all through my study. Here in Makassar they employ the local people. And Muslim religion is important. But in Java, employment is based on skills. Skill is considered the most important thing. Not ethnicity, religion or the like (Rudi, an accountant in a private firm, Sulawesi, 2002, author's translation).

Rudi's point holds true for the implicit local pre-selection of ADS candidates. The most academically able Christian students complete undergraduate study at the northern university. If they come south to Universitas Hasanuddin for postgraduate study they are relatively unknown and have no kin contacts among university staff. Addressing large gatherings of potential ADS awardees at Universitas Hasanuddin over a number of years, this author was aware that all but a few were Buginese Muslims, despite the diversity of students in the postgraduate centre. While all ADS applications go to Jakarta for evaluation, it was clear that in South Sulawesi certain applicants are encouraged over others to apply. Whether open category or public sector, the candidate must feel that he or she has a good chance of success. Many instances of mentoring were observed and all of these involved Buginese Muslim academics encouraging and informing students from the same ethnic and religious background. In Indonesia, patronage is a very important factor in any career or pathway to upward social mobility. This patronage extends beyond mentoring to financial support, which is important because there are substantial costs in applying for ADS awards. The only acceptable English language test is expensive, as is the formal medical examination. High costs for an uncertain outcome tend to favour candidates from homes with better incomes, or with better lateral kin connections to obtain loans. There is also a certain measure of skill and cultural capital in locating the ADS website, determining deadlines, accessing relevant information and filling out forms properly. So even the process of applying is facilitated by appropriate family background, mentoring, and lateral kin/religious links. Finally, there is the question of English language competency. If the candidate does not have sufficient language skills, which many outside the disciplines of Arts/Humanities do not, then he or she must take intensive language classes, which are very expensive.

In short, successful ADS candidates from Universitas Hasanuddin were observed to be helped and encouraged over quite a long period of time by sympathetic lecturers or mentors who had studied overseas themselves. It seemed unlikely, given the ethno-religious local loyalties of South Sulawesi, that mentoring by senior university academics and public servants from a Muslim, Buginese background would be given to candidates from other faiths and from other racial or ethnic groups. It is important not to misunderstand this phenomenon as simple prejudice. Patronage is a cultural and moral expectation on the part of Buginese of all ages and backgrounds (Robinson 2002: 155). However, the effect of these "asymmetries of information" (Stieglitz 2002: xi), and the specificity of local ethno-religious patronage, is sufficient to create a situation where Muslim Buginese candidates tend to be the ones who submit winning ADS applications to Jakarta. They then go to Australia and return metaphorically crowned with laurels to eventually take up governance positions in education, politics, the local public service, and even religion, thus reinforcing Buginese hegemony in South Sulawesi. In this way, ADS awards at the local level can operate to favour the consolidation of an ethnic elite, strengthening social capital bonds that tend to exclude others.

Building Social Capital and Australia's Foreign Policy

Indonesia is strategically important in Australia's regional foreign and trade policy. Patrick argues that the focus of Australian aid is "largely influenced by trade, commercial and strategic factors" (1999: 91). Agafonoff (1994: 72) argues that political objectives often override development objectives in the allocation of funds for aid programs. Guthrie describes the ADS scheme as a diplomatic exercise of limited value (2002: 328). Yet the scholarships are extremely well-regarded by the Indonesian government, even though the aid money really flows back into Australia in the end. It is obviously a significant public relations exercise to annually fund 360 ADS awards for Indonesia, since this is important symbolic evidence of Australia's continuing commitment to friendly relations between the two countries, despite tensions and flare-ups.

Nevertheless, Australia is not only trying to directly stimulate economic capital, but seeking to implicitly reinforce lateral or 'bridging' social capital through the ADS scheme. Social capital in global aid discourse is defined as "the institutions, relationships and norms that shape the quality and quantity of a society's social interactions" (World Bank 2001: 1). It is further defined as 'social cohesion' which lies at the heart of civil society and good governance. We can see that the idea of promoting social capital can be logically linked to the objective of good governance in developing nations. Hadiz (2002) expresses this logic as follows: good governance arises from rational choice which is facilitated by 'good' social capital, which is inclusive rather than exclusive (see the Universitas Hasanuddin example above). Education theoretically provides the knowledge sets and ways of thinking that favour rational over non-rational ways of thinking. The effect should be even better (theoretically) if the educative process takes place in the setting of an ideal example of good governance in practice – a western democracy. Indonesian civil society is imagined to be strengthened by "students carrying home favourable impressions of Australia" (Guthrie 2002: 330).

Unfortunately, this reassuring chain of logical outcomes does not always follow from developing country students studying in western countries. Falk and Kanach (2000) give the example of Iran. Under the regime of the United States-backed Shah (1941-1979), modernization was the main thrust. Students were sent away to Europe and North America to gain the skills and training needed for Iran's rapid industrialization and expansion into the world market economy. In fact, the educational experience outside Iran largely encouraged the Islamic revolutionary zeal which eventually brought down the Shah. The young people "became highly politicized while outside their country" (Falk & Kanach 2000: 2). After the Islamic revolution (1979), the majority seem to have enthusiastically endorsed the "education of Iranians at home under a strict religious and cultural tutelage" (Falk & Kanach 2000: 2). Of course, by virtue of their western education, returning graduates took a prominent, and probably lucrative, role in this tutelage. Falk and Kanach (2000: 2) conclude that "it seems desirable to reformulate the goals and benefits of study abroad in a manner that is sensitive to the altered conditions brought on by globalization". This example is interesting because, although currently a secular state, Indonesia is the largest Islamic nation in the world, and the anti-western backlash alluded to in the Iranian example is strongly prevalent in many quarters of Indonesian society (Nilan 2003), and implicated in the recent terrorist attacks on western targets. Although Indonesia seems unlikely to ever follow the Iranian example of a single fundamentalist Islamic state, it does serve as a reminder that familiarity with the West may breed contempt as well as the comforting bonds of enhanced social capital.

This example also demonstrates the fallacy of assuming that education and training can ever, in themselves, provide a quick solution. As Chapman (2002: 35) states, in developing Asia, education and training are often "offered as a remedy for problems that arise from deterioration of political influence or lack of needed funds to make the necessary changes". It is doubtful whether the vast and complex issues which underlie the economic and political crisis currently facing over 200 million Indonesians will be alleviated much at all by an external agent such as Australia offering 360 overseas study scholarships a year to candidates who already enjoy some measure of privilege.

Conclusion

Despite the assertions made above, this paper is not arguing for a cessation, or even a redirection, of aid funding away from education in Indonesia. On the contrary, education remains not a short term quick-fix solution to the ills of a nation, but an excellent long-term investment in future economic prosperity and political stability, as long as it is relevant, and perceived as fairly distributed. In its optimum form, education builds both appropriate cultural capital and positive (bridging) social capital. This paper has examined some of the questions that might be asked about the extent to which the current ADS scheme is contributing effectively to reducing poverty and achieving sustainable development in Indonesia. The tentative conclusion offered here is that the current scheme of scholarships for overseas study is not the optimum program for achieving these goals. ADS awards are costly, and only 360 candidates in Indonesia a year are selected. A tentative proposal is for at least some of the AUS$30 million dollars worth of travel costs, tuition fees and stipends which currently get paid back into Australian universities and the Australian economy per year on behalf of Indonesian scholarship students instead be paid into Indonesian universities through in-country support for education, including internal scholarships. For example, in the early 1990s an AusAID project set up significant resources and staff for the teaching of 'polytechnics' (Nurhadi 1998: 181) at Universitas Hasanuddin. More of this kind of direct funding for higher education needs to occur. There is also the issue of increasing access to higher education. The Virtual Colombo Plan (VCP), a distance education scheme developed by AusAID and the World Bank, already hints at the possibilities for increased in-country postgraduate education using information technology, even though, as Ninnes (2004, this volume) demonstrates, the framing rhetoric of VCP encodes many of the same faults of colonialist logic that inhere in the ADS scheme. Finally, it is clear from a recent *Bappenas* (Indonesian Ministry for National Development Planning) initiative for a 'sandwich' postgraduate program in local planning and policy offered between selected Australian and Indonesian universities (Coelen 2003), that the Indonesian government wants to see many more Australian-Indonesian joint tertiary programs offered in-country.

There is a danger that any move away from ADS-style scholarships might be seen as a backward step in Australia's foreign relations, since they are popular with the Indonesian government, and Indonesian candidates are very enthusiastic about study overseas. Yet as we move into an era characterized by deeper, and yet more complex, regional relationships (Sulaiman & Sofyan 1998: 4), it is vitally important that Australia, as a privileged and wealthy Asia-Pacific nation, really does give substantial aid to the higher education sector in the region, especially if "accessing the benefits of globalisation" (AusAID 2003: 12) is a real foreign aid objective. In the current world economy, facilitating the competitive advantage of enterprises in developing countries such as Indonesia demands the education of a workforce capable of rapid and flexible responses to market change. It is also necessary for culturally and locally appropriate processes of good governance to be developed that ensure stable conditions for economic growth. It is argued here that much of this capacity-building toward economic sustainability should be undertaken in local contexts, so that the content is directly relevant and can be flexibly adapted to new laws and regulations as these evolve. However, this can only happen on a wide scale in Indonesia if the training and education institutions are capable of delivering the goods. It is therefore most important that countries like Australia develop aid schemes which can build up the educational access and resources in Indonesian tertiary institutions.

References

Adams, D. & Chapman, D. 1998. "Education and National Development in Asia: Trends and Issues." *International Journal of Educational Research* 29(7): 583-601.

Agafonoff, A. 1994. "Contribution to Panel Discussion: Future Directions for Australian Aid." In *Retrospective on Australian Aid: Looking Back to Improve the Future,* no editor. Canberra: Australian Development Studies Network, ANU.

Antlov, H. 2002. "Not Enough Politics? Regional Autonomy and the Democratic Polity." Paper delivered to the Indonesia Update Conference – Local Power and Politics. Canberra: Australian National University, 27-28 September.

Antweiler. C. 2001. "Transethnic Identity and Urban Cognition in Makassar: Regionalism and the Empowering Potential of Local Knowledge." *Antropologi Indonesia* 25(65): 13-39.

Appadurai, A. 2001. "Introduction." In *Globalization,* edited by A. Appadurai. Durham: Duke University Press.

Apple, M. 2001. "Comparing Neo-liberal Projects and Inequality in Education." *Comparative Education,* 37(4): 409-423.

Aronowitz, S. & Giroux, H. 1991. *Postmodern Education.* Minneapolis: University of Minnesota Press.

Auletta, A. 2000. "A Retrospective View of the Colombo Plan: Government Policy, Departmental Administration and Overseas Students." *Journal of Higher Education Policy and Management* 22(1): 47-58.

AusAID. 2001a. *Reducing Poverty: The Central Integrating Factor of Australia's Aid Program.* Canberra: Australian Agency for International Development.

AusAID. 2001b. *AusAID Strategic Plan.* Canberra: Australian Agency for International Development.

AusAID. 2002. *Snapshot of Training as of March 31, 2001.* Canberra: Australian Agency for International Development.

AusAID, 2003. *AusAID Annual Report 2003.* Canberra: Australian Agency for International Development.

Back, K. 1994. "Education in the Aid Program." In *Retrospective on Australian Aid: Looking Back to Improve the Future,* no editor. Canberra: Australian Development Studies Network, ANU

Bayhaqi, A. 2000. "Social Aspects of Higher Education: The Case of Indonesia." *Ekonomi dan Keuangan Indonesia* 68(3): 215-252.

Binsardi, A. & Ekwulugo, F. 2003. "International Marketing of British Education: Research on Students' Perception and the UK Market Penetration." *Marketing Intelligence and Planning* 25(5): 318-327.

Bourdieu, P. 1984. *Distinction: A Social Critique of the Judgement of Taste.* Translated by Richard Nice. Cambridge: Harvard University Press.

Bourdieu, P. 1985. "The Forms of Capital." In *Handbook of Theory and Research for the Sociology of Education,* edited by John Richardson. New York: Greenwood.

Bourdieu, P. & Passeron, J-C. 1990. *Reproduction in Education, Society and Culture.* Second Edition. London: Sage.

Butcher, A. 2002. "A Grief Observed: Grief Experiences of East Asian International Students Returning to their Countries of Origin". *Journal of Studies in International Education* 6(4): 354-368.

Castells, M. 1996. *The Rise of the Network Society: The Information Age: Economy, Society and Culture.* Volume One. Oxford: Blackwell.

Chapman, D. 2002. *Management and Efficiency in Education: Goal and Strategies.* Volume 5, series *"Education in Developing Asia".* Hong Kong: Comparative Education Research Centre, University of Hong Kong and Manilla: Asian Development Bank.

Coelen, R. 2003. *Bappenas* Scheme for Joint Masters Degree Programs. Personal communication.

Coleman, J. 1988. "Social Capital in the Creation of Human Capital." *American Journal of Sociology* 94 (Supplement): S95-S120.

Colongan, A. 2002. "What's Happening on the Ground? Findings from the Indonesia Rapid Decentralisation Appraisal." Paper delivered to the Indonesia Update Conference – Local Power and Politics. Canberra: Australian National University, 27-28 September.

Daroesman, P. & Daroesman, R. 1992. *Degrees of Success: A Tracer Study of Australian Government Sponsored Fellowships 1970-1989.* Canberra: Australian National University, Australian International Development Assistance Bureau, and the International Development Program of Australian Universities.

Djelantik, A. A. M. 1997. *The Birthmark: Memoirs of a Balinese Prince.* Hong Kong: Periplus Editions.

Downer, A. 1997. "Better Aid for a Better Future. Seventh Annual Report to Parliament on Australia's Development Cooperation program and the Government's Response to the Committee of Review of Australia's Overseas Aid Program." Accessed December 10, 2003 from http://www.ausaid.gov.au/publications

Everingham, C. 2002. "Rediscovering 'the Social' Through the Concept of Social Capital." Newcastle: Centre for Asia Pacific Social Transformation Studies University of Newcastle.

Falk, R. & Kanach, N. 2000. "Globalization and Study Abroad: An Illusion of Paradox." *Frontiers: The Interdisciplinary Journal of Study Abroad* 4: 1-8 [online]. Accessed 30 July, 2002. Online. http://www.frontiersjournal.com/ back/six/falk.htm

Fox, J. 2002. "Beyond Jakarta: Contemplating Indonesia's Possible Futures." In *Beyond Jakarta,* edited by M. Sakai. Bathurst: Crawford House Publishing.

Guthrie, G. 2002. "Crumbs from the Table: The Impact of Globalisation and Internationalisation on the Poverty of Third World Universities." In *Internationalizing Education in the Asia-Pacific Region: Critical Reflections, Critical Times, Proceedings of the 30th Annual Conference of the Australian and New Zealand Comparative and International Education*

Society (6-8 December), edited by P. Ninnes & L. Tamatea. Armidale, NSW: School of Education, University of New England.

Hadiz, V. 2002. "Power and Politics in North Sumatra: The Uncompleted *Reformasi.*" Paper delivered to the Indonesia Update Conference – Local Power and Politics. Canberra: Australian National University, 27-28 September.

Hassan, R. 2002. *Faithlines: Muslim Conceptions of Islam and Society.* Oxford: Oxford University Press.

Hellstén, M. 2002. "Internationalizing the Curriculum: The Student Experience." In *Internationalizing Education in the Asia-Pacific Region: Critical Reflections, Critical Times, Proceedings of the 30th Annual Conference of the Australian and New Zealand Comparative and International Education Society* (6-8 December), edited by P. Ninnes & L. Tamatea. Armidale, NSW: School of Education, University of New England.

Heyneman, S. 2003. "The History and Problems in the Making of Education Policy at the World Bank 1960-2000." *International Journal of Educational Development* 23(3): 315-337.

Hull, T. 2001. "First Results from the 2000 Population Census." *Bulletin of Indonesian Economic Studies* 3(1): 103-11.

Ikhsan, M. 2002. "Economic Update." Paper delivered to the Indonesia Update Conference – Local Power and Politics. Canberra: Australian National University, 27-28 September.

IMF. 2002. *International Financial Statistics: Country Analysis.* New York: International Monetary Fund.

Jalil, A. 2002. "Australian-Indonesian Education Links." Paper delivered to Autonomy in Education in the Indonesian Context Conference. Canberra: ANU, 29 September.

Kian Wie, T. 2001. "Reflections on the New Order 'Miracle'". In *Indonesian Today: Challenges of History,* edited by G. Lloyd & S. Smith. Singapore: Institute of Southeast Asian Studies.

Kingsbury, D. & Aveling, H. 2002. "Introduction." In *Autonomy and Disintegration in Indonesia,* edited by D. Kingsbury & H. Aveling. London: RoutledgeCurzon.

Lay, C. 2002. "The Politics of Regional Autonomy under Megawati's Presidency." Paper delivered to the Indonesia Update Conference – Local Power and Politics. Canberra: Australian National University, 27-28 September.

Livingstone, D. 1999. "Beyond Human Capital Theory: The Underemployment Problem." *International Journal of Sociology* 36(2): 163-192.

Mackie, J. 1999. "Tackling the Chinese Problem". In *Post-Soeharto Indonesia: Renewal or Chaos?* edited by G. Forrester. Bathurst: Crawford House Publishing.

Malley, M. 2002. "Historical Patterns of Centralisation and Decentralisation." Paper delivered to the Indonesia Update Conference - Local Power and Politics. Canberra: Australian National University, 27-28 September.

May, M. & Bartlett, A. 1995. "'They've got a Problem with English': Perceptions of the Difficulties of International Postgraduate Students." In *Teaching for Development,* edited by P. Thomas. Canberra: CPN Publications.

Mietzner, M. 2002. "Business as Usual: The Territorial Command System and Regional Autonomy." Paper delivered to the Indonesia Update Conference – Local Power and Politics. Canberra: Australian National University, 27-28 September.

Nesdale, D., Simkin, K., Sang, D., Burke, B. & Frager, S. 1995. *International Students and Immigration.* Canberra: Australian Government Publishing Service.

Nilan, P. 2003. "Young People, Politics and Religion in Indonesia." *The International Scope Review* 4: 8 Online. Available from http://www.tisr.com

Nurhadi, M. 1998. "Cooperation in Higher Education and Development of Human Resources". In *Bridging the Arafura Sea: Australia-Indonesia Relations in Prosperity and Adversity,* edited by I. Sulaiman, H. Sofyan & S. Smith. Canberra: National Centre for Development Studies.

Patrick, I. 1999. "Why Foreign Aid?" *Kritis: Jurnal Studi Pembangunan Inter-Disiplin.* Edisi 1/TTh 12(1): 68-98.

Phillips, M. & Stahl, C. 2001. "International Trade in Higher Education Services in the Asia-Pacific Region, Trends and Issues." *Asian and Pacific Migration Journal* 10(2): 273-301.

Pinches, M. 1996. "The Philippines New Rich: Capitalist Transformation amongst Economic Gloom." In *The New Rich in Asia: Mobile Phones, McDonalds and Middle Class Revolution,* edited by R. Robison & D. Goodman. London: Routledge.

Putnam, R. 1993. *Making Democracy Work: Civic Traditions in Modern Italy.* Princeton NJ: Princeton University Press.

Putnam, R. 2000. *Bowling Alone: The Collapse and Revival of American Community.* New York: Simon and Schuster.

Raffer, K. & Singer, H. 1996. *The Foreign Aid Business: Economic Assistance and Development Co-operation.* Cheltenham: Edward Elgar Publishing.

Rasyid, R. 2002a. "An Evaluation of Decentralisation: The Background and the Score Sheet so Far." Paper delivered to the Indonesia Update Conference - Local Power and Politics, Canberra: Australian National University, 27-28 September.

Rasyid, R. 2002b. "Autonomy of Education and Politics in Indonesia." Paper delivered to the Conference on Autonomy in Education in the Indonesian Context. Canberra: ANU, 29 September.

Rizvi, F. & Walsh, L. 1998. "Difference, Globalisation and the Internationalisation of the Curriculum." *Australian Universities Review* 41(2): 7-11.

Robinson, K. 2002. "Inter-ethnic Violence: The *Bugis* and the Problem of Explanation." In *Beyond Jakarta,* edited by M. Sakai. Adelaide: Crawford House Publishing.

Robison, R. 1996. "The Middle Class and the Bourgeoisie in Indonesia." In *The New Rich in Asia: Mobile Phones, McDonalds and Middle Class Revolution,* edited by R. Robison & D. Goodman. London: Routledge.

Robison, R. & Goodman, D. 1996. "The New Rich in Asia: Economic Development, Social Status and Political Consciousness." In *The New Rich in Asia: Mobile Phones, McDonalds and Middle Class Revolution,* edited by R. Robison & D. Goodman. London: Routledge.

Schapper, J. & Mayson, S. 2002. "Internationalisation of Curricula: An Alternative to the Taylorisation of Academic Work." In *Internationalizing Education in the Asia-Pacific*

Region: Critical Reflections, Critical Times, Proceedings of the 30th Annual Conference of the Australian and New Zealand Comparative and International Education Society (6-8 December), edited by P. Ninnes & L. Tamatea. Armidale, NSW: School of Education, University of New England.

Smith, G. Morey, A. & Teece, M. 2002. *How International Students View their Australian Experience.* Canberra: Australian Education International and Department of Education, Science and Technology.

Stieglitz, J. 2002. *Globalization and its Discontents,* New York: Allen Lane/The Penguin Press.

Sulaiman, I. & Sofyan, H. 1998. "Introduction." In *Bridging the Arafura Sea: Australia-Indonesia Relations in Prosperity and Adversity,* edited by I. Sulaiman, H. Sofyan & S. Smith. Canberra: National Centre for Development Studies, Australian National University.

Sulaiman, I. & Smith, S. 1998. "Australia and Indonesia: A Maturing Partnership in an Open Region." In *Bridging the Arafura Sea: Australia-Indonesia Relations in Prosperity and Adversity,* edited by I. Sulaiman, H. Sofyan & S. Smith. Canberra: NCDS.

Surakhmad, W. 2002. "Decentralizing Education: A Strategy for Building Sustainable Capacity for Regional Development." Paper delivered to the Conference on Autonomy in Education in the Indonesian Context. Canberra: ANU, 29 September.

The Jakarta Post. 2002. "UNDP Report Finds Indonesia More Democratic but Nothing Else." *The Jakarta Post,* 25 July.

Tiedeman, K. 2002. "Conversations with Australian Development Scholarship (ADS) Recipients from Indonesia." Paper delivered to the 30th Annual Conference of the Australian and New Zealand Comparative and International Education Society, University of New England, New South Wales, 6-8 December.

Tin Hta Nu. 1995. "Impact of Australian Education: A Burmese Experience." In *Teaching for Development,* edited by P. Thomas. Canberra: CPN Publications.

UNDP. 2002. *The Indonesian Human Development Report 2001.* Jakarta: United Nations Development Programme.

Welch, A. 2002. "Blurring the Borders: Finding a New Balance in South East Asian Higher Education." Paper delivered to the 30th Annual Conference of the Australian and New Zealand Comparative and International Education Society, University of New England, New South Wales, 6-8 December.

Wiryono, S. 1998. "Indonesia-Australia: An On-going Process." In *Bridging the Arafura Sea: Australia-Indonesia Relations in Prosperity and Adversity,* edited by I. Sulaiman, H. Sofyan & S. Smith. Canberra: NCDS.

Woolcock, M. 1998. "Social Capital and Economic Development: Towards a Theoretical Synthesis and Policy Framework." *Theory and Society* 27(1): 151-208.

World Bank. 1999. "Indonesia: Country Profile." Online. Accessed 7 May 1999. http://www.worldbank.org.

World Bank. 2001. "What is Social Capital? In *PovertyNet* Online. Accessed 9 May 2001. http://www.worldbank.org/poverty/scapital/whatsc.htm.

World Bank. 2002. *Engendering Development.* New York: Oxford University Press.

Ziegler, O. 1973. *The World and South East Asia.* Sydney: Oswald Ziegler Enterprises.

9

Managerialism, Internationalization, Taylorization and the Deskilling of Academic Work: Evidence from an Australian University

Jan Schapper and Susan Mayson

Introduction

Australian universities have undergone very substantial change over the last ten to fifteen years. Globalization and its attendant forces for internationalizing education, technological change enabling mass delivery of education and shifts in political ideology surrounding the governance and funding of higher education have wrought changes to the structure and context of academic work. It is within this context that we, and others before us (see for example, Deem 2001, Marginson & Considine 2000, Marginson 2002, Welch 1998), point to effects of managerialism and internationalization on academic institutions and those who work within them. The erosion of academic freedoms, alienation from university decision-making processes, accompanied by large class sizes, student diversity and the administrative and pedagogical demands of new modes of curricula delivery, characterize the academic's everyday working environment.

   As academics we reflect on the impact of these forces for change on our working lives and on our roles as teachers and researchers. We are not alone in our reflections. A growing number of papers and studies document the many ways in which the university experience of students, academic and administrative staff has been radically transformed (see, for example Barry, Chandler & Clark 2001, Coaldrake 1999, Deem 2001, Marginson 2000a, Parker & Jary 1995). Much about the changes in higher education brought about by managerialism and internationalization is to be applauded. Many papers celebrate the opportunities and practice of what is variously called multicultural, cross-cultural, intercultural, or culturally inclusive education in universities (see Beamer 1992, Gudykunst & Kim 1997, Peoples Wessinger 1994, Prescott & Hellstén this volume). And, while managerialism or, to use Welch's (1998: 4) phrase, the "cult of efficiency" has its critics (see for example, Bellamy, Morley & Watty 2003, Marginson & Considine 2000, Parker & Jary 1995, Welch 1998, Winter, Taylor & Sarros 2000), managerialist policies and practices have fostered more effective and transparent management practices within our universities. For example, recently introduced human resource management policies and procedures such as performance management criteria and workloads models provide criteria for transparent performance measures and allocation of work.

As we prepared for this chapter we noted that although we shared many of the sentiments of the critics of internationalization and managerialism, we felt that too much of the generalized commentary surrounding internationalization sanitized the realities faced by academic staff engaged in implementing an internationalized curriculum in a large Australian university. Although words such as "massification" (Coaldrake 1999, Scott 1998), the "homogenisation" of curriculum (Marginson 2000a, 2000b) and the "commodified curriculum" (Lewis 1998, Welch 2002) resonate with our recent experiences, they do not adequately capture the grinding and intellectually deskilling circumstances faced by academics, at least in our university and within our Department. We are struck by what we experience as the very normative idealizations provided by supporters of internationalized curriculum development and think it worthwhile to provide some details of our experience of internationalization. In the spirit of adding to the intellectual debate on internationalization of higher education we invite comment not necessarily on our current practise but on the context and practices through which internationalization is planned, developed and implemented.

In this chapter, we begin by describing the context in which we work and argue that internationalization and managerialism have transformed academic work in ways that devalue academics' contribution to teaching and learning and threaten academic autonomy. In order to make sense of our experience and the broader changes that shape the context in which we work, we draw on our discipline of management to describe what we call the 'Taylorization' of academic work. We outline Frederick Taylor's principles of scientific management and argue that the growing trend towards centralized management decision making and standardization, key elements of Taylor's scientific management, are readily identified in the pedagogical processes and expected academic practices in higher education. We illustrate our arguments and the utility of the 'Taylorization' framework by presenting a case study constructed from our experience as participants in one of our university's projects to develop and deliver an internationalized common curriculum to students in Asia, South Africa and Australia. Finally, as a way forward we offer some insights from the internationalization literature that provides a pedagogically focused and inclusive approach to developing internationalization strategies.

The Context: Internationalization, Managerialism and Higher Education

Internationalization and managerialism are highlighted in the literature as two fundamental forces for change in Western universities across the globe (Marginson 2002, Marginson & Considine 2000, Deem 2001). While these forces for change have operated in tandem within universities in recent times, many writers interested in analysing the effects of neo-conservative ideologies in higher education institutions and the rise of managerial power in universities have done so without reference to particular kinds of strategies developed by university decision-makers (see for example Bellamy, Morely & Watty 2003, Winter, Taylor & Sarros 2000, c.f. Welch 1998). For the purposes of our chapter, we see internationalization and managerialism as two powerful and intersecting forces that shape academic work in higher education.

Internationalization is not new to Australian universities (Knight & de Wit 1995, Welch & Denman 1997). From the 1950s onward, foreign affairs initiatives and aid programs opened Australian universities up to international students from across the Commonwealth through government hosting and scholarship schemes. In the late 1980s access to Australian higher education broadened when the Government abolished aid-based educational programs and permitted universities to charge full-fees to overseas students (Marginson 1997, 2000b). Internationalization is now a strategic corporate activity for Australian universities that provides an important source of non-government funding and the capacity for universities to expand activities across national borders (Welch 2002). Australia is currently the third largest provider of university education for overseas students after the United States and the United Kingdom, and overseas students represent one-fifth of total enrolment of students in Australian universities (Marginson 2002).

While Australian universities continue to intensify their engagement with external markets, various writers point to the contradictory nature of globalization and the ways in which interdependent global systems have shaped institutional responses to global and local markets in education (Marginson 1997, 2000a, 2000b, Marginson & Considine 2000, Porter & Vidovich 2000). Most significantly, there have been profound changes to university structures and governance and a reshaping of academic work brought about by the ways in which universities responded to the opportunities and threats presented by global education markets (Marginson 2000a, Marginson & Considine 2000, Porter & Vidovich 2000, Rizvi & Walsh 1998, Welch & Denman 1997).

For the purposes of our argument we highlight the influence of managerialist practices and values in the development of internationalization strategies. For example, the tendency towards the 'massification' of education is not just an institutional response to falling government support for university activities and universities' need for rapid growth and global integration into world-wide economic, cultural and knowledge systems in order to maintain competitive advantage in global education markets (Marginson 2000a, 2000b, Marginson & Considine 2000, Porter & Vidovich 2000, Scott 1998). It is a response based on the demands and requirements of managerialism in terms of effectiveness and efficiency and the need to measure broad outcomes across a range of standardized activities. Within this context, universities face contradictory tendencies. They must market and deliver their educational services across the globe while simultaneously accommodating diverse, localized and de-centred needs of specific student groups. In order to participate in these markets, universities, such as the one we work for, respond most readily to universalizing forces by relying on modes of economic rationality such as centralized strategic planning (supported by centralized government planning and policy) and economies of scale to maintain competitive advantage in markets which are themselves very localized and de-centred (Pratt & Poole 1999/2000, Welch & Denman 1997). Education becomes a commodity (see Lewis 1998), delivered to 'customers' in rationalized and economical ways, with only lip service paid to the learning outcomes or educational objectives of diverse student groups (see also Jamieson & Naidoo this volume).

Managerialism and the influence of new public management practices in the higher education sector have operated in tandem with internationalization as a fundamental force for change in modern universities in Australia and the UK (Barry, Chandler & Clark 2001, Bellamy, Morley & Watty 2003, Deem 2001, Marginson & Considine 2000, Winter, Taylor & Sarros 2000). The rise of managerialist ideology and increased power of university managers has created an alienated and demoralized academic workforce and a climate of resentment and resistance, even among academics who have become academic managers and who have benefited from managerialist policies (Bellamy et al. 2003, Chandler, Barry & Clark 2002, Gleeson & Shain 1999, Taylor, Gough, Bundrock & Winter 1998). From the perspective of these writers, managerialism has centralized decision-making, increased workloads, fragmented work tasks and diminished academic autonomy by alienating academics from the decision making structures within universities (see also Coaldrake & Stedman 1999).

Addressing the shift to the managerialist or corporate approach to higher education, Marginson and Considine (2000: 5) provide an insight into the purpose and ethos of what they have termed the "Enterprise University":

> In the Enterprise University, the economic and academic dimensions are both subordinated to something else. Money is a key objective, but it is also the means to a more fundamental mission: to advance the prestige and competitiveness of the university as an end in itself. At the same time, academic identities, in their variations, are subordinated to the mission, marketing and strategic development of the institution and its leaders.

The Enterprise University represents a "reworked" university structure (Pratt & Poole 1999/2000: 18) which is reliant on entrepreneurial activities, centralized planning and an increasingly independent (of government and collegial control) corporate structure (Marginson & Considine 2000, Pratt & Poole 1999/2000, Welch &

Denman 1997, Welch 2002). Academics are squeezed by the competing demands of entrepreneurial marketing and quality educational outcomes and academic standards (Bellamy et al. 2003, Chandler et al. 2002, Welch 1998, Winter et al. 2000).

Such universities rely on the flexibility of personnel and resources (Marginson & Considine 2002). As academics, flexibility means increased demands on our time but with limited access to scarce departmental resources to support our international activities. For example, in our experience the role of 'travelling faculty', which potentially provides valuable international experience and enhances our ability to deliver an internationalized curriculum (see also Welch & Denman 1997), is not shared across all staff that have international responsibilities. And, for those academics that do travel at the university's expense, concerns of efficiency and effectiveness over-ride the needs of the travelling academic and the provision of quality teaching outcomes. For many travelling staff the hours are long with an expectation of multiskilling. Not only must they teach, they also engage in marketing and recruitment activities at education fairs. Despite the importance of these roles to the university's future enrolments (and business), our experience tells us there is little provision of intercultural training or training in student selection methods. Development of flexibility might be the key to an enterprise university's success in maintaining its market share but the pressures for flexibility clearly exploit the goodwill of academic staff.

Those academics whose productive time is filled with either administrative demands or international travel find it increasingly difficult to engage in research (Pratt & Poole 1999/2000). University entrepreneurial activities encourage a shift away from basic research to more lucrative commercial consulting activities and links with industry to increase revenue flows and institutional prestige (Marginson & Considine 2000, Pratt & Poole 1999/2000). Academic involvement in these activities comes with a cost of added stress and time pressures leading to less time spent preparing for teaching, less personal time and scarce academic resources being consumed on non-academic activities.

Not surprisingly, the shift from local academic autonomy to corporate control has created a climate of academic discontent within universities (Coaldrake 1999, Taylor et al. 1998, Welch 2002). Internationalization of Australian higher education along with the introduction of managerialist practices has challenged and changed university structures, the nature of academic work and the meaning of what it is to be an academic. As Marginson and Considine (2000) and others argue, 'Enterprise Universities' seek to maintain their competitive advantage in global education markets by developing universalized and commodified mass education programs. Driven by market forces with an emphasis on cost minimization these programs cannot adequately serve the diverse needs of international student groups (Welch 2002). The effect of these changes on academic work is profound. Academic autonomy is lost as courses are developed and marketed centrally. Identities as academics are under constant challenge as academic staff take on multiple and often conflicting roles as consultants, researchers, teachers, counsellors and international marketers. Support for academics involved in international activities is scarce and the central and strategic control of resources with its demands for flexibility compromises the quality of academic life.

Taylorization of Education

Disaffection with our experience of academic life and the need to offer some form of challenge and resistance to managerialist policies and practices served as the catalyst for developing this analysis. To provide a framework to help us make sense of the cause of our dissatisfaction, we turned to a theory from our discipline of management that has underpinned much management ideology and practice since the turn of the twentieth century – Taylorism or scientific management. We chose to use the principles of scientific management in preference to the popular critique of modern society by Ritzer (1993) who gave the label of 'McDonaldization' to the application of the principles of fast-food outlets in the dispensing of health, education, and travel in modern society. Although McDonaldization with its emphasis on efficiencies, predicability and control does capture some of the features of mass production relevant to our experience it does not address what we feel to be the greatest attack on contemporary academic work within an international program. This we have identified as the wresting of intellectual labour from academic staff by corporate decision makers thereby casting academics in the role of process labourer. Because we are also loathe to perpetuate, even unconsciously, the implied suggestion that the primary task of higher education is business (see Prichard & Willmott 1997) we have also, despite their provocative and popular appeal, rejected the use of the labels McDonaldization and McUniversity (Parker & Jary 1995) in this chapter.

In referring to our industrial past, we are nonetheless continuing a considerable tradition of educators who have done similarly to make sense of current academic labour in higher education (eg. Parker & Jary 1995, Willmott 1995). For instance, the metaphors of the academic labour process as the academic assembly line (Barry et al. 2001) and the academic production line (Parker & Jary, 1995) and more recently the mill (Winter et al. 2000) are used to convey the sense of de-skilling and de-professionalization of academics in today's factories of learning. During the mid-1990s, this was exemplified by the debate waged by academics about the Fordist climate within distance education in general, and United Kingdom Open University (UKOU) in particular (see Stevens 1996 for an overview of the debate). It has been noted that Fordism is a term used quite loosely to describe the labour processes demanded by mass production as well as national and global regulation (Sayer 1996). It is the labour process described as Fordist (Amin cited in Holmer Nadesan 2001) that is of relevance here. Scientific management, an essential platform of Fordist ideology, refers specifically to that labour process, which for the purposes of this chapter, provides the boundary to our discussion.

The founder of scientific management, Frederick Winslow Taylor, an engineer, developed his particular theory of labour process in the late 1800s and early 1900s following his intense interest in workplace productivity and efficiency (Jaffee 2001). At a time when production was increasingly socialized into large-scale organizations, Taylor noted the increasing control skilled workers and not the owners had over the pace and organization of work (Hatch 1997). Taylor believed worker control and know-how placed owners at a disadvantage because production depended on workers' discretion to determine their own efficiencies (Jaffee 2001). In order to overcome this, Taylor, concerned by the lack of rational work systems within manufacturing, developed principles for establishing independent estimations of optimal inputs and outputs.

The systems Taylor implemented were designed to wrest control of production from workers in order to give control back to the employers. Having gained that control, Taylor then instituted the means to increase the pace of work and increase efficiencies (Thompson & McHugh 1990). To gain control over work processes, employers had to diminish workers' power vested in their knowledge of work processes based on experience and traditions of their various trades. Taylor identified this knowledge as the 'rule of thumb' and contrasted it with the application of rational scientific processes developed and controlled by managers. He argued "the management must take over and perform much of the work that is now left to the men" (Taylor 1911, cited in Jaffee 2001: 51). Taylor's other concern was the irregularity and unreliability of production, and again, it was only through the application of scientific methods to production that standards could be regularized and instituted. Idiosyncratic work patterns and methods were to be replaced by the "one best way" (Taylor 1912, cited in Locke 1982: 15) determined by the manager. Adopting principles of standardization, tools and procedures were also developed by management in accordance with designs that experiments had shown to be the most effective in a given context (Locke 1982: 15). In this way, managers assumed control over workers and production.

According to Morgan (1997), scientific management offered the promise of consistency, efficiency, standardization and predicability of products and services. Through the separation of the planning and design of work from those who perform the work, managers established controls over workers. Jobs were to be designed by the managers that could by their nature control, without the necessity of close supervision, the pace and execution of the work.

It is not, we believe, an exaggerated claim that the principles of scientific management are currently enacted in our university's approach to internationalizing the curriculum. Consistent with the principles of scientific management, the move to internationalization has emerged from centralized corporate decision makers who have done the thinking, designed the processes, developed the policies and informed the teaching staff of their tasks. That is, the serious business of knowledge creation is now the privilege of corporate decision makers far removed from teaching contexts, displacing academic staff, the previous custodians of teaching and learning in higher education. Academic teaching staff in this context are no longer valued for their intellectual contribution to student learning but for their ability to deliver pre-packaged education with efficiency and economy.

This Taylorized approach to education can accommodate and indeed encourages over-enrolments of students. Fewer academics are required to address the learning requirements of a growing and diverse student population (Allport 2000, Coaldrake 1999). Recent figures released by the Australian Vice Chancellors' Committee (AVCC 2001) highlight this trend. The ratio between students and teaching staff has "worsened substantially, rising from 12.9 per cent of students for each university teacher in 1990 to 18.8 students for each teacher in 2000". The figures for Business, the faculty to which we belong, together with Law and Administration are even higher with a student staff ratio of 28.3 in 2000. This chapter is not arguing that inter-nationalization strategies are the sole contributors to this worsening ratio, and the AVCC papers detail many other factors. Nonetheless, the AVCC does note that even those universities and disciplines successful at attracting full-fee paying students, who at undergraduate level tend to be overseas students, experience worsening ratios.

The growth in student teaching ratios has been made possible by the widespread availability of telecommunication technologies. So too, is the current strategy of internationalization dependent on these technologies. For the majority of students, interaction with the academic occurs electronically, either through web-based discussion groups or by email. There is an expectation that on-campus students attend tutorials and lectures but because their teaching staff are often sessional and not available outside their limited teaching hours, they too require these communication technologies. Although online education is expensive to establish and maintain (Allport 2000, Welch 2002), senior administrators and academics champion the availability of virtual and flexible learning wherever a student may be living and working. Significantly, the promise of flexibility provided by learning technologies have exacerbated stresses on staffing by allowing universities do more with less – increase enrolments, resist the hiring of new tenured teaching staff and substitute tenured staff with casualized teaching-only positions (Welch 2002). Allport (2000) notes however that students will not be satisfied with an education that is little more than the downloading of notes.

Case Study: Teaching an Internationalized Curriculum in a Managerialist Context

The strategy of internationalization taken by our university is a combination of twinning in Singapore and Hong Kong, the establishment of teaching campuses off-shore in Kuala Lumpur, Malaysia and Johannesburg, South Africa and extensive efforts to attract overseas students, especially at post-graduate level, to study at one of the six Victorian-based campuses. Until the departure of the university's previous Vice Chancellor in 2002, plans were in place to open further campuses in South East

Asia and the Indian sub-continent (Monash University Office of International Development n.d.). Research sites additional to those based in London, UK and Trento, Italy were to be opened in Germany and in North America (Monash University 2002a).

Within the Monash Teaching and Learning Plan 2003-2005 (Monash University n.d.), considerable attention is paid to the requirements of an internationalized institution with a number of objectives detailed for the internationalization of the curriculum, greater sensitivity to cultural diversity and encouragement to staff and students to study and work in other countries. In recognition of the need for the internationalization of the curriculum a project called the Curriculum Internationlisation and Flexible Delivery Project was undertaken within the Faculty of Business and Economics (see Monash University 2003). This was a pilot project designed to develop internationalized course materials and flexible delivery options for two core first year undergraduate units taught within the Bachelor of Business and Commerce Degree, one of which was the core first year management unit in which we teach.

Within our department, those involved in the project problematized the internationalization aspects of the project because of staff concerns about Western-centric focus of the management discipline. However as the project progressed, it was clear that internationalization issues were subordinated to issues of flexible delivery of materials to large numbers of students. Eventually, in line with Taylorist principles of efficiency through standardization, the objectives of the project were modified to include the design of standardized subject content for delivery to students enrolled in the Faculty's global degree. As part of the push for standardization, the 'one hundred per cent rule' was introduced. Like Taylor's mantra of the 'one best way', the rule stipulated that students enrolled within the Bachelor of Business and Commerce degree, irrespective of the campus on which they are located or mode through which they participated in study, received the same curriculum, completed the same assessment tasks, sat the same examinations and were assessed by the same criteria (Monash University 2002b).

Contrary to expectations, the one hundred per cent rule does permit some flexibility. Different texts may be chosen to suit local circumstances and there is some provision of local references and readings to suit local needs. In the main though, academic staff generally adhere to the rule for reasons of convenience and consistency and most students use the same text and references regardless of their location. Because of the cultural origin of much of the course content within management courses the rule creates problems for staff and students. Far from being culturally neutral (DeBry 2001) the content and ideology of the Management texts are predominantly developed in the United States with a few modified by the addition of local case studies provided by Anglo-European authors based in Australia (see for example, Bartol, Martin, Tein & Matthews 2003; Robbins, Bergman, Stagg & Coulter 2003, Waddell, Cummings & Worley 2000).

We are acutely aware of the irony that we not only experience cultural domination by United States of America in our discipline (see also Clegg, Linstead & Sewell 2000) but we perpetuate this domination in the broader international context.

Course content experienced by all students could be typified as overwhelmingly Western in orientation, and almost exclusively US in content. References to other cultures are in the main, incidental, anecdotal and from the position that suggests North American culture is the norm. Examples and language relevant to the United States such as "minorities", Hispanics, people of colour and so on highlight the extent to which the materials are culturally grounded in North American language and culture (see, for example, Managerial Communication texts such as Daniels, Spiker & Papa, 1997, Gamble & Gamble, 1999). This homogenization of course content along with the Taylorist pressures of standardization militate against any benefits derived from teaching in an internationalized context.

To administer the common curriculum, and in an effort to maintain standardization, the Department of Management has adopted a model in which each subject is allocated a Coordinator/Chief Examiner who is responsible for curriculum development, curriculum maintenance, establishment of assessment tasks, setting of examinations, and the moderation of assessments, and who is the final point of accountability for the distribution of results across the campuses and to all students. The Chief Examiner's brief is to consult with academic staff over teaching and pedagogical issues. However, for the academic staff teaching within this degree, academic independence and autonomy is very limited by this level of centralized decision making. In practice, Chief Examiners (who get a time allowance for their role) become managers. They make most of the decisions to ensure the standardized delivery of course content with varying levels of consultation with other academic staff. Tightly controlled by common learning objectives, assessments and examinations that ensure that the curriculum conforms to the one hundred per cent rule, the only autonomy accorded to academics is in the development of lecture and tutorial materials for one's campus.

As our case study demonstrates, the Taylorized approach to international education has many attractions for an 'enterprise university'. It offers guarantees of standardized curriculum and standardized assessments, and the reassurance to students and employers of the consistency of the degree irrespective of where that degree is completed. More importantly, efficiencies can be expected with the standardization of courses. Only one set of materials is required, the longer life of materials allows larger print-runs of print materials and other materials can be made available electronically. This point in particular was made in a university document in which the author noted "Standardisation of content facilitates the use of flexible learning support materials in a wider range of teaching situations and therefore *reduces the average cost of using them*" (emphasis added) (Monash University 2003: 3). Further efficiencies can be expected from this Taylorized approach as teaching duties such as marking and student support can now be outsourced. There is an assumption that freed from the necessity to develop curricula that addresses the particular circumstances of their students, academics can churn through increased student numbers. As we indicated earlier, this Taylorized approach accommodates and indeed encourages over-enrolments of students.

Some Thoughts for a Way Forward

Although we are very critical of the quality of education provided to students in the name of internationalized curriculum our concern in this chapter is to comment on the Taylorist assault on the professionalism of academic staff (Danaher, Gale & Erben 2000), teaching autonomy and intellectual freedom. Allport (2000: 43) describes intellectual freedom as "the rights of academic staff to freely discuss, teach, assess, develop curricula, publish research and engage in community service." The university's approach to internationalization has, in its execution, seriously eroded a substantial component of the recognized basic rights of academic staff. In our experience of internationalization, academics are no longer in control of curriculum development, teaching or assessment, and are facing what Marginson (2000a) refers to as the deconstruction of the academic profession. Standardized courses rob academics of professional autonomy, professional judgement and intellectual engagement. This loss of engagement has been exacerbated by the increasing casualization of academic staff to service the internationalized curriculum, which not only offers a serious challenge to service quality but also undermines academics' capacity to engage in open and robust debate.

From our perspective, internationalization, like the globalizing forces from which it emanates, creates a complex and ambiguous context for teaching and learning. On the one hand, internationalization exerts a centralising and homogenizing influence on academic work illustrated by the strengthening of the cultural hegemony of Anglo-American thinking in both the content and teaching approaches of our courses. At the same time, our academic labour is increasingly shaped by Taylorist methods developed to overcome the problems of providing educational services to students separated by time and geography. Taylorization has stripped us of our autonomy as teachers and researchers because the relationship between the thinkers (academics as researchers) and the doers (academics as teachers) has been displaced.

In contrast to this experience of internationalization, there are approaches that offer greater potential for positive changes to teaching and learning by creating the possibility of multiple viewpoints, new ideas and the intellectual space to challenge the values and assumptions that underpin our discipline. There are a number of writers in the area that offer a pedagogical (as opposed to a managerialist) rationale for an internationalized curriculum that enhances academic autonomy and promotes student participation in their own learning program (see for example Schoorman 2000, Whalley 1997).

Indeed, our own university, in its literature on internationalizing the curriculum, refers to guidelines from a document titled *Best Practice Guidelines for Internationalizing the Curriculum* (Whalley 1997). With the stated objective of creating intercultural/international literacy, the guidelines seek to 'concretize' the internationalization project. Drawing on the work of two European scholars (Bremer & van der Wende 1995, cited in Whalley 1997: 2) an internationalized curriculum is described as:

Curricula with an international orientation in content, aimed at preparing students for performing (professionally/ socially) in an international and multi-cultural context, and designed for domestic students and/or foreign students.

The Whalley (1997) document provides extensive detail in areas of curriculum development at the program and unit level, identifying necessary support activities to the process of internationalization of the curriculum. Although the guiding principles are recommended reading by the professional Teaching and Learning specialists in the university, they cannot yet be integrated into teaching practice by academic staff while the standardization approach to internationalization imposed at the operational level by the university managers remains in place.

Similarly, Schoorman (2000), while arguing for a more overtly political conceptualization of internationalization than Whalley, clearly establishes ground rules for curriculum development and provides a creative direction for academic teaching practice. The key components of Schoorman's vision of internationalization include the requirement to be a) counter-hegemonic, b) on-going, c) comprehensive, d) multifaceted and e) integrated (Schoorman 2000: 6). It is clear that unlike those who manage internationalization in our university, Schoorman's (2000) model of inter-nationalization is one that focuses on pedagogical issues of teaching and learning and not just administrative solutions and outcomes. For Schoorman (2000), internationali-zation demands curriculum change to accommodate multiple perspectives implicit within a global model. She embraces diversity brought about by internationalization and recognizes the multifaceted ways (compared to the Taylorist ideal of 'the one best way') in which internationalization can be addressed in university lecture theatres and classrooms. Of particular value in Schoorman's (2000) model is the critical perspective on internationalization that recommends a counter-hegemonic orientation to education and the importance of returning the responsibility of internationalizing curricula to teachers and learners.

For us, this model, if even partially implemented, signals an end to the Taylorist approach to education we describe above. It points to the value of a multifaceted program of action, compared with the homogenized delivery of commodified teaching materials, designed by curriculum developers far removed from teaching and learning contexts. Interestingly, some of the ideas outlined in Schoorman resonate with the recent statements by policy makers in the Australian higher education bureaucracy. To quote a recent Australian Minister for Education, Brendan Nelson (2002: x):

Student-centred learning environments should serve the needs of an increasingly diverse group of students without compromising the effectiveness of learning or adversely affecting the working environment for academics and other staff. This will require consideration of the timing and structure of learning experiences and the feasibility of customised or individualised approaches to higher edu-cation curricula.

Should this policy on internationalization be implemented, there would be the requirement that time and money be allocated to local academics and students to develop course materials that provide global perspectives and incorporate intercultural approaches to understanding key concepts within different subject areas. There may even be resources allocated to programs such as teaching exchanges so that academics can gain international experience working beside overseas colleagues and students in class rooms in Hong Kong, Malaysia, Singapore and China.

Despite our enthusiasm for Nelson's rhetoric, Whalley's practical good sense and Schoorman's vision of internationalization, we are sufficiently pragmatic to be aware that others within our university may be less excited by the proposal. We are currently in an era in higher education where all staff are exhorted to do more with less. More teaching hours, more students, more courses, more subjects, more majors and of course more research, more publications, more grants and not forgetting more administration, more committees, and more accountability. Clearly, the models of internationalization presented by Whalley and Schoorman and the one mooted by the current education bureaucracy require considerable resources to flow to the contexts in which teaching and learning occur. Again, pragmatism tells us this is unlikely.

It is generally accepted wisdom that universities are "in crisis" and their contributions to the societies within which they are located are increasingly under challenge (see Blackmore 2001 for a review of many recent books on the issue). The Federal Government that once provided 85 per cent of funding for higher education in Australia now provides only 48 per cent (Marginson 2002). Recent geopolitical events following acts of terrorism on symbols of Western capitalism in the United States and Indonesia are being held responsible for falling enrolments of international students to our university. With fewer students, falling income and growing debt we anticipate greater pressure on academic staff to produce more materials for distribution as efficiently and cheaply as possible. With more emphasis on reducing costs and less on pedagogical excellence we know internationalization as we have experienced it will continue.

Conclusion

While managerialism is alive and well in our university, managerialist practices are not uncontested by those within it. University staff have responded to changes in their work environments in a variety of ways including collusion, resentment and resistance (see, for example, Chandler et al. 2002, Gleeson & Shain 1999, Parker & Jary 1995). This chapter has been our response. It offers not only a challenge to our university's managerialist response to internationalization, but also a way forward. Scholars such as Whalley (1997) and Schoorman (2000) remind us of the 'business' of diverse educational institutions such as ours – teaching and learning – and the importance of pedagogical issues and individual needs rather than efficiency and standardization.

Despite the pressures of contemporary academic work, we must continue to engage in argument and be willing to contest the managerialist practices that threaten to separate the thinking from the doing of teaching practise, particularly in the current internationalized environment in which we teach. As our chapter demonstrates, there are alternative approaches to the managerialist 'one best way', for developing a more inclusive, democratic and multi-faceted approach to teaching in an internationalized context. Internationalization has the potential to open up learning opportunities for staff and students, particularly within our management discipline with its Western-centric assumptions and US-based interpretations of cultural diversity. Without such approaches, the discipline of management is in danger of becoming irrelevant to our students as they seek employment in increasingly globalized and internationalized workplaces.

We are critical of the quality of education provided to our students and the practices that rob us, and our colleagues, of our professional autonomy and devalue our intellectual endeavours. To make sense of this we turned to our management discipline and the ideas of Frederick Taylor to argue that current practices constitute the Taylorization of higher education, exemplified by centralized corporate planning and the push to provide educational courses in the most efficient and effective way through common curricula and standardized course materials. The pressures of internationalization and managerialist responses to falling government funding have compromized our academic autonomy, threatened our profession and increased our teaching workloads. Nonetheless, despite our understanding of the current financial pressures on the university we call for an approach to internationalization that recognizes the important link between academics' research activities and the contribution these activities make to the pedagogical soundness of the courses we offer students in an internationalized context.

References

Allport, C. 2000. "Thinking Globally, Acting Locally: Lifelong Learning and the Implications for University Staff." *Journal of Higher Education Policy and Management* 22(1): 37-47.

Australian Vice-Chancellor's Committee (AVCC). 2001. *Fact Sheet 4: The Worsening Student Teacher Ratio.* [online] Retrieved 22 Aug 2002. Available from http://www.avcc.edu.au/policies_activities/international_relations/internationalisation_initiatives/offshor.htm.

Barry, J., Chandler, J. & Clark, H. 2001. "Between the Ivory Tower and the Academic Assembly Line." *Journal of Management Studies* 38(1): 87-99.

Bartol, K., Martin, D., Tein, M. & Matthews, G. 2003. *Management: A Pacific Rim Focus (International Edition).* New York: McGraw-Hill Inc.

Beamer, L. 1992. "Learning Intercultural Communication Competence." *The Journal of Business Communication* 29(3): 295-293.

Bellamy, S., Morley, C. & Watty, K. 2003. "Why Business Academics Remain in Australian Universities Despite Deteriorating Working Conditions and Reduced Job Satisfaction:

An Intellectual Puzzle." *Journal of Higher Education Policy and Management* 25(1): 13-28.

Blackmore, J. 2001. "Universities in Crisis? Knowledge Economies, Emancipatory Pedagogies, and the Critical Intellectual." *Educational Theory* 51(3): 353-369.

Chandler, J., Barry, J. & Clark, H. 2002. "Stressing Academe: The Wear and Tear of the New Public Management." *Human Relations* 55(9):1051-1069.

Clegg, S., Linstead, S. & Sewell, G. 2000. "Only Penguins: A Polemic on Organization Theory from the Edge of the World". *Organization Studies* 21: 103-117

Coaldrake, P. 1999. "Rethinking University Work" Paper presented at the Higher Education Research and Development Society of Australasia Annual International Conference, Melbourne, 12-15 July.

Coaldrake, P. & Stedman, L. 1999. "Academic Work in the Twenty-first Century: Changing Roles and Policies." Occasional Paper Series no. 99H. Canberra: Higher Education Division, Department of Education, Training and Youth Affairs.

Danaher, P., Gale, T. & Erben, T. 2000 "The Teacher Educator as (Re) Negotiated Professional: Critical Incidents in Steering between State and Market in Australia." *Journal of Education for Teaching* 26(1): 55-71.

Daniels, T., Spiker, B. & Papa, M. 1997. *Perspectives on Organisational Communication (4th Edition).* Boston: McGraw Hill.

Deem, R. 2001. "Globalisation, New Managerialism, Academic Capitalism and Entrepreneurialism in Universities: Is the Local Dimension Important?" *Comparative Education* 37(1): 7-20.

DeBry, D. 2001. "Globalizing Instructional Materials: Guidelines for Higher Education." *TechTrends* 45(6): 41-45.

Gamble, T. & Gamble, M. 1999. *Communication Works (6th Edition).* Boston: McGraw-Hill.

Gleeson, D. & Shain, F. 1999. "Managing Ambiguity: Between Markets and Managerialism - A Case Study of 'Middle Managers' in Further Education." *The Sociological Review* 47(3): 461-490.

Gudykunst, W. & Kim, Y. 1997. *Communicating with Strangers: An Approach to Intercultural Education.* New York: McGraw-Hill.

Hatch, M. 1997. *Organization Theory Modern, Symbolic and Postmodern Perspectives.* Oxford, England: Oxford University Press.

Holmer Nadesan, M. 2001 "Post Fordism, Political Economy, and Critical Organizational Communication Studies." *Management Communication Quarterly* 15(2): 259-264.

Jaffee, D. 2001. *Organization Theory Tension and Change.* New York, NY: McGraw Hill.

Knight, J. & de Wit, H. 1995. "Strategies for Internationalisation of Higher Education: Historical and Conceptual Perspectives" in *Strategies for Internationalisation of Higher Education: A Comparative Study of Australia, Canada, Europe and the United States of America* edited by H. de Wit. Amsterdam: European Association for International Education.

Lewis R. 1998. "Commodified Curricula: The Coursebook." *Australian Universities Review* 41(2): 3-4.

Locke, E. 1982. "The Ideas of Frederick W. Taylor: An Evaluation." *The Academy of Management Review* 7(1): 14-24.

Marginson, S. 1997. *Markets in Education*. St Leonards, NSW: Allen and Unwin.

Marginson, S. 2000a. "Rethinking Academic Work in the Global Era." *Journal of Higher Education Policy and Management* 22(1): 23-35.

Marginson, S. 2000b. *Monash: Remaking the University*. St Leonards, NSW: Allen and Unwin.

Marginson, S. & Considine, M. 2000. *The Enterprise University: Power, Governance and Reinvention in Australia*. Oakleigh, Victoria: Cambridge University Press.

Marginson, S. 2002. "The Phenomenal Rise of International Degrees Down Under." *Change* 34(3): 34-43.

Monash University. 2002a. "Global Development" [online]. Melbourne: Monash University Website. Retrieved October 30 2002. Available from http://www.monash.edu.au/intoff/global development/index2.html.

Monash University. 2002b. *Undergraduate 2002*. Clayton: Monash University.

Monash University. Office of International Development. n.d. "Monash in 2006" [online]. Melbourne: Monash University Website, retrieved August 19 2003. Available from http://www.monash.edu.au/international/oid/pandp/d.../monash2006.html.

Monash University. n.d. "Teaching and Learning Plan 2003-2005" [online]. Melbourne: Monash University Website. Retrieved August 19 2003. Available from http://www.adm.monash.edu.au/dvcap/ltp/LTPoverview.html.

Monash University. 2003. "Strategic Innovations Fund, Final Report" [online]. Melbourne: Monash University Website. Retrieved August 18 2003. Available from http://www.adm.monash.edu.au/dvcap/grants/00_13fin.htm.

Morgan, G. 1997. *Images of Organizations*. Thousand Oaks, CA: Sage Publications.

Nelson, B. 2002. *Striving for Quality: Learning, Teaching and Scholarship*. Canberra: Australian Government Publishing Service.

Parker, M. & Jary, D. 1995. "The McUniversity: Organization, Management and Academic Subjectivity." *Organization* 2(2): 319-338.

Peoples Wessinger, N. 1994. "Celebrating Our Differences: Fostering Ethnicity in Homogenous Settings." *Journal of Physical Education, Recreation and Dance* 65(9): 62-69.

Porter, P. & Vidovich, L. 2000. "Globalization and Higher Education Policy." *Educational Theory* 50(4): 449-453.

Pratt, G. & Poole, D. 1999/2000. "Global Corporations 'R' Us? The Impacts of Globalisation on Australian Universities." *Australian Universities Review* 42(2)/43(1): 16-23.

Prichard, C. & Willmott, H.1997. "Just How Managed is the McUniversity?" *Organization Studies* 18(2): 287-317.

Ritzer, G. 1993. *The McDonaldization of Society*. Newbury Park, CA: Pine Forge Press.

Rizvi, F. & Walsh, L. 1998. "Difference, Globalisation and the Internationalisation of the Curriculum." *Australian Universities Review* 41(2): 7-11.

Robbins S., Bergman, R., Stagg, I. & Coulter, M. 2003. *Management* (3rd Edition). Frenchs Forest, NSW: Prentice Hall Australia Ltd.

Sayer, A. 1996. "Book Review – Post-Fordism: A Reader, Edited by Ash Amin." *Capital and Class* 59 (Summer): 151-153.

Schoorman, D. 2000. "What Really Do We Mean by 'Internationalization'?" *Contemporary Education* 71(4): 5-11.

Scott, P. (ed.) 1998. *The Globalization of Higher Education*. Buckingham, UK: Open University.

Stevens, K. 1996. "Have the Shifting Sands of Fordism Resulted in Ground Lost or Ground Gained for Distance Education?" *Distance Education* 17(2): 247-258.

Taylor, T., Gough, J., Bundrock, V. & Winter, R. 1998. "A Bleak Outlook: Academic Staff Perceptions of Changes in Core Activities in Australian Higher Education, 1991-1996." *Studies in Higher Education* 23(3): 255-268.

Thompson, P. & McHugh, D. 1990. *Work Organisations: A Critical Introduction*. London: Macmillan.

Waddell, D., Cummings, T. & Worley, C. 2000. *Organization Development and Change (Pacific Rim Edition)*. Melbourne: Nelson Thompson Learning.

Welch, A. 1998. "The End of Certainty? The Academic Profession and the Challenge of Change." *Comparative Education Review* 42(1): 1-10.

Welch, A. 2002. "Going Global? Internationalizing Australian Universities in a Time of Global Crisis." *Comparative Education Review* 46(4): 433-471.

Welch, A. & Denman, B. 1997. "Internationalisation of Higher Education: Retrospect and Prospect." *Forum of Education* 52(1): 14-29.

Whalley, T. 1997. *Best Practice Guidelines for Internationalizing the Curriculum*. Victoria, BC: Ministry of Education, Skills and Training, and the Centre for Curriculum, Transfer and Technology. Retrieved December 15 2003. http://www.ctt.bc.ca/curric/BP.

Willmott, H. 1995. "Managing the Academics; Commodification and Control in the Development of University Education in the UK." *Human Relations* 48(9): 993-1028.

Winter, R., Taylor, T. & Sarros, J. 2000. "Trouble at Mill: Quality of Academic Worklife Issues within a Comprehensive Australian University." *Studies in Higher Education* 25(3): 279-294.

10

International Policy Convergence in Higher Education: An Analysis from the Periphery

Katarina Tuinamuana

Introduction

In response to international developments in educational policy discussions, higher education institutions and governments on the periphery are changing the way that they articulate policy. Although local institutions and governments may appear to have autonomy in educational policy formulation and practice, international trends have had a wide-ranging impact on peripheral systems of education. This chapter analyses the convergence of educational policy across international borders (Ball 1998) by examining the 'new managerialism' in higher education in Fiji, looking in detail at how international trends in educational policy are being adopted at the national level in Fiji and how they are being played out in the local, peripheral setting of a Fiji teacher education institution.

The international context of education has changed significantly over the last decade, and in today's more globalized world it is no longer possible to ignore the effects of global macro socio-economic changes on both national and local education systems. The influence of these changes on national education systems is widely acknowledged with, for example, an increase in privatization and market driven reforms (Dale 1997, Elliot 1999, Smyth, Dow, Hattam, Reid & Shacklock 2000, Whitty 1997, Woods & Jeffrey 1996). Furthermore, according to Ball (1998: 122), concepts such as the 'learning society', the 'knowledge-based economy' and the 'new managerialism' are policy 'condensates' which "serve and symbolise the increasing colonization of education policy by economic policy imperatives".

Emerging as part of the trend brought about by economic globalization is the focus on the internationalization of higher education. The internationalization of higher education might be understood as a response of higher education to globalization. More specifically, it could be seen as "a systematic, sustained effort by

199

government to make higher education institutions more responsive to the challenges of globalisation of the economy and society" (Elliot 1999: 32).

The internationalization of higher education in this sense is examined here in relation to secondary teacher education policy and practice in Fiji, a country that has one national institutional provider of secondary teachers, namely, the Fiji College of Advanced Education (FCAE). The Ministry of Finance in Fiji has required that all Ministries produce new policy documents including Mission Statements and Strategic Plans along the lines of the new managerialist style. Thus the Fiji Ministry of Education (MoE) has recently developed three new policy documents: *Education Fiji 2020*; The *Strategic Plan 2000 – 2002*; and the *2001 Corporate Plan*. These policy documents are used to plan and monitor educational processes at all levels of the education system, including higher education. As a consequence, and as I discuss in this chapter, the FCAE has now developed its own Mission Statement and Strategic Plan complete with performance indicators.

There is a clear appropriation of economic discourses in the new FCAE documents. Defining education in terms of economics "means that economic interests dominate content and process in education, and that in turn requires that what counts as knowledge is redefined, for practitioners as well as pupils" (Ozga 2000: 56). This knowledge and reality are largely defined in a meaning-deficient new managerial style, and this should be a crucial matter for debate (Loughlin 2002).

Of added interest, however, is how these new, globally recognizable policies are implemented by the FCAE, and this chapter reports on some research findings based on a study of teacher education in Fiji (Tuinamuana 2002). I argue that although the new global educational discourses might have the potential to contribute to the construction of a new reality of education in Fiji, the way in which the new managerialist policy is perceived and acted upon by the players on the ground adds complexity to the situation.

The New Managerialism

The new managerialism is a form of management that emphasizes efficiency and effectiveness using techniques and values appropriated from the business sector. Ball (1998: 123) suggests that in practice, there is an "insertion of the theories and techniques of business management and the 'cult of excellence' into public sector institutions".

There is very little doubt that the new managerialism has become a part of the way in which education is conceptualized within institutions and at local, national and global policy levels. Loughlin (2002) discusses some of the new language associated with the quality reforms introduced in the United Kingdom. He very aptly entitles his article with the words: "Assurance, effectiveness, ownership, empowerment, auto-nomy, dynamic, learning curves, a continuum of quality-awareness, self-actualisation and enhancement ... whatever that means". Loughlin (2002: 20) is critical of the culture of "perpetual linguistic innovation" evident within contemporary management practice suggesting that, first, this new terminology is inadequately explained by its promoters, except in superficial and circular ways, and second, that the purpose of the new jargon is really to deliver support for existing government policies.

Moreover, the new managerialism is seen as a way to devolve responsibility (that is, power), at a very superficial level, to practitioners. Thus, in this situation practitioners might attain a sense of empowerment, whereas in reality control and power remain at centralized locations. Hartley (1997: 48) outlines the UK experience with the new managerialism:

> How can the costs of the welfare state be pruned so that both professionals and clients lend their approval to the cuts? The preferred solution is to assign control of strategy to government, but to devolve to institutions and to individuals the control over tactics which will implement that strategy. Funding now follows performance, as a reward; hitherto funding preceded performance as an investment.

In this sense, within the new managerialism, there is now a new form of employee involvement. Ball (1998: 123) calls this the cultivation of "corporate culture" a development that is "deeply paradoxical. On the one hand . . . managerial response-bilities are delegated and initiative and problem solving are highly valued. On the other hand, new forms of surveillance and self-monitoring are put in place, for example, appraisal systems, target setting, and output comparisons."

Thus the new managerialism, replete with its own jargon, seems to be function-ing in support of neo-liberal global economic agendas in its appropriation of the technicist language typically used in the business sector. That Fiji is not exempt from these international trends is evident in the directions that she is now taking in matters to do with educational policy both at a general level and more specifically in terms of teacher education. The next section illustrates this point further.

The New Managerialism in Fiji

Fiji is currently going through an unprecedented phase of educational policy docu-ment production, with the new-style policy documents now gaining a unique currency of authority and prestige. This phase commenced at the beginning of 1999, when the MoE developed a strategic plan to "provide greater focus and direction on educational planning in government" (Kotobalavu 2000: i). This plan was called the *Education Fiji 2020 Strategic Plan*, and was developed during the reign of the newly elected Labour/Peoples' Coalition Party Government. It was later supplemented by the

Strategic Plan 2000 – 2002, and the *2001 Corporate Plan: Putting the 'Strategic Plan 2000 – 2002' into Action.*

It might be asked from what impetus did these documents suddenly appear? It is evident that the preparation of the new set of planning documents was initiated by the economic requirements set up within the Fiji Ministry of Finance. In a section on "Internal Outputs" the 2001 MoE Corporate Plan lists as the number 1 output, "Prepare Corporate Plan". The quality of this Plan is to be assessed in terms of how far it complies with the "requirements of (the) Public Service Act and (the) Finance Management Act" (Fiji Ministry of Education 2001: 37). There are thus very clear links between the new policy documents and the macroeconomic policies that successive governments in Fiji have been pursuing since the onslaught of neo-liberal ideals (Prasad 1998). Fiji is not exempt from the influence of the International Monetary Fund (IMF) and World Bank directives, and is now integrated with the global structural adjustment policies that are encouraged by these institutions and their subsidiaries. Commentators have suggested that the Bank has "abandoned its role as a development bank to become a policy-making institution that intervenes in the internal affairs of countries" (Ugarteche 1997: 201).

The current economic emphasis on the principles of neo-liberalism affects education in 'developing' countries in a number of significant ways. The most visible influence has been one of intervention in the supply of teaching personnel, transferral of curricula from the centre to the periphery, sharing of examinations and the growth in the number of external consultancies carried out. However, the underlying influence can be better articulated in terms of the role of education in being a tool for integration of Fiji as a 'junior' player into the wider regional and global economy.

It is significant, therefore, that the push for policy formulation seems to be coming from outside the education sector. This of course is not a phenomenon restricted to Fiji's situation. Furthermore, there is some feeling in the education sector that the MoE might not have acted on its own accord in following the new managerial trend if there had not been an impetus from the Finance Ministry for development of the new plans. A senior academic member of staff working at the management level at the FCAE commented on these developments, tying them in with the reforms that Fiji is currently undergoing:

> It's all tied up with these public sector reforms that we are inheriting, or borrowing from Australia. And it's all tied up with Performance Management Systems where you have to have a Vision, a Mission, you have to have a Strategic Plan, and your Annual Plans and all that. If it weren't for that I don't think that the ministry would ever dream that that's the way they'd like to go. That's a very recent thing and only because they've been forced to be able to think ahead. Otherwise they're very reactive and never proactive (Interview with Lecturer A, 2000).

The next section analyses this new managerial-style policy development.

Education Fiji 2020

This document is the first in the series of 'new style' policies, and the language employed within the text of the policy tends toward the new managerialist style as discussed above:

> *Education Fiji 2020* denotes the beginning of an increased focus on planning at all levels of education, providing a framework for strategic and management planning which will ensure that the efforts of all partners in education are integrated for the benefit of our students, the community and the nation ... This analysis identified a number of changes and challenges which were the starting point for developing the objectives and planned outcomes for education to the year 2020. The outcomes describe the desired features of education by the year 2020 and give us reference points from which we can measure our success (Fiji Ministry of Education 1999: 2).

Almost at the outset, *Education Fiji 2020* uses the language typical of the discourse of the new managerialism. There are strong tendencies towards a behaviouristic perspective, with an uncritical emphasis on outcomes and measurement. After an introduction to the tradition of education in Fiji and an examination of changes and challenges, the *2020* document goes on to discuss 10 objectives for planning in education to the year 2020. Each of these objectives is followed by a set of "desired outcomes", which are to act as sources of measurement of achievement of these objectives. Both the objectives and the outcomes are replete with the exhortation to develop quality and excellence. Objective 6 is, "To establish standards, monitor, account for and seek continuous improvement in the performance of our learners, our staff and our education system" (Ministry of Education 1999:11). The document buttresses this economic terminology with appeals to the participatory nature of education with objective 10, which states, "To increase educational participation at all levels, encouraging a learning culture with community recognition of the importance and value of education and training throughout life" (Ministry of Education 1999:11). These two objectives taken together aptly illustrate Hartley's point about the two sets of vocabulary evident in the new managerialism:

> Before us, therefore, is the discourse of the new managerialism. It comprises two sets of vocabulary, the one replete with the industrial metaphors of the rationally structured machine, the other suffused with the appeals to empowerment and ownership. The former is the discourse for strategy; the latter for tactics. Somehow, we, the professionals ... are meant to mix these two contradictory vocabularies in our minds, as if they are of a piece, devoid of

contradiction, logically coherent. In our attempt to bring their contradictory logics together, we are left with confusion and not a little cynicism. It just does not feel right. And it does not feel empowering (Hartley 1997: 48).

Strategic Plan 2000 – 2002

The *Strategic Plan* provides detailed strategies for the achievement of the objectives outlined in *Education Fiji 2020*. As with the latter document, The *Strategic Plan* continues with the use of the new managerialist discourse. There is an emphasis on outcomes and performance indicators, and the associated discourses of measurement and accountability. The idea that educational outcomes can and should be predicted and then measured seems to be the logical and sensible thing to do. However, the adoption of the rhetoric of outcomes and performance is, again, indicative of the move toward viewing education in entrepreneurial terms, supporting a broader thesis about the economizing of education that is now a significant part of international developments in higher education. Furthermore, as with the *Education Fiji 2020* document, there are appeals to "empowerment", "partnership" and "ownership" of education processes (Fiji Ministry of Education 2000: 7-9). These more humanistic concerns are placed alongside the economic rhetoric that is implicit as a techno-rational discourse of control from the central policy-making body; or as Hartley puts it, there is a contradiction between the central controlling discourse of strategy as is evident in the metaphors of industry, and the discourse of tactics that promotes a façade of policy ownership by the practitioner (Hartley 1997: 48). As will be evident from the response of teacher educators in Fiji to the new policy, the rhetoric of empowerment and ownership does not devolve into local cultures of practice in Fijian teacher education.

2001 Corporate Plan

The managerialist language continues in the *2001 Corporate Plan,* the third major policy document produced by the Fiji MoE in line with the requirements of the Fiji Finance Management Act.

> The Ministry of Education is declaring 2001 as the Year of Breakthrough ... We have analysed our inputs, outputs and desired outcomes for the Year 2000 and have mapped out in this Plan a more decisive and focused pathway for education in Fiji in 2001. Our primary focus is to realise set accountabilities and targets in partnership with our stakeholders (Fiji Ministry of Education 2001:1).

The focus in this particular document is on the ministry outputs for 2001. In its review of the 2000 outputs there are 11 pages of a tabulated assessment of delivery of outputs, with a separate column for "If Not, Why?" cases. There is a strong tendency towards a ticking off of achievements with the inclusion of a separate entry each for bureaucratic items such as: "Payment of salary", "Payment of accounts", "Payment of government grants", and "Issue of revenue and trust fund receipts".

Although these are extreme examples of the more bureaucratic aspects of the outputs, what is of interest here is that they are tabulated alongside more professional issues such as: "Provision of teaching services", "Provision of pre-service teaching services", "Strengthening of Fijian education", "Conduct research when necessary on above issues and use finding as basis of advice". The juxtaposition of two very diverse sets of outputs in this contrived manner is, again, reflective of an underlying techno-rational ideology.

The New Managerialism in Teacher Education

The FCAE has recently developed a Mission Statement and a Strategic Plan. The directive for this initiative came from the MoE via the Ministry of Finance. As with the MoE *2020* document, the FCAE planning documents are assessed in terms of how satisfactorily they comply with the Fiji Finance Management Act (Government of Fiji 1999).

In essence, the new FCAE planning documents do not differ from the three new Fiji MoE documents described above. For example, the FCAE Strategic Plan is structured according to the very same objectives contained in the *Education Fiji 2020* policy document. It outlines strategies and performance indicators that will be used to achieve and assess the defined objectives. There is an emphasis on excellence and quality. In addition, the economic terminology is, as for *Education Fiji 2020*, buttressed by an appeal to the participatory nature of education in several of its objectives and strategies.

The development of the three new policy documents *Education Fiji 2020*, *Strategic Plan 2000-2002*, and the *2001 Corporate Plan*, along with the new FCAE planning documents, is an important moment for Fiji. Their production is indicative of a strong centralized attempt to take a more proactive stance on matters to do with education. However, as has been suggested above there are a number of matters of concern that need to be noted. First, the fact that the directives for this policy development emerge from the finance sector should not be seen as an unimportant issue. The dictates of the financial sector through a wider economic rationalist culture of cost cutting, downgrading, objective measurement, and monitoring and account-ability should be noted for its effects on educational and other social institutions in the country. Second, there is a need to separate the professional matters from the more mundane bureaucratic matters in a consideration of what are called outputs. Education is primarily a human endeavour and designing policy for its own sake considerably denies this factor. Third, it is clear that the language of the new managerialism has emerged in the new policy documents, and there are indications that much of this language is imported from the economic sector. Again, a view of education as an overtly technicist endeavour induces a tendency towards a meaninglessness and a decontextualization of policy matters.

This flurry of paperwork in planning the education system is, of course, not happening in a vacuum. A planning document is only as good as the community that it was written for, and therefore we must ask the question: what do teacher educators make of this new-style managerialist documentation?

Practitioner Responses to the New Policy: Who Owns Teacher Education?

Data collected by Tuinamuana (2002) as part of a larger research study point to a contradiction between the set of new official policy discourses and that of context-bound discourses. Context-bound here refers to discourses articulated by those directly involved with teacher education on the ground. In effect, teacher educators generally did not feel that they owned teacher education, a situation that further confirms the workings of a technocratic ideology at work. This issue can be illustrated with the analogy of car factory workers who work on one isolated part of the product and receives little intrinsic personal satisfaction from their labour. Similarly, if the ownership of teacher education practice becomes externalized and alienated from personal experience then there is a sense of disengagement from practice. Practice becomes routinized and takes on a hue of artificiality and automaticity.

The data shows that there is very little fit between the official policy discourse and the response from those more directly involved with teacher education. As might be expected in a system where the perception is that, over the years, very little has changed in the education system, there is also a significant degree of scepticism about what the officially sanctioned policy is able to achieve at the level of implementation. Further, there was a general lack of awareness of what the policy is, and sometimes there was almost apathy about what it might mean for future changes and developments. The dominance of a discourse of educational practice that has become routinized over the years suggests that that this lack of interest in larger issues might be part of the process of alienation that separates educational practice from any meaningful and dynamic contextualization.

In trying to effect educational change through new policy formation, the mistake is often made of not including those on the 'shop floor' in decision-making. Fullan (1991: 38) suggests that the implementation of educational change involves "change in practice". However, the data suggests that the changes that the new policy directions are designed to effect would actually make very few inroads into educational practice. The bureaucratic inertia and personal apathy that seems to dominate local culture/s of educational practice make significant contributions to widening this space between policy and implementation. This inertia and apathy is, of course, not presented to lay blame at any personal level. Rather, the objective is to draw attention to this situation as it exists in a wider context of a dominant techno-rational culture of teacher education. An articulation of this point, conversely, also assists in clarifying the possibilities that lie in a teacher education policy and practice that works, not in the form of alienation, but as a form of educational change (Fullan 1991).

Below, I discuss in some detail the responses of teacher education personnel to the issue of policy. These responses illustrate the sense of disengagement from policy issues that was evident in local cultures of teacher education practice. Despite the rhetoric of decentralization and local empowerment that imbues neo-liberal approaches to governance (McGinn 1997), the picture that emerged from interviews with teacher education staff suggested that national policy development at the governmental level was something that 'they' did. Very few staff members were aware of the existence of the new MoE policy documents. Where there was awareness, there seemed to be some consensus in the perception that the MoE tended to focus on issues of numbers rather than quality of teachers.

At the senior administrative level, the principal of the FCAE suggested that, in his opinion, the FCAE was happy to work within the MoE requirements. This is not surprising since the FCAE is a government institution and is funded and run by the central management at the MoE headquarters. In response to the question "Is teacher education policy formalised in any way here [at FCAE]?", the principal observed:

> For the college how it all started here, the policy for teacher education institutions are formulated by the ministry. They initiate policy, of course, through the influence of the government of the day .... So in terms of policy guidelines we are going along with the major policies set by the MoE. We do not deviate but we want to make sure in what way we can help the MoE achieve the major goals and the vision of the MoE. So we have a vision statement, we have strategies, and because of that without these plans how can we justify what we are doing? Because in there we have different programmes there we are following so we can justify for budget allocation.

However, in interviews with FCAE lecturing staff, the question of policy initiated some interesting discussion. The following extract is typical (K is the researcher, C1 is the respondent):

K	As far as you are aware, what are the written policy documents that guide teacher training in Fiji?
C1	I've seen only education ones. I haven't seen any teacher training policies.
K	The College has a vision statement? How widely was it discussed here at FCAE?
C1	It wasn't really discussed it came from the top [i.e. from the MoE] to the administrators here and then it was brought up at the staff meeting, and it was decided that this was going to be our mission statement.

K   How is it brought down to the school [ie. Faculty] level?

C1   When you have meetings with the schools, reviewing of courses and all that, the mission and the statement is there. And you check what you have been practising to see whether it is in line with the statement.

K   Is it a useful thing to have?

C1   I suppose it's good to have a mission statement in that you have a goal, but the only time I even know that they ever talk about it was for the Performance Management System.

K   What are some of the factors that restrict the potential for change?

C1   We don't have good governance. We have never had a good minister. We have ministers who talk about goals and visions. The government of the day has to mean it and be serious about improving education. Just paying lip service to it doesn't work.

In light of the data collected from the FCAE, a comment from the MoE seemed necessary. When interviewing a senior manager at the MoE, I asked the question, "How does the MoE direct, if it does direct, the work of the FCAE?" The response was:

> Well [the MoE and FCAE] have a board on which we are represented. And [the MoE and FCAE] also have an examination board on which the senior staff sits as well …. Also we dictate in terms of the budget, we dictate in terms of the course to be run … dependent on the needs. For some years we have had enough language teachers for example, so we changed the enrolment to lessen the numbers in the area and move to technical vocation, if we found that there were more vacancies in that area then we will increase the number.

This comment is quite telling especially in the light of other comments made by teacher education staff on the preponderance of issues of quantity over those of quality. Furthermore, the MoE, in its managerial role with the FCAE, seems to focus on a technical role. My interview with the senior management at the MoE continues thus (K is the researcher, M1 is the respondent):

M1   So in a sense because [the FCAE is] a government institution there is some direction, or control from the ministry and the way it goes. It appoints the staff, it determines the budget, the capital programmes, by capital I mean building of new facilities, and other assistance that comes with it.

K   And how do you get feedback from them to you?

M1   Um …

K   In terms of the things that they … what *they* want?

M1   Like in the government system we have an annual budgeting system. So the principal and the staff if they want to put forward certain projects what they want, their needs, they have to put in their annual requests.

K   What about at the level of the professional needs of teachers, or curriculum discussions. Is there a section in the ministry that deals directly with FCAE or are they sort of autonomous?

M1   They are autonomous in that, but they may consult with the Curriculum Development Unit (CDU) officers, they deal more with the professional side of things.

However, my own discussions with both FCAE staff and CDU staff suggested that contact between them was minimal. This was partly due to both groups of staff being overworked, and also to the fact that there were very few workable structures set up for more liaising between the FCAE and the CDU.

The following interview response creates a direct link between teacher education policy and the lack of interaction between the CDU and the FCAE (where C3 is the FCAE respondent):

K   Are you aware of any formal secondary teacher education policy for Fiji? Have you ever seen anything on paper?

C3   No. With CDU, by right, there should have been a lot of interaction with us [on this matter]. But it seems that they are in a world of their own, But only when we need help, then we go out [to them]. But with them they really wouldn't seek our help. They are probably more concerned with teachers in the field, rather than teachers who are coming to the field. They are forever going out on school visits. They don't realise that if they come here [FCAE] they will make more impact.

The above discussion indicates that there is a significant degree of scepticism about the policy relationship between central policy defining bodies, and those that participate at the level of implementation. The new policy documentation produced by the MoE through its *Education 2020* policy has permeated into the FCAE via their own policy documents, as discussed by the Principal of the college. The lecturing staff themselves differ in their level of awareness, with some maintaining what might be considered to be a healthy scepticism. However, the existence of an overt apathy about the meaning of policy for teacher education in Fiji is significant. Although the following response was not typical of FCAE lecturers' comments on policy related issues, it still represents a considerable segment of opinion in the college:

K   Are you aware of any formal secondary teacher education policy?

C4   No ... I am quite ignorant

K   Do you think there might be one?

> C4   There should be.
>
> K   What kinds of things do you think this policy should emphasize?
>
> C4   I think the hours of teaching should be looked at. Some schools have one-hour periods, some have 40 minutes. Because one hour ... imagine for students' level of concentration. So such things should be standardised from the ministry.
>
> K   Did you have a chance to look at the Fiji Education Review Report?
>
> C4   I wasn't interested.
>
> K   Is there a reason for your not being interested?
>
> C4   I have so many things to do, like me studying, and my family, and I am running all new courses this year. I just didn't have the time to do it.
>
> K   What about from what you've read in the papers? What did you think about the way that the review was carried out?
>
> C4   I think reports like this, there's a big hue and cry, a lot of money is put in, it's made and it's shelved, then nothing happens.

The following extract provides a further example of the lack of interest in matters pertaining to policy:

> K   Do you have an opinion on the Fiji Education Review commission?
>
> C5   Actually I haven't gone through the review. So I won't be able to comment.
>
> K   Did your school make a contribution to the submission from here?
>
> C5   Yes, um ... Actually I'm not aware of what contributions were made. I'm not really aware of that. It happened beginning of last year, and was mostly compiled by our head of school [faculty head].

It is debatable whether the lack of interest in wider matters impacting on teacher education is due to a lack of time, or whether it is indicative that educators just become accustomed to matters such as a lack of policy ownership as they progress in their careers. That there is a lack of sense of ownership in the policy process is, however, very evident, and it is clear that there is a developing sense of apathy in the way that policy issues are being addressed. This might be due to the centralized nature of policy making in Fiji. The development of the new planning documents does not seem to have altered the situation for the better.

    The above discussion has shown the scepticism with which teacher educators view the top-down approach to policy making, whether it is at the governmental level or the institutional level. There was also concern shown that the implementers of the policy did not have more of a voice in the policy making process. For example, a teacher educator sitting on the Education Forum (a forum set up by the MoE to discuss new initiatives in education that would then be presented to the cabinet for ratification) was less than flattering about its role. The interviewee makes specific comments about the top-down nature of proceedings of the Education Forum:

> This body [the education forum] is only a rubber stamp at the moment.... Because at the moment whether you agree or disagree to what is being proposed you just go there. In other words it is just a rubber stamp. But the proposal, where did this proposal come from? We're not part of the initial process, where these needs come from.

The understandings expressed in the interview with this Education Forum member are supported by data from interviews with other teacher educators. The following interview extract, focussing on the policy making process, provides an example of this (where K is the researcher and L1 is the lecturer):

K   What kinds of considerations do they take into account when they make policy? Perhaps think of something that you were involved in?

L1   Some policies came from the Education Forum members although that body is just a showpiece for the ministry people ... I personally feel that every thing comes from the Permanent Secretary (of Education), they decide on something and then they do it.

K   Who influences the Permanent Secretary now?

L1   Actually, he should be influenced by the people but at the moment, uh honestly, it is more political decisions, it is the political masters who call the tune. The other people who call the tune is the employers.

K   What do you think about that?

L1   It's good and bad. Because they provide employment so we must train them to fit there. The bad thing is that they are money-makers, and they are going into one direction and therefore we are not able to prepare the human resource.

Thus there are strong implications here that the role of the Fiji Education Forum in formulating policy needs to be re-assessed. If there continues to be a limited sense of dialogue between policy makers and practitioners then, as discussed earlier, the gap between official policy discourses and context-bound discourses will widen further.

The role of the Education Forum was also critiqued in the report of the Fiji Education Review Commission 2000:

> The Forum is required to meet three times a year but in reality it does not meet this requirement. It is an advisory body, and has no powers as such. Its role is to advise the Minister on organisation and policy matters, and any matter raised by the Permanent Secretary. Ideally, the Education Forum should fulfil the role of a

'Think Tank'. It appears, however, that it has become a forum for stakeholders to express grievances and the MoE to defend itself (Tavola 2000: 31).

As the discussion with the Education Forum member (cited above) progressed to the specific issue of teacher education, s/he talked more directly about the FCAE. When questioned about the role of policy in teacher education, the interviewee makes specific comments about the FCAE:

> Yes but those people [FCAE] are the implementers, they don't really know how come they're doing what they're doing, 'why am I doing what I'm doing? Where does this originate from? Whose idea was this, where did the process start?'

This is a strong indication of the urgent need for more participation at the level of policy development. However, although this is a worthy call there is some doubt that, within current organizational structures of teacher education in Fiji, policy formulation can work in any other way.

In concluding this section on the issue of ownership of teacher education in Fiji, it would seem that, in spite of there being immense amounts of documentation generated by the development of new policy, there is very little meaningful or willing engagement concerning how this new policy might be usefully applied to Fiji's education system. Rather, the policy seems to just 'sit there', on display as it were, and the main function that it has served to date has been to do with planning for future teacher requirements, and for bureaucratic functions of resource allocation. These functions are of course very important, but it is clear that further steps have not been taken to ensure a closer link between official policies and context-bound settings.

Conclusion

The teacher education policy-practice context in Fiji is shaped by a complex interplay of local and external factors, and can be described as currently being in a state of unprecedented flux. Policy is being disseminated and discussed in new ways, and the indication is that much of this is in the form of the new managerialism that is part of the techno-rational discourse associated with economic globalization. Certainly there is scope for further research into how policy plays out in particular contexts of implementation. This chapter has drawn out some of the contextual factors that are important to an enhanced understanding of these new policy developments, and for any educational reform to be successful, a socio-economic and historical assessment should be made of the major issues. Otherwise, the impact of the new policy will inevitably be reduced.

It might be argued that the techno-rational approach to education in Fiji is not new; in fact it developed as part of the history of the introduction of colonialist education (Whitehead 1981). However, it could also be argued that the intensity and pervasiveness of neo-liberal, managerialist approaches to educational policies are unprecedented in Fiji. Furthermore, if the new policy proceeds to underpin the introduction of educational reforms into Fiji, the particular problems surrounding education in Fiji, such as the lack of ownership of reform on the part of practitioners, will become masked by policy innovations.

It is clear that there is a strong and urgent need for a well-articulated philosophical and theoretical direction for teacher education. As I have shown in this chapter, higher education in Fiji is becoming internationalized in the sense that there is a rise to prominence of international administrative and policy approaches derived from managerialist discourses associated with globalization. If educators are to avoid the negative consequences of these approaches, including alienation and the marginalization of educational concerns, then educationists must be allowed to take a stronger proactive professional role. As Ilon (2000: 281) suggests:

If we are unwilling or unable to rapidly adapt to the dynamics of a knowledge-based economy, we may forgo our chance to become proactive agents of change. Fields far less capable of developing our diverse and contextually driven productive capacities may well influence the design of education. The possibility for a radically improved future will be diminished.

References

Ball, S.J. 1998. "Big Policies/Small World: An Introduction to International Perspectives in Education Policy". *Comparative Education* 34(2): 119-130.

Dale, R. 1997. "The State and the Governance of Education: An Analysis of the Restructuring of the State-Education Relationship." In *Education: Culture, Economy and Society*, edited by A.H. Halsey, H. Lauder, P. Brown & A. Wells. Oxford: Oxford University Press.

Elliott, D. 1999. "Internationalising British Higher Education: Policy Perspectives". In *The Globalisation of Higher Education*, edited by P. Scott. Buckingham: Society for Research into Higher Education & Open University Press.

Fiji Ministry of Education. 1999. *Education Fiji 2020*. Suva, Fiji: Ministry of Education.

Fiji Ministry of Education. 2000. *Ministry of Education Strategic Plan 2000-2002: Putting Education Fiji 2020 into Action*. Suva, Fiji: Ministry of Education.

Fiji Ministry of Education. 2001. *2001 Corporate Plan: Putting the Strategic Plan into Action*. Suva, Fiji: Ministry of Education.

Fullan, M. 1991. *The New Meaning of Educational Change*, 2nd edition. New York: Teachers College Press and Toronto: OISE Press.

Government of Fiji. 1999. *Public Finance Management Act, 1999*. Suva: Government Printer.

Hartley, D. 1997. "The New Managerialism in Education: A Mission Impossible?". *Cambridge Journal of Education* 27(1): 47-57.

Kotobalavu, J. 2000 "Foreword". In *Learning Together: Directions for Education in the Fiji Islands*. Report of the Fiji Islands Education Commission/Panel. Suva: Government Printer.

Ilon, L. 2000. "Knowledge, Labour and Education". *Compare* 30(3): 275-282.

Loughlin, M. 2002. "Assurance, Effectiveness, Ownership, Empowerment, Autonomy, Dynamic, Learning Curves, a Continuum of Quality-Awareness, Self-Actualisation and Enhancement ... Whatever That Means." *The Times Higher Education Supplement*, March 22.

McGinn, N. 1997. "The Impact of Globalization on National Systems of Education." *Prospects* 27(1): 41-54.

Ozga, J. 2000. *Policy Research in Educational Settings: Contested Terrain*. Buckingham: Open University Press.

Prasad, B.C. 1998. "The Woes of Economic Reform: Poverty and Income Inequality in Fiji". *International Journal of Social Economics* 25(6, 7, 8): 1073-1094.

Smyth, J., Dow, A., Hattam, R., Reid, A. & Shacklock, G. 2000. *Teachers' Work in a Globalizing Economy*. London: The Falmer Press.

Tavola, H. 2000. "Status Report". In *Learning Together: Directions for Education in the Fiji Islands*. Report of the Fiji Islands Education Commission/Panel. Suva: Government Printer.

Tuinamuana, K. 2002. *Global Discourses and Local Culture/s of Practice: A study of policy and practice in secondary teacher education in Fiji*. PhD thesis, University of Edinburgh.

Ugarteche, O. 1997. *The False Dilemma: Globalisation – Opportunity or Threat?* Translated by Mark Fried. London and New York: Zed Books.

Whitehead, C. 1981. *Education in Fiji: Policy, Problems and Progress in Primary and Secondary Education, 1939-1973*. Canberra: Australian National University.

Whitty, G. 1997. "Marketisation, the State, and the Re-Formation of the Teaching Profession." In *Education: Culture, Economy and Society*, edited by A.H. Halsey, H. Lauder, P. Brown & A. Wells. Oxford: Oxford University Press, 1997.

Woods, P. & Jeffrey, R. 1996. "A New Professional Discourse? Adjusting to Managerialism." In *Contemporary Issues in Teaching and Learning*, edited by P. Woods. London: Routledge/Falmer in association with The Open University.

Notes on Contributors

Catherine Doherty is a Doctoral student in education at the Queensland University of Technology, Brisbane, Australia. Her doctoral project explores the production of cultural difference in online internationalized higher education programs. Her research interests include literacy practices in technological environments and how pedagogies accommodate cultural difference. Address: School for Cultural and Language Studies, Queensland University of Technology, Victoria Park Rd, Kelvin Grove, QLD 4059, Australia. Email c.Doherty@qut.edu.au

Grant Harman is an Emeritus Professor of educational management at the University of New England (UNE), Armidale, Australia. He was Professor of educational management at UNE from 1985 to 2001 and his special research interests are in educational planning and management, higher education policy, comparative studies, the academic profession and research policy and training. He is coordinating editor of the refereed journal *Higher Education* published by Kluwer Academic Publishers in the Netherlands. Address: School of Professional Development and Leadership, University of New England, Armidale, NSW, 2351, Australia. Email gharman@pobox.une.edu.au

Meeri Hellstén is a Lecturer in education at Macquarie University, Sydney, Australia. Her research interests are located in the fields of cross-cultural and comparative education, socio-cultural and identity issues in education, e-learning pedagogies and effective teaching and learning in higher education. She is currently chief investigator of two funded research projects documenting the international student experiences of Australian higher education and self-esteem learning programs for adolescents. Meeri convenes and teaches on a large undergraduate unit in educational psychology. Address: Email meeri.hellsten@mq.edu.au

Ian Jamieson is Professor of Education, Dean of the Faculty of Humanities and Social Sciences and Pro-Vice Chancellor for Learning and Teaching at the University of Bath, UK. His main research interests include the relations between schooling and work, educational evaluation, school effectiveness and improvement, and higher education. He was the founding editor of the *Journal of Education and Work*. He is an auditor for the UK Quality Assurance Agency, and has been a non-executive director

215

of UCAS, the UK higher education admissions service. Address: Faculty of Humanities & Social Science, University of Bath, Claverton Down, Bath, BA2 7AY, United Kingdom. Email: I.M.Jamieson@bath.ac.uk

Susan E. (Hinton) Mayson is a Lecturer in management at Monash University, Melbourne, Australia. Her research interests include gender inequalities and work organisations; diversity issues in organisations; women in management; human resources management and recruitment on the world wide web; postmodern organisation theory; and organisation behaviour. Department of Management, Monash University, PO Box 1071, Narre Warren, VIC, 3805, Australia. Email: susan.mayson@buseco.monash.edu.au

Rajani Naidoo is a Lecturer in the Department of Education and a member of the International Centre for Higher Education Management in the School of Management at the University of Bath, UK. She sits on the governing council of the Society for Research into Higher Education (SRHE) and is a member of the editorial board of the *British Journal of Sociology of Education*. She has been involved in directing a range of innovative higher education developments in South Africa and in the United Kingdom. Address: Department of Education, University of Bath, Claverton Down, Bath, BA2 7AY, United Kingdom. Email: R.Naidoo@bath.ac.uk

Pam Nilan is a Senior Lecturer in sociology in the School of Social Sciences at the University of Newcastle, Australia. She has been researching young people and social change, including change in education, in Australia and the Asia-Pacific since 1991. She is currently working on a book on cultural trends and patterns among global youth. Address: School of Social Sciences, University of Newcastle, University Dve, Callaghan, NSW, 2308, Australia. Email: Pamela.Nilan@newcastle.edu.au

Peter Ninnes is a Senior Lecturer in sociology of education in the School of Education, at the University of New England, Armidale, Australia. His research interests include comparative and international education, the discursive constitution of academic fields, "post" perspectives in education, education in post-conflict contexts, and science education and diversity. He is currently President of the Australian and New Zealand Comparative and International Education Society. Address: School of Education, University of New England, Armidale, NSW, 2351, Australia. Email: pninnes@pobox.une.edu.au

Anne Prescott is a Lecturer in the teacher education program at the University of Technology, Sydney, Australia. Previously, she worked at two other universities in Sydney. As part of that work, Anne has come in contact with international students leading to her research in this area. Email: Anne.Prescott@uts.edu.au

Jan Schapper lectures in the Department of Management at Monash University, Melbourne, Australia. She teaches in the areas of general management, human resource management and management theory. Jan's research interests include academic teaching and learning issues surrounding internationalization and transition, and research in the area of organisational change. Address: Department of Management, Monash University, PO Box 1071, Narre Warren, VIC, 3805, Australia. Email: j.schapper@buseco.monash.edu.au

Michael Singh is a Professor in the School of Education at the University of Western Sydney, Australia. His research interests include applied socio- linguistics; cross-cultural communication; cultural diversity; cultural politics of globalization; global English; intercultural education; internationalization of higher education; internationalization of the curriculum; sustainability of linguistic diversity; race class and national identity; teaching English to speakers of other languages (TESOL); transnational cultural and intellectual flows; and globalization, new technologies and education. Address: School of Education and Early Childhood Studies, University of Western Sydney, Darug Country, Locked Bag 1797, Penrith South DC, NSW, 1797, Australia. Email: m.j.singh@uws.edu.au

Parlo Singh is an Associate Professor in the School of Cultural and Language Studies in Education, Queensland University of Technology, Brisbane, Australia. Her research interests include sociology of education with a specific focus on the formation of cultural identity in and through schooling practices. Parlo Singh is currently writing a book on Globalization, Cultural Identity and Pedagogies contracted with Lawrence Erlbaum, Associates, Mahwah, New Jersey, USA. Address: Centre for Language, Literacy and Diversity, Queensland University of Technology, Victoria Park Rd, Kelvin Grove, QLD, 4059, Australia. Email p.singh@qut.edu.au

Katarina Tuinamuana has worked as a Lecturer in Education since 1992 at the University of the South Pacific, Suva, Fiji. Prior to this, she taught English and Social Science in Fiji schools. She was awarded a PhD from the University of Edinburgh in 2002, working in the area of the sociology of education. Her current research interests are: the process of educational policy development and implementation in the Pacific region, issues in international education, epistemology and teacher education, the changing discourses used to describe education processes, the design and implementation of educational reform, and issues surrounding 'relevance' and 'indigenizing' of learning and teaching. Address: School of Humanities, University of the South Pacific, PO Box 1168, Suva, Fiji. Email: tuinamuana_k@usp.ac.fj

Rui Yang was an associate professor at a Chinese university before he commenced his doctoral studies in 1996. He received a PhD from the University of Sydney in 2001. After working for two years as a lecturer in comparative and international education at the Graduate School of Education, The University of Western Australia in Perth, he joined Monash University in 2003, and then the University of Hong Kong in 2004. He has written extensively in the field of comparative education. His current interests are focused on comparative and global studies in education and higher education internationalization. Address: Comparative Education Research Centre, Faculty of Education, The University of Hong Kong, Pokfulam Road, Hong Kong, China. Email: cerc@hku.hk

Index

Other Books Published by the Comparative Education Research Centre

1. Mark Bray & R. Murray Thomas (eds.) (1998): *Financing of Education in Indonesia*. ISBN 971-561-172-9. 133pp. HK$140/US$20.

2. David A. Watkins & John B. Biggs (eds.) (1996, reprinted 1999): *The Chinese Learner: Cultural, Psychological and Contextual Influences*. ISBN 0-86431-182-6. 285pp. HK$200/US$32.

3. Ruth Hayhoe (1999): *China's Universities 1895-1995: A Century of Cultural Conflict*. ISBN 962-8093-81-9. 299pp. HK$200/US$32.

4. David A. Watkins & John B. Biggs (eds.) (2001): *Teaching the Chinese Learner: Psychological and Pedagogical Perspectives*. ISBN 962-8093-72-X. 306pp. HK$200/US$32.

5. 貝磊、古鼎儀編 (2002)。《香港與澳門的教育與社會：從比較角度看延續與變化》。ISBN 962-8093-94-9. 250pp. HK$200/US$32.

6. Mark Bray with Roy Butler, Philip Hui, Ora Kwo & Emily Mang (2002): *Higher Education in Macau: Growth and Strategic Development*. ISBN 962-8093-60-6. 127pp. HK$150/US$24.

7. Yoko Yamato & Sally Course (2002): *Guide to International Schools in Hong Kong*. ISBN 962-8093-62-2. 82pp. HK$72/US$12.

8. Ruth Hayhoe (2004): *Full Circle: A Life with Hong Kong and China*. ISBN 962-8093-31-2. 261pp. HK$200/US$32.

9. 貝磊、丁小浩、黃平 (2004):《減輕貧困人口的經濟負擔：在中國甘肅省降低基礎教育的家庭成本》。ISBN 962-8093-33-9。53pp。HK$50/US$10 [Also available in English]

Series: Education in Developing Asia

1. Don Adams (2004): *Education and National Development: Priorities, Policies, and Planning*. ISBN 971-561-529-5. 81pp. HK$100/US$12 each or HK$400/US$50 for set of five.

2. David Chapman (2004): *Management and Efficiency in Education: Goals and Strategies*. ISBN 971-561-530-9. 85pp. HK$100/US$12 each or HK$400/US$50 for set of five.

3. Mark Bray (2004): *The Costs and Financing of Education: Trends and Policy Implications*. ISBN 971-561-531-7. 78pp. HK$100/US$12 each or HK$400/US$50 for set of five.

4. W.O. Lee (2004): *Equity and Access to Education: Themes, Tensions, and Policies*. ISBN 971-561-532-5. 101pp. HK$100/US$12 each or HK$400/US$50 for set of five.

5. David Chapman & Don Adams (2004): *The Quality of Education: Dimen-sions and Strategies*. ISBN 971-561-533-3. 72pp. HK$100/US$12 each or HK$400/US$50 for set of five.

Series: CERC Monographs

1. Yoko Yamato (2003): *Education in the Market Place: Hong Kong's International Schools and their Mode of Operation*. ISBN 962-8093-57-6. 117pp. HK$100/US$16.

2. Mark Bray, Ding Xiaohao & Huang Ping (2004): *Reducing the Burden on the Poor: Household Costs of Basic Education in Gansu, China*. ISBN 962-8093-32-0. 67pp. HK$50/US$10. [Also available in Chinese]

3. Maria Manzon (2004): *Building Alliances: Schools, Parents and Com-munities in Hong Kong and Singapore*. ISBN 962-8093-36-3. 117pp. HK$100/US$16.